Bill

I really "!!" and
All your help
guidance,
Wish you the
best of success!

CREATING EQUITY

AN INVITATION

If you found this book helpful in building your business, you might be interested in learning about other financial information products published by Securities Data Publishing. Join other savvy professionals using these publications to stay ahead of their competition by keeping up with the latest news and important trends.

To receive our current product catalog, please call our Customer Service Department at 1-800-445-5844 or 212-765-5311, or write to Customer Service, Securities Data Publishing, 40 W. 57th Street, 11th Floor, New York, NY 10019 or send an e-mail to sdp@tfn.com. For up-to-the-minute financial news and information on the Internet, please sign on to our *FP Online* web site at http://www.fponline.com.

CREATING EQUITY

HOW TO BUILD A HUGELY SUCCESSFUL
ASSET MANAGEMENT BUSINESS

by

JOHN J. BOWEN, JR.

SDP
BOOKS

THIS BOOK IS PUBLISHED BY
SECURITIES DATA PUBLISHING BOOKS

This publication is designed to provide accurate and authoritative information in regard to the subject matter covered. It is sold with the understanding that neither the author or the publisher is engaged in rendering legal, accounting, or other professional service. If legal advice or other expert assistance is required, the services of a competent professional person should be sought.

From a Declaration of Principles jointly adopted by a Committee of the American Bar Association and a Committee of Publishers.

ISBN 0-914470-88-4

Manufactured in the United States of America
First Edition

*To my wife Jean for her encouragement,
love and support.
To my parents, who taught me to live life
with passion and perseverance.
To my friends everywhere who have made
this ongoing journey worthwhile.*

CREATING EQUITY

TABLE OF CONTENTS

ACKNOWLEDGEMENTS

T his book is the result of over 20 years of learning and having fun. Along the way, we have received a lot of help.
Almost all of what we've learned in the business has been
learned from our strategic alliance partners.

This book will help financial advisors to build hugely successful
asset management businesses for their clients and themselves, by applying the frontier of investment business knowledge. It is a roadmap,
clearly illustrating how advisors, by establishing trust and truly impressing their clients, can create equity worth millions of dollars.

We would like to begin by thanking three leading members of
the financial economic community, Harry Markowitz, Merton Miller
and William Sharpe, whose research was rewarded with the Nobel
Prize in Economics and which provides the foundation for the
investment section of this book. In addition, we would like to thank
Eugene Fama, Ken French and Meir Statman, for their academic
research and guidance in applying these principles.

No one deserves more credit for the application of this research
than the principals at Dimensional Fund Advisors, David Booth and
Rex Sinquefield. They were early pioneers in the development and

application of investment strategies for the institutional investor. They joined with us to bring these same strategies to private clients. Dan Wheeler, one of the directors at Dimensional, worked closely with us to make the establishment of our turnkey asset management program a reality. We would also like to thank Gene Fama, Jr., Art Barlow, David Plecha, Truman Clark and Jeanne Sinquefield, for their continued guidance in the application of these investment theories.

One of the missing links to the establishment of financial advisors was the technology necessary to implement these strategies with private clients. Charles Schwab & Co. made this possible. We would like to thank Charles Schwab, John Coghlan, Dennis Clark, Linnet Diely, Nick Georgis, Jeff Roush, Jim Hackley, Gerald Graves, Nancy Baker, Scott White, and Chip Roame, for their contributions and insights into our business development.

Michael Gerber has been leading a Small Business Revolution before anyone knew there was one. He called it The E-Myth Revolution. The E-Myth is a process, a system, a model, which can be implemented in any small business, and once implemented provides freedom and joy for those who own the business, as well as those who work in it. Michael's insights have helped us tremendously in creating our turnkey business model.

We are deeply grateful to Bruce Morris, CEO of our publisher, Securities Data Publishing, who saw the value that financial advisors would receive from this book and gave us the opportunity to complete it; to our editor, Evan Simonoff, for his patience, editorial guidance and encouragement; to Sue Fredrick for the development of our marketing plan; to Carl Sullivan for line editing; to Melanie Bracken for production support; to Erin Wright for her production assistance; to Sharon Pollack for her book jacket design; to Ladi Odeku for book design; and to Mark Fadiman for his insights on the industry.

We want to thank Larry Chambers, of Chambers & Associates, our writing coach, for acting as a guide and sounding board to make this book a reality.

This book would not have been possible without the independent financial advisors who chose to work with us in bringing these strategies to individual investors. Their best practices have been incorporated in this book and their willingness to share their best practices has made both their businesses and Reinhardt Werba Bowen successful. We incorporate many of their strategies in this book. We'd particularly like to thank Betty Albitz, Harold Anderson, Donald Bailey, Jeffrey Berg, Doug Bergman, Gordon Bernhardt, Kenneth Boone, Joseph Bowie, Jon Brandes, Curt Bryant, John Burroughs, John Byrd, Eileen Clune, John Cooke, Melvin Cooper, Barbara Davis, Joanne Deaton, John Deaton, Max DeZemplen, Michael Dixon, Stanley Dorrance, Theodore Dumas, Bob Ericson, Lucinda Fairfield, Jeff Forman, Richard Fremd, Rob Kemp, Gerald Gasber, Dan Goldie, Richard Graham, Dennis Greene, Anthony Hannon, Michael Irving, Marv Kaye, Russ Ketron, Robert Kresek, Robert Lacy, John Lindsey, Darla Main, Craig Martin, Lynn Mathre, Stanley McCormack, Robert Newell, Dennis Park, Kathleen Peer, Paul Pennington, Gary Pia, Charles Putney, Michael Ritchie, Michael Severance, Jeffrey Shoffer, Mark Sievers and James Suellentrop

Thanks to the staff of Reinhardt Werba Bowen Advisory Services for their tireless effort in making this book happen; Mark Mushet for his diligent review of all data and graphs; Jan Garred, who assists us through each revision; Marlene Bass, for maintaining our schedules; and Ben Bingaman, Rich Boone, Stan Carson, Bill Finn, Ron Howard, Betty Kabanek, Laurie Nardone, Alex Potts, Ron Reynolds, Dave Richardson and Guy Ridout for their insights into refining our message; and to our board members, Ken Koskella, Chuck Masters, Carl Reinhardt, Joe Shepela, Mike Weakley and Alan Werba, for their wisdom.

Thank you to our special good friends, Steve Moeller with American Business Visions; Bill Bachrach with Bachrach & Associates; Jeff Saccacio with Coopers & Lybrand; Michael Lane and Bob Saunders with Providian; Jim Jorgensen of *It's Your Money*; Keith Clark with Lawco Wealth & Benefits; The International Association for Financial Planning; the Institute for Certified Financial Planners; and the Institute for Investment Management Consultants, for their assistance.

Most of all, we want to sincerely thank our thousands of clients who have entrusted us with their life savings. They have placed their confidence in us and allowed us to pioneer these strategies for private clients.

John J. Bowen, Jr.
July 4, 1997

CHAPTER ONE

INTRODUCTION

If we could show you how to build an asset management business worth well over a million dollars by following the steps illustrated in this book, would you read it?

Good! You have purchased the right book.

My name is John Bowen. I am CEO and President of Reinhardt Werba Bowen Advisory Services (RWB), an independent investment asset management firm located in the heart of Silicon Valley in San Jose, California. Our business is helping financial advisors build hugely successful turnkey asset management businesses. Our advisors have followed the steps we are about to show you, and they tell us the approach has not only been liberating, but also exciting and profitable. We believe you will feel the same way. That's why we've written this book. We will show you how to walk the talk each step of the way. You will learn from our successes and avoid our mistakes. I know, because the following steps have helped many advisors build a million-dollar asset management business in less than five years. Our advisors help us and, in turn, we help them build their own businesses. With their help, we have built a billion dollar asset management business.

We've written this book for five different types of readers. If you are already a successful advisor, this book will make you more successful. If you are a stockbroker contemplating leaving your firm, this book will help you make a smooth transition. If you have been in the financial planning business and have been struggling along for years, we will teach you a better way. If you have always been interested in your own personal finances, are currently in a career transition, and have the desire to build a substantial business, this is the road map you've been looking for. And lastly, for those of you just starting out in the financial planning arena, this can be your primary guide to success for your clients and yourself.

This book was designed to nurture you, encourage you, and give you confidence to set out on your own path. Your guides will be the most successful people in the asset management industry. You will meet top producers, top academicians, and top marketing people, and learn their personal insights. You will find out the inside story, and be able to use financial experts' experiences to create your own success.

Before we get started, I would like to address the biggest challenge financial advisors face in their careers: How to offer the best available investment advice to clients and, at the same time, create their own business equity. That, in a nutshell, is the challenge of our industry.

If you are already in the investment business, would your business sell for what you think it's worth? Almost all financial advisors who answer that question honestly must reply, "No." That's not because they haven't worked hard to develop their businesses. These advisors may have built businesses that earn well over a million dollars a year, but they can't sell their businesses for its inherent worth. The painful truth is they don't own businesses, they "own" jobs.

No matter how hard they work or how hard they plan, their underlying investment process cannot produce consistent returns. If their investment process is not producing consistent results, results are not replicable. If results are not replicable, there is little or no equity value inherent in the business.

In the 1980's, dramatic changes affected the investment community. The quantity of investment products available to the public increased exponentially while, at the same time, quality diminished significantly. These were very frustrating times for financial advisors. As a successful financial planning firm working to help our clients reach their financial goals, we would prepare an elaborate financial plan for each client that clearly laid out the road to successful attainment of those goals, including investment recommendations. Here was the central problem—we used outside investment professionals to implement our recommendations. When these outside vendors performed up to their stated expectations, our clients would achieve their financial goals. However, in many cases, the results of actual investments were disappointing. An investment firm could spend years building a practice, but with a few missed expectations of bad performance, or a change in tax laws, the practice could shrink dramatically. You may have had similar experiences with your own practice.

When we decided to explore selling our financial planning practice in 1985, what we discovered shocked us. Although we were grossing over $7 million a year in commissions and fees, our practice couldn't command anywhere near what we thought it was worth. Compared to other businesses, ours was nearly worthless; we had built zero equity in our business. The highest all-cash offer was $120,000. We could have made that delaying the escrow 45 days.

But as fate would have it, our discouraging experience turned out to be the most enlightening of our business careers. We had discovered that what we owned were high paid jobs that no one wanted to purchase. The practice was not transferable. We did not own a business.

The discovery that our business was worth far less than we ever imagined was very demoralizing. I experienced a major crisis of confidence. I knew our clients wanted and needed our help, but I wasn't sure whether our professional advice was worth the commissions we were charging. More and more new prospects were bringing *Money* magazines and *Forbes* to their initial appointments. They had the audacity to ask why they should pay us when they could buy top-rated, no-load mutual funds directly. I tried to explain why, but most of them just did not see the added value. When we did make a sale, we earned about half of what we had formerly made as commissions continued to go down. We received a one-time commission for a lifetime of service commitments; our income dropped through the floor. My partners and I had to lay off half our office staff and bills were piling up. I knew there had to be a better way.

One day while I was teaching graduate school at our local business college, I suddenly experienced the dichotomy between what I was teaching as the ideal and what was actually being implemented in the financial services industry.

I was teaching a class on investment theory in the Masters Business Administration program at Golden Gate University and a major part of the curriculum covered Modern Portfolio Theory, the Nobel Prize-winning investment strategies developed during 40 years of research conducted primarily at the University of Chicago. The concepts and strategies were well-known in academic and institutional circles. They were taught in the finance departments of nearly every major university in America. By 1988, over half a trillion dollars was invested by institutions using these concepts, but less than 1% of the investing public used such strategies to manage money.

During a class, one of my students asked me, "Mr. Bowen, do Modern Portfolio Theory strategies really maximize expected returns and reduce volatility?"

"Yes, of course they do," I replied.

He continued his questioning, "The people who developed Modern Portfolio Theory are the best and brightest in the investment industry today, aren't they?"

"Yes, they certainly are."

6

Then he asked, "Are you using Modern Portfolio Theory to manage your clients's money?"

"Uh, no . ."

"Well if these strategies are so great, why aren't you using them for your clients?"

I was embarrassed; I didn't know what to say. Of course, I had a lot of excuses and rationalizations for why we didn't use the theories, but the bottom line was we weren't using the principles that actually work.

His questions kept me thinking all night. Why was I settling for second best when I knew a better investment methodology? I decided right then and there that I was going to use Modern Portfolio Theory to manage my clients' money. I wouldn't be satisfied with anything but the best for my clients.

I had a meeting with my partners the very next day and told them that the student's questions made a lot of sense. We all agreed I should find a way to implement these strategies in our business. That student's questions ultimately led me on a crusade to identify the best strategies in the investment world. And, the search for a way to put these strategies into practice became our company's driving force.

However, after extensive, time-consuming research, we found it wasn't so easy. Modern Portfolio Theory was great in theory, but it was very difficult to apply in practice. At that time, only large institutional investors with hundreds of millions of dollars had access to the people and technology necessary to apply the concepts. But we were committed to bringing these Nobel Prize-winning investment strategies to the general public—because they worked. You see, we really wanted to help our clients; we wanted to see their money grow and we wanted to provide them with the very best investment methodology available.

Our quest led us to the most brilliant minds in the field of financial economics, people who actually had the answers to many of our questions. At first, many of these top academics— who had developed the concepts that won the Nobel Prize in

Economics in 1990, known collectively as Modern Portfolio Theory—attempted to discourage us from trying to communicate these concepts to our clients. They were used to dealing with fellow academicians or the investment committees of large pension plans, and they thought these strategies were too complicated for private investors and would only confuse them. So we ran a pilot program to introduce these concepts, and we discovered that the logic was so compelling that our clients were quick to grasp it. In fact, investment professionals had the hardest time of all grappling with the concepts! Individual investors knew that there had to be something better than what they were doing. They just did not know what it was until we told them how Modern Portfolio Theory worked.

To our own amazement, these new investment strategies actually simplified the investment decision-making process for our clients and freed them to focus on other aspects of their lives. Once it was clear that our clients actually understood the strategies, we wanted to communicate the concepts to as many people as possible.

Along the way, something else happened—the focus of our business began to radically shift. Rather than attempting to do everything as we had done before—whether it was tax planning, estate planning, insurance planning, etc.—we began to focus on the right solutions in investment. We found that we had fewer clients coming to us, but they were the right clients.

As we started achieving moderate success, it became evident there was still something missing: We needed to design our practice to be a viable business.

A successful business is the only way to assure your clients they are in successful hands. It is in your best interest, as well as in your clients' best interest, to create substantial equity in your business—even if you have no plans to sell it.

Unfortunately, we all know all too well that most financial planning practices have little equity value. A recent study reported by the International Association for Financial Planning (IAFP) showed that the average financial planner makes only about $55,000 annually. My guess is they put in many hours over the standard 40-hour workweek. To be candid, the average financial planner has a terrible job.

How do you redesign your business model? Start with a clean sheet of paper and look at the most successful model for a business today—the franchise. Of every retail dollar spent, 45¢ passes through a franchise business. The most successful franchise, McDonald's, now accounts for over 6¢ of every dollar spent in restaurants. What are McDonald's customers buying? Hamburgers and french fries? No, they're buying consistency.

Think about the last time that you visited a McDonald's. Seven percent of all Americans will visit McDonald's on an average day. Ninety-five percent of all Americans have eaten at a McDonald's during the last 12 months. McDonald's consistently delivers on its promises. The company does not promise to give you the best food; only to give you "a break today." They consistently deliver that break. They manage their customers' expectations well.

When consistency is missing, your clients don't know what to expect. The secret of creating equity in your business is to develop a system that consistently delivers the same high quality services, time and time again. Let me explain how systems can dramatically increase value by contrasting two hamburger stands on the same city block with the same gross revenue. One is a McDonald's; the other is a mom-and-pop stand.

Assuming that this McDonald's is average, it will have gross revenue of over $2,000,000 and a pre-tax profit of over $300,000. Not bad for selling hamburgers and french fries. The mom-and-pop stand is unlikely to be anywhere close to these numbers. To complete this research, I stopped by a local mom-and-pop operation and asked about their business. To make sure I caught them, when did I need to stop by? Anytime they are open; mom and pop are there. Plus, I could count on them being there a couple hours before they opening and a couple of hours after closing. For all this work and much better hamburgers, they earn much less than a third of the McDonald's numbers. When I asked how often the mom and pop take vacations, they answered about every three years. But because they cannot afford to go on vacation together and leave the business, they alternate between husband and wife every third year.

But make the assumption, just for illustration, that both the mom-and-pop operation and McDonald's have the same gross revenue, which one would have more net income? The mom-and-pop store would, due to their lower costs and no franchise fee. However, which business would sell for more? McDonald's would sell for a substantial premium. The reasons are simple: All of McDonald's systems are in place; the training is systematic; and if the owners don't show up, it hardly makes a difference. On the other hand, if mom and pop don't show up, no one eats and the dollars don't come in. Mom and pop own a job and it is a terrible job. It is extremely difficult to sell a terrible job. Unfortunately, many in the financial services industry own terrible jobs, as well; they just don't know it.

Let's examine some of the biggest mistakes we made on our journey from owning a job to owning a business and how we overcame these challenges through systems. Systems are the solution.

Mistake #1: Too busy trying to be all things to everyone.

Solution: Decide what specific business you're in. Financial planning sets you up for failure because you need to be an expert in everything. You know you can't be everything to everyone and, even more important, your clients know this, too. Pick the area that you most enjoy and focus on that. Document the process each step of the way. Do this and you will be able to repeat these steps—you will build consistency.

We decided we were in the business of delivering a Turnkey Asset Management Program (TAMP) to financial advisors. While we enjoyed working directly with investors, we saw a tremendous need for many advisors to have a turnkey system. By helping many advisors to be hugely successful, we could help many more investors reach their financial goals. You may decide that the asset management business is not right for you, and that's okay. Follow what you have a passion for.

Mistake #2: No written procedures to benchmark for continuous improvement.

Solution: Put everything in writing and go step by step, making constant improvements. Once we decided what business we were in, we were able to create an equity building enterprise. We documented the process for others in our company to follow. Unless it is in writing, you do not own it. More importantly, you cannot benchmark your performance to determine how you are doing. If you carry everything in your mind, you need to be physically present all the time. None of your knowledge is transferable. More importantly, your operations cannot be systematically improved.

Mistake #3: Limited client-tracking systems.

Solution: Take a step back and stop recommending every promising investment that comes your way. Prepare an Investment Policy Statement (IPS) for each client and recommend appropriate investments to meet that policy statement. Focus on a few chosen investments and track them. Make it your job to know everything about those investments and meet every portfolio manager.

Before our company implemented an effective tracking system, we were recommending too many investments. We now handle and track only 12 investments. We know everything about these investments and we're personally acquainted with every portfolio manager. We know these managers as well as we know our own company.

Mistake #4: No consistent marketing plan.

Solution: Become strategic first, before becoming tactical. Strategy is the big picture; tactics carry out the detailed objectives of the overall strategy. Develop strategic marketing programs within your firm. In our company, we work with top marketing consultants to develop our marketing programs. Now if something doesn't fit our overall plan, we don't do it.

Most of us have had at least one successful marketing campaign. Unfortunately, we often move on to the next opportunity without fully developing the current success. One of the most powerful words in the English language is "No." As you become more successful, more opportunities will tempt you. Unless you have your marketing plan, you will be constantly changing directions, frustrating your efforts to reach your next level of success.

Mistake #5: Different investment experience for each prospect.

Solution: Be consistent. No matter who a prospect is, or whom that prospect talks to in our firm, he or she will have the same experience as the next person. This also gives clients the confidence to refer substantial new business to you.

Mistake #6: Not enough time to think. You are overloaded with work and spend most of your time just trying to keep up.

Solution: Take time out to be introspective. Make sure everything in your business is consistent with what you want to accomplish. Most of us do what is urgent, but not what's important. Prioritize the importance of your actions. It is so easy to answer that next phone call, go through the latest mail or read *The Wall Street Journal* and think you are being productive.

You are making a big investment in time to read this book. But what is the chance that when you get back to your office on Monday, you will begin implementing some of our suggestions? It's much more likely that you will get caught up in voice-mail messages, e-mail and answering your employees. Strategic planning often takes a back seat to the many little crises of the day unless we schedule time for it. After you have completed your business plan, schedule a minimum of two hours each week to reflect on whether you are still on track. Examine last week's calendar. Were your activities consistent with the goals you set for yourself and your business? Do not forget to schedule quality time for your family and for yourself.

Each week, look ahead to the next few months to see that what you've scheduled is consistent with your plan; if not, make changes. Promise not to make the same mistakes again. Remember, balance is important. So often we forget that we are in business so that we have the opportunity for more life.

Mistake #7: Focus on delivering performance and not on managing expectations. Most financial planners promise exceptional performance which they can't deliver, but have caused their clients to expect it.

Solution: Stop promising to outperform the market. Instead, promise to deliver market returns. By doing that, you'll deliver exactly what you have promised your clients. You'll never again have to apologize for performance that's lower than your clients' expectations. How many times have you had to apologize for something unanticipated and out of your control? Do not set up false expectations that you know in your heart you cannot deliver. There is no quicker way to lose the confidence of clients.

Mistake #8: Providing free financial planning services, in hopes of gaining business.

Solution: Build outside strategic alliances to provide extra services. At one time, we had four full-time financial planning case writers working for us. We believed we were adding value. However, when we discontinued this approach, we became more focused and stopped being overloaded. Instead, we built strong strategic alliances with outside CPA firms that could help us address financial planning issues.

We co-sponsored, with a "big six" CPA firm, a workshop entitled "Maximizing Wealth for Shareholders," where the audience was composed of CEOs and CFOs of small publicly traded companies. During the presentation, one of our advisors explained the benefits of executive financial planning. As a result, a CEO asked us if we would be willing to hold a one-day workshop for his top ten executives. He pointed out that his firm had gone public recently and the selling restrictions for his executive group were soon to expire.

The CEO asked our CPA co-sponsor what he would charge for a one-day workshop. We waited with trepidation for his response; knowing that, in the past, we would have gladly done it for free. What financial advisor would not give up a day for the potential of ten new clients, each with millions to invest? We certainly didn't want to lose this opportunity due to charging too much. When the CPA answered that they could probably do it for $25,000, our hearts sank.

The CEO thought for a moment and stated that seemed reasonable. On the spot, we scheduled a date for one of our most profitable workshops ever; even though the CPA firm received most of the $25,000 for their work developing material for the presentation. The increased credibility added much to our success. The workshop was also much better, since everyone was highly motivated because of the fee. The best part was, the CPA firm did the financial plans, and we prepared the Investment Policy Statement for each client. Focus and strategic alliances do work.

Mistake #9: The business is focused on you. If you are not there that day, you don't make money.

Solution: Get the focus off yourself. If your business is focused around you, then every client expects to see only you. There's no leverage. By creating a collective group of people providing a service, your clients will be more willing to meet with anyone in your firm. In the past, we didn't know where our business lives stopped and our personal lives began. A person buying such a practice would discount it heavily or, more likely, not even consider buying it. Now, we surround ourselves with the best and brightest people in investment management—on the academic and research side, and in marketing, public relations and software development—thus, increasing our credibility dramatically.

Mistake #10: Focusing on gross revenue, not on net income.

Solution: It's what you take home that counts. Shift your focus to producing profitability. Early on, we discovered that gross revenue meant very little in terms of building equity. We then focused on building a business that had a recurring revenue stream and, more importantly, a predictable bottom line net profit. The prime determinant of equity value is your sustainable profitability.

As advisors, we consistently won the award for top producer at our broker/dealer's annual convention. We can recall wondering why we didn't feel great about it. The answer was, while we had a great gross income, the costly methods of mass marketing and of providing complete financial planning left us pretty lean on the net income. We did not feel we deserved any award.

Even worse, if we were getting the award for top production, how was everyone else doing? Obviously, not well. Most of us had dysfunctional businesses and just didn't know it. Knowing what we now know, we will never again lose sight of the importance of net income.

Mistake #11: Not using technology effectively.

Solution: Take advantage of the new paradox. Small companies have a competitive advantage over large companies because they can more easily apply new technology. They do not have to convert cumbersome old legacy systems to new. We now use state-of-the-art technology and upgrade regularly. Today's client-server technology allows you to accomplish, relatively cost effectively, anything you can clearly imagine. Use your lack of systems to leapfrog over the competition.

Mistake #12: Few cost controls.

Solution: Design your systems with cost in mind. In the beginning stages, we focused entirely on the growth of our business. We thought that as long as a new project or a new person would bring in more revenue than it cost, we'd do it. This incremental revenue based planning led us to severely over-expand during our financial planning days.

Later, by designing a financial management system with cost uppermost in mind, we became cost effective. Now we can successfully budget and track costs for each specific project and person to determine what actions are appropriate to the most cost-effective achievement of our goals.

Mistake #13: Being dependent or independent.

Solution: There are three ways you can relate to your business—as dependent, independent, or interdependent. Dependence is totally relying on the support and direction of another firm. Most of us have learned the hard way that to put our total trust in another firm just doesn't make good business sense. Our experiences have made us skeptical of promises made to us by others. Many who have experienced the bust of firms like Southmark and Integrated Resources firsthand like us have moved to an even higher level of cynicism. These experiences have led many to strike out on their own. It's unlikely, however, that you can do everything well by yourself.

The successful way to create equity in business is to become interdependent. In an interdependent business relationship, duties are shared between you, others in your firm, and your business partners, such as your broker/dealer and TAMPs. Everyone benefits by creating a win-win-win environment.

By getting your systems in place—documenting each step of your operation, taking the focus off yourself, putting in cost controls, being consistent in your marketing plan, and taking the time to be introspective - you can maximize your journey to success in building a million dollar fee-based practice. The opportunities for you to do well, by doing well by your clients, are endless.

I

BUILDING A HUGELY SUCCESSFUL
ASSET MANAGEMENT BUSINESS

We started by examining the challenges financial advisors face and barriers that must be overcome. It is easy to get locked inside these challenges and never reach your next level of success. To accomplish the next level, you will need to move from being a technician with an entrepreneurial seizure to being a truly effective businessperson, as Michael Gerber states in his book, *The E-Myth*. To make this real, you must leave your old company behind and begin to build a "New Co." The foundation of your New Co. will be the endless opportunities that the asset management business presents. In Part I, you will see why no other industry has as much promise as the asset management business to do well by doing good.

CHAPTER TWO

THE OPPORTUNITIES FOR SUCCESS IN THE
INVESTMENT MANAGEMENT BUSINESS

The asset management industry is one of the few industries in America today in which an individual can get started with almost no capital. In a short period of time, an investment advisor can build a substantial income and a lucrative business, establishing the foundation for personal wealth and family security. The best part is this can all be accomplished while doing well by your clients.

Our message is simply that you can build an asset management business worth well over a million dollars, plus a great lifestyle full of fun, friendships, personal time, and job satisfaction from helping clients realize their financial dreams. That is, if you know what to do to grow a successful business in this field. That's just what you'll learn in this book.

If you don't approach the establishment and growth of your business correctly, the experience can be a nightmare—long hours, a grueling schedule, and no personal time. In fact, this industry has such a high burnout rate that 80% of those who enter the financial services industry are gone within the first five years. Of those who do survive the first five years, another

80% leave the business in the next five. So what separates the burned out or mere survivors from the truly successful?

After 12 years as an advisor and six years of running an asset management business, plus making it our business to observe what the best and brightest have done, we think we have a good idea of what it takes to be successful in this field. Success leaves behind a trail of clues. If you follow that trail, and systematically and consistently replicate it, your business will be prosperous. If you go off the trail, you'll waste valuable time and energy, and your business will most likely never achieve the level of success possible. You owe it to yourself, your family and your clients to be the best you can be. Now let's look at the opportunities our industry presents.

Last year, 1996, was a banner year for Wall Street firms, with record earnings. We will soon see more investment advisors exploring new options and going independent will become easier. Technology is also expanding, which makes the independent investment advisor's job even more efficient and effective. Successful advisors will become less like employees and more like entrepreneurs. The turnover of registered representatives on Wall Street will continue to increase.

Affluent investors want a seasoned professional who will help them reach decisions, provide information and contacts for products, and make judgments about investments particularly appropriate for them. In building your business, you must effectively deliver what investors perceive as value to attain real success.

To better understand the affluent, we will explore a number of interesting findings, primarily provided to us by Charles Schwab & Company of San Francisco. Schwab conducted a telephone survey of 575 participants and four focus groups, with two on each coast. Charles Schwab has allowed us to share some of the highlights from this recent research which focuses on three major areas: U.S. Wealth and Investors, Competitor Approaches, and Customer Needs and Behaviors. This division will provide you with a framework to better understand both the opportunities and challenges of the asset management industry.

Concentration of U.S. Wealth and Investors
You Should Target

There is a high concentration of wealth among the 260 million people in the U.S. living in 91 million households. Today, Americans have $13.3 trillion total in investable assets. Much of that is concentrated in what we will call the "super affluent" market of households with over $5 million of investable assets, but an even greater amount of wealth is tied up in what we will call the "affluent" market of households with over $500,000 but less than $5 million of investable assets. It's this affluent market that we think is the key to your success.

Discounters are aimed at the mass market of households with under $500,000 of investable assets, but that's not your market, unless you want to compete primarily on price and high volume. Neither is the super affluent market your target, because there are so few of them—and most of those are tied up in bank trust departments and other high-end providers. Approximately 3 million of "affluent" households have 42% of the wealth. The average affluent household's investable assets are $1.8 million. In total, this segment represents $5.6 trillion of investable assets. It's these households that make up your ideal market. Your marketing plan should be to go out into the local community, find the affluent, identify a specific target niche, get to know them, and begin building trust. You will soon develop a solid client base.

Both recent trends, increased savings and the liquefaction of existing wealth, present great opportunities for financial advisors. Schwab predicts consumers will increase savings because consumers perceive that two of their "traditional pillars" are disintegrating—one, faith in Social Security being available for their retirement; and two, the drying up of defined benefit plans. As consumers become increasingly cognizant of these pillars crumbling, they'll increase their search for a new savings vehicle.

Increased savings is one reason why there will be more assets for financial advisors to manage in the future. The other is that consumers have large amounts of money tied up in non-liquid forms of investments, such as real estate and small businesses, that they will liquidate as they age. As the Baby Boom population gets older and heads for retirement, they're going to sell their big houses and small companies, roll out of their 401(k) plans, etc. All that money becomes viable for financial advisors to manage.

These trends indicate that the number of households with between one and five million in investable assets will be the fastest growing, at an estimate of 19% over the next five years. This is not the investor with $50,000 and it's not the investor with $25 million. It's the middle affluent market, made up of the rich but not the super rich. That's the clientele you want to target.

WHAT ARE YOUR COMPETITORS DOING?

There is no shortage of competitors for this $13.3 trillion. In the chart below, we see a snapshot of where money is today. The majority of investable dollars, surprisingly, is in full commission brokerages and retail banks. The wirehouses have 38%, a commanding lead. New York-based Merrill Lynch, by itself, has $750 billion. Our niche of investment managers has only $767 billion, or 6%. It is surprising that with all the publicity discount brokerage firms receive, they have even less of the pie than investment managers—only $550 billion, or 4% of the total.

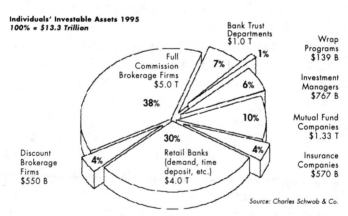

Figure 2-1:   A Snapshot of US Wealth by Channel is Revealing

While many of us consider discount brokerage firms to be our primary competitors, they're not. If we focus on the target market of affluent investors, the competition becomes clear: the full commission brokerages.

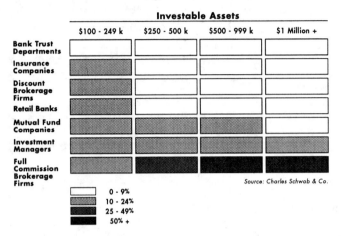

Figure 2-2:   Percentage of Affluent Investors Using Institution as Primary Investments Provider

Bank trust departments nationally have less than 9% of the affluent household market; for most of us, they are not serious competitors at this time. The discount brokerage firms have had little success beyond those households with under $250,000 in investable assets. The same can be said for both insurance companies and retail banks. The action is in these three types of firms: mutual fund companies, investment managers, and full commission brokerage firms. Mutual fund companies are significant participants in the accounts below $1 million. Investment managers are significant players in all size accounts, but the full commission brokerage firms command over 50% of the investable assets in accounts of over $250,000. We have some room to grow in market share.

Merrill Lynch, with its 13,000 "financial consultants," has begun to focus attention on competing more effectively with the financial advisor community with increased emphasis on financial planning, discretionary investment management, and asset-based pricing. With their mutual fund discretionary products, this one firm has collected over $7 billion.

Merrill Lynch has recently introduced a non-discretionary asset-based pricing program entitled "Financial Advantage" that includes no-load funds. In the chart below, we have listed the services offered by Merrill Lynch from marketing information provided to us. The annual fees are over any additional fees earned for selling syndicated products.

	Bronze	Silver	Gold	Platinum
Assets Required	$100 - 250 K	$250 - 500 K	$500 k - 1 MM	$1 - 5 MM
Annual Fee	150 bp	138 - 150 bp	119 - 138 bp	84 - 119 bp
Transactions Per Year Included	12	25	40	50 - 75
Added Features	· Visa Classic	· Online Access	· Global Gold Program	· Preferred Pricing on Trust Services
	· Research Mailings	· ATM Use	· Electronic Bill Payment	· Unlimited Banking Services
	· 25 bp Off Margin Loans	· Wealth Transfer Analysis	· Qualified Plan Analysis	· Charitable Remainder Trust Review

Source: Merrill Lynch

Figure 2-3:   Financial Advantage

Unfortunately, not just Merrill Lynch sees the opportunities. The most effective full commission brokerage firm to date has been Smith Barney of New York, with its 11,000 representatives. Today over half of Smith Barney's income comes from asset-based fees. They have recently announced an asset-based pricing program, which will offer no-load funds in a 1.5% wrap program for accounts less than $200,000.

Historically, banks have attracted the assets of affluent households through their trust departments. They now control $950 billion, which is more than half the discretionary market. Banks are now attempting to use this approach on the retail end. While still a small player, banks' assets have grown at 142% to $1.3 billion. This is double the wirehouses' wrap program growth rate of 60%. Retail banks are likely to pose significant competition in the future due to their comparative advantages of branch networks, broad customer bases, and widely recognized brand names. If they ever do get it right, they're going to be a real threat.

Mutual fund companies and discount brokers are looking to gain greater access to the affluent household market by offering a broad range of services and tools, with varying results.

	Discretionary Money Management Offers	Help & Advice Tools	Affluent Service Offer
Vanguard	· Personal Advisory Service wrap account ($500,000 minimum*) · Star Portfolios (Fund-of-Funds) · Asset Allocation Funds	· Workbooks · Planning/investigating software · Online rep advice aid · Personal financial planning service- $500 financial plans	· Flagship Services (>$500,000) - Individual service
Fidelity	· Portfolio Advisory Service wrap account · Freedom Funds (Fund-of-Funds) · Asset Allocation Funds	· Workbooks · Planning/investing software · Online rep advice aid	· Premium Services (>$200,000) - Team service
Schwab	· Advisor Source · OneSource Portfolios (Fund-of-Funds) · Asset Allocation Funds	· Workbooks · Investing software · Online rep advice aid	· Priority Access (>$1 Million) - Team service for the self-directed investors
	* Personal Advisory Service has a minimum of $2,500		

Source: Charles Schwab & Co.

Figure 2-4: Mutual Fund Companies and Dicount Brokers are Providing a Variety of Tools and Services

To compete effectively with the competition, advisors need to understand the services various providers offer, the tools they utilize, and at what cost to the consumer.

There is a high concentration of success among financial advisors. As of June 1996, there were 44,777 Registered Investment Advisors (RIAs), of which only 24,010 were active. If we pull out the 7,583 who earned commissions and other income, we find 16,427 who are fee-based or fee-only. For the purpose of this book, we are focused on individual assets. So, if we separate the 1,376 institutional managers, we find there are 15,051 managers of fee compensated, individual assets. These 15,051 financial advisors control $870 billion of assets under management. These assets are not evenly divided. Only 175 advisors have assets under management of over a billion dollars. A larger number, 812, have assets totaling $200 million to $1 billion. Collectively, advisors with over $200 million control 72% of the individual managed assets. The remaining 14,064 managers, with between zero and $200 million of assets under management, have total assets of $240 billion. This averages approximately $17 million per advisor in the below $200 million group—certainly nowhere near what it takes to run a successful business.

No one knows for sure which industry segment will be the ultimate winner of the affluent households' investable assets, but the most likely winner will be those who deliver the highest perceived value on the most cost-effective basis.

Your Clients' Unique Needs and Behavior

Investors' households can be divided into two segments: self-directed and delegators. Self-directed investors want to handle their own investments. They typically enjoy spending time on their investments, with the average time being seven hours per month. This segment has an average age of 48 with the median of investable assets being $84,000.

Delegators by contrast, usually do not enjoy managing their investments, spending only four hours a month on average. They tend to be older, with a median age of 58, and have more assets, on average $200,000. The larger investable asset base appears to be primarily due to the increase in age. Clearly, our target is the delegator, and delegators have strong views of what they deem important:

- 84% of delegators prefer to deal with a single individual.
- 73% want to consult with an expert.
- 72% like to plan ahead five to 10 years.
- 70% would like to become more knowledgeable.
- 70% want to deal with people who know them by name.
- 63% prefer to invest through a large nationally known firm.
- 63% prefer to spend as little time on their investments as possible.
- 53% need help preparing a plan.

- 53% do not trust stockbrokers.
- 52% are not sure if their own financial decisions are right.

Reviewing the results of the survey, it's obvious that affluent delegators are a great market for financial advisors. Unfortunately, your competitors see the same opportunities. Don't spend a lot of time worrying what the discounters are doing on the retail side in the area of help and advice. If you were to visit a discounter's branch, you'd probably be disappointed at the relatively low level of help and advice provided to clients. Schwab has established a Help and Advice Tools hotline at (800)435-4000 for the self directed investor that does an admirable job of assisting investors with less than $100,000 investable. If the caller has over $100,000, he is asked if he would like to consider a financial advisor and, if so, he is referred to a financial advisor working with Schwab. To participate in this referral program, you must join Schwab AdvisorSource^{tm} program. Investment advisors can easily differentiate themselves by giving personalized and ongoing financial advice. Your targeted clients are delegators with $100,000 or more to invest.

Discounters receive an incredible flow of transfers from the full service brokerage firms. The small number of accounts that do leave discounters are primarily the large accounts. These customers didn't leave for cheaper pricing, but rather for more personal advice than discounters offer.

Schwab, Fidelity, Vanguard and other discounters go after the "self-directed" types, investors who do it themselves. Let the discounters take care of the self-directed investor; it's your job to take care of the delegator. Therein lies tremendous opportunity for you as a financial advisor. You're better equipped to handle the delegator-type consumer than you are the self-directed. Don't worry about trying to compete with Schwab, Fidelity or Vanguard; you don't have to. Delegators are more than half the market, 56% of the U.S. population, and they have 62% of the wealth. What you have to do is differentiate yourself from the competitors who also serve this affluent market.

You do need to compete with the major wirehouses. Their national brand names give them a significant competitive advantage. When consumers were asked if they'd be more likely to sign on with a national well-known name such as Merrill Lynch or a local, independent money manager, half went for the well-known name. There was a big "don't know" contingency that probably wants both. You need to develop a business that consistently delivers more value-added than your wirehouse competitors.

In the past, most advisors have chosen to go it alone. The traditional model has been the advisor doing everything: asset aggregation, investment policy statements, asset allocation, investment selection, performance reporting, customer service, and, oh yes, running the business. That's the popular model, but we think there is a better way.

Turnkey Asset Management Programs (TAMPs) like the one we offer at RWB are growing rapidly. Many advisors prefer to remain "asset gatherers" in partnerships with money management firms. In matching up with a TAMP, make sure you share the same investment philosophy. (If you do not, the partnership will not be tenable.) Look to the TAMP to take over all responsibilities other than asset aggregation and client service. Ideally you want to work with only one TAMP to get the maximum leverage from that firm's support systems. It is important for both parties to choose their partner well.

Turnkey Asset Management Programs:

Company	Phone Number
ADAM Investment Services, Inc.	*800-753-2326*
Advisory Consulting Group (AIMS)	*800-553-2326*
Brinker Capital	*800-333-4573*
Callan Associates, Inc.	*415-541-4000*
Centurian Counsel	*800-878-8536*
Clark Capital Management	*800-766-2264*
Clarke Lanzen Skalla	*800-635-3427*
Frank Russell	*206-572-9500*
FundMinder, Inc.	*800-343-3677*
LBS	*800-477-1296*
Lockwood Financial Group, Inc.	*800-467-6134*

Matrix Asset Allocation	*513-563-8015*
Meridian Investment Management	*800-828-4881*
Portfolio Management Consultants, Inc.	*800-852-1177*
R.Meeder Advisory Services	*800-377-8796*
Reinhardt Werba Bowen	*800-366-7266*
RTE Asset Management	*800-552-0551*
Schield	*800-275-2382*
SEI Investments	*800-SEI-1003*

The investment management industry has grown dramatically over the last five years. The future looks even brighter. Consider the following:

1) Enormous consumer wealth. Investment advisors are in the best position to work with private individual wealth, a $13 trillion industry that's segmented and accessible.

2) Money flooding into the industry, due in large part to an expected increase in the savings rate. Savings rates have gained a few digits over the last two years—up from the 4.3% we saw a couple of years ago, and the bottoming out at 3.8%. Rates have been coming back slowly and are expected to continue to rise.

3) The huge liquefaction of wealth in an aging population approaching retirement.

The world has changed from when the asset management business was just a small niche of the industry and few paid it much attention. Merrill Lynch is trying to reinvent itself as a firm delivering financial planning. Prudential Securities of New York runs an ad that reads, "No-loads doesn't have to mean no advice." This is an increasingly competitive industry that's well aligned with consumer interests. We think that fee based financial advice is the best way to get financial advice, and that the industry is going to continue to grow significantly.

One of the biggest challenges is that there are too many opportunities. The secret of business success is focus. In the next chapter, we will show you that by focusing on creating equity, you can begin the journey of building a hugely successful asset management business.

CHAPTER THREE
_____

CREATING EQUITY IN A HUGELY SUCCESSFUL
ASSET MANAGEMENT BUSINESS

W hen we ask advisors in our QuickStart training pro-
gram to tell us what they were promised upon get-
ting their first position in the financial services
industry, they have no problem remembering. The list usual-
ly looks something like this:
- Financial freedom to build wealth by creating equity
- Unlimited income—you can write your own paycheck
- Be your own boss
- Flexibility to take time off
- Help clients achieve financial success

When we ask how many had achieved all the items on the
list during their careers (averaging 15 years), usually no one
raises their hand. The comments are more often that they have
created no equity, that the unlimited income was unrealized,
that being their own boss wasn't what they thought it was, and
that the job flexibility was that they had to work only part
time—12 hours a day. The only promise that most felt they
had realized over their careers was that they had helped their
clients—although there was often some disagreement here.

The greatest challenge the recruiter had told them they would have was to decide just how much money they wanted to make and how soon. Just a little hard work and you'd achieve the good old American dream. Many of us have realized one part of that dream—the *work* part. Perhaps while you have been helping your clients reach financial independence, you have been ignoring your own. Even if you are doing a good job for your clients and making a large income for yourself, you may not be building equity in your business or realizing the quality of life you want. If you continue to do what you are doing now, you will not get the same results. With the competition increasing, your results will decrease unless you work harder or smarter. It's your choice.

There are a lot of you out there, which means lots of competition. Even so, not quite 8% of the registered investment advisors control 95% of all managed assets. A natural process of consolidation is beginning to take place. You are going to have to build value in your business just to compete effectively. Competition is starting to come from a variety of fronts. You need substantial resources to compete and succeed.

RECAPTURING THE AMERICAN DREAM

It's not going to come from just adding more clients. The real change will come from creating value inside your business. You do that by making your business worth buying. Even if you have no desire to sell your firm, you want to build up your firm *as if* you are going to sell it, because that strategy will maximize its value while improving your quality of life. The secret is to create the best systems around. Systems not only make your business profitable and build value, they also benefit your investors. We used to think only about the investors; the idea was always to focus on their needs. But to remain competitive today, you're going to have to think of both your investors and yourself. What you need is a quick and easy template to follow.

If you wanted to sell your asset management business, could you? Do you know how much it's worth? Do you have transferable systems in place? There really isn't a lot of history of firms buying firms. The biggest buyer of institutional money management firms is Boston-based United Asset Management, listed on the New York Stock Exchange. They share some interesting information on pricing a business.

They use three primary factors to determine value in a financial advisory firm: assets under management, gross revenue, and free cash flow.

The first two factors are pretty straightforward. The third, free cash flow, needs an explanation. Free cash flow is net profitability adjusted by fair market compensation for the principals and other non-cash adjustments. Most financial advisors for tax reasons bonus all profits in their business to maximize their after-tax income. For example, one financial advisory business paid $300,000 to its key officer, yet the fair market wage for his position was $150,000. The free cash flow in this case would be $150,000 in profit.

There are variations; for instance, financial planning revenue has little to no value because it's expensive to service, whereas revenue from asset management is highly valued. The following is the average of all transactions publicly available in 1995, provided by United Asset Management:

• 2.1% times the total of assets under management.
• 2.7 times gross revenue.
• 9.7 times free cash flow.

Let's take a closer look: Bob Wilson is sole proprietor of a $100 million financial advisory firm with a gross revenue of $800,000. Wilson pays himself $300,000. He can hire someone to replace him at $150,000, the market wage. So there's a $150,000 free cash flow. Let's use the ratios to give Wilson's business a value.

Start with the assets under management: $100 million times 2.1%, or $2.1 million. Next, gross revenues: $800,000 times 2.7, or $2.16 million. (Almost the same.) Last, free cash flow: $150,000 times 9.7, which works out to $1.455 million. If we calculate a weighted average, the business is worth about $1.9 million. Not bad. He has fulfilled the entrepreneurial dream of creating value. You can do this, too. Unfortunately, it is not this easy to value a business. These are only averages and in almost all cases these are firms with substantially more assets and systems.

BUILDING SUBSTANTIAL EQUITY VALUE

One of our consultants, Mark Tibergien with Management Advisory Services of Moss Adam LLP, located in Seattle, worked with us to develop these 10 key value building strategies you will want to implement:

1. *Plan ahead.* Whether you're going to sell or not, by understanding how firms are valued and designing your business accordingly, you can create huge value for your investors, your employees, and yourself. By planning to create equity, you can more easily accomplish it.

2. *Maintain good financial records.* There is nothing that will kill a sale quicker than the lack of good financial records. From the standpoint of an ongoing business, there's nothing that will kill it more quickly either. We are always surprised when financial advisors don't even produce simple monthly reports of what they've budgeted, what was actually spent, and what was at variance. Who prepares your financial records is important as well. Potential buyers will determine how credible your financial statements are by the firm that prepared them.

3. *Be profitable.* Remember that you're running a business for profit. You can't help anyone if you are out of business. There is no problem in doing *pro bono* work, but understand when it is *pro bono*. Make sure to do most of your work at a competitive rate. Think long-term profits versus short-term transactions. Free cash flow is the primary determinant of value. To maximize your creation of equity you need to be solidly profitable.

4. *Make yourself dispensable.* Build a transferable client base. There's nothing more important than this in both creating equity and improving your quality of life. If you build a system that revolves around you, it will be impossible to transfer the business to anyone else. I had a large client base. I put systems in place to deliver a consistent experience and then turned over my clients to key staff members. We were concerned that clients would leave if they couldn't work with the president of the firm. Instead, I got thank-you notes saying the service had never been better.

Clients wanted a high level of service; that's what they continued to get. You cannot focus all the attention on yourself as the investment guru and expect to be able to make this transition. If you want to grow the firm and/or sell the firm, you must create something larger than just you.

This can be done by forming an alliance with a TAMP. In addition, if you are going it on your own, you should consider establishing an investment committee that you chair which will review all recommendations. This will set the stage with your clients for you to ultimately transfer quarterly meeting responsibility to staff, while you are still involved with their investments.

5. *Monitor key ratios.* Focus on the three ratios: assets under management, revenue, and net profitability. Every month review with your staff other ratios important in your business. Other key indicators would include number of new accounts, any closed accounts, additions, withdrawals, average fee, errors, and your cash position. When examining your key indicators, your reports should be graphed over time so that you can see if any trends are developing that require action.

6. *Apply business management techniques.* You can create tremendous value if you build in the right systems. You have to provide communication, both internal and external. The most valuable assets you have are your employees. Most financial advisors are so busy trying to build their business that they all but ignore their staff. To help your employees help you, they need to be informed. You must create systems that provide for this and they will reward you.

7. *Maintain service, responsiveness, and consistency.* This business is all about strong client relationships. Hold client meetings on a regular basis, at least quarterly. A buyer has to depend on those established relationships. Many financial advisors have grown up in the transactional commission side of the business. Here they were rewarded for doing as many transactions as possible but not for service. If you sold a mutual fund and the client later wanted out; fine, you had already been paid.

Clients often were never contacted unless they initiated the contact. This is the "kiss of death" in the asset management business. It is a "pay-as-you-go" system; if you are not providing added value, there is no reason for the client to continue to pay you. If there is no reason for the client to continue to pay you, there is no reason for a buyer to pay much of a premium for your business.

8. *Identify the right buyer.* Make sure that you understand who the buyer is. How will the buyer add value for your investor clients? Make sure you are not taking all the risks in the transaction. Often a buyer will try to shift all the risk of purchase to the seller through workouts. This is frequently the case when local financial planning firms are acquired. They often do not have the capital to make any significant down payment. Instead they use your cash and cash flow to finance the transaction while taking little or no risk. Each buyer will have its own agenda. You need to understand his or her motivation to make sure it is closely aligned with yours.

9. *Facilitate the transfer.* This is a long-term decision. Don't kid yourself that you can sell a business and be out in 90 days. Figure on a minimum of two years, or no one's going to be interested. More often it will be four years. If you're thinking about selling, make sure you plan out the timetable.

10. *Get help.* These are big, important decisions. If you choose to pursue that full entrepreneurial dream, get professional help. Align yourself with a CPA who does business valuation and is familiar with mergers and acquisitions. Get to

35

know people who have had experience, which you can tap into before you consider any transaction.

To summarize, you have a huge opportunity. Whether or not you are ever going to sell your company, focus on creating maximum value *as if* you are going to sell it. By following certain rules of enhancement and using established ratios for selling an investment, you can design your business to maximize value and achieve everything you've ever dreamed about. And all that is by serving your clients well.

Everyone wants to create equity—few do. To distinguish yourself from the rest of the herd of investment advisors, you must effectively differentiate yourself with a unique message. In our industry, truth can be a unique selling proposition.

II

ESTABLISHING YOUR FIRM'S INVESTMENT PHILOSOPHY

B efore beginning to build your asset management business, you must identify clearly the services you want to offer. Fundamental to your services is your investment philosophy. This will provide the foundation for building your asset management business.

In establishing your firm's investment philosophy, it is critical that you provide value added service. Many financial advisors mistakenly believe their value-added is beating the market averages. Nothing could be further from the truth. In the next three chapters, we explore how you can differentiate yourself from your competitors and add value in what your investors truly need: prevention of costly mistakes and peace of mind. This will provide the foundation for your hugely successful asset management business.

CHAPTER FOUR

SEPARATING NOISE FROM INFORMATION FOR YOUR CLIENTS

The main challenge every financial advisor faces today is to deliver a consistent investment experience to their clients. You will set yourself apart by following investment strategies that are academically grounded. Your job is to help your clients become *informational* investors who understand how markets work and how to apply this understanding so they do not fall prey to the costly mistakes of *noise* investors.

Unfortunately, the vast majority of individual investors are noise investors without even knowing it. What is a noise investor? Noise investors believe that, by regularly reading the many financial publications, they can become insiders to information that gives them some advantage. In our office, we refer to this material as *investment pornography*. It gets investors all excited and confused. Not surprisingly, most noise investors significantly underperform the market.

Let's look at how investment noise causes confusion. Many advisors continue to sell the "hot" mutual funds—the ones with the best performance or track record. They tell their clients that their portfolios are best diversified with many investments. We believe the primary reason that many advisors recommend many mutual funds is that, if they select several funds, at least one is certain to look good. The likelihood of losing their client to disappointment is at least reduced, but this strategy sets up both the advisor and their clients for future failure.

What most advisors don't realize is that the mutual fund manager's main goal is to become the "hot" fund that raises more money. They tend to focus on stock selection and/or market timing—in essence, making bets. Unfortunately, these management strategies are costly to implement, have an extremely low probability of success, and are ineffective in adding value. In fact, these strategies contribute less than 6% of a portfolio's profit determination. Academic studies have found that 94% of returns are generated from making the right asset allocation decisions.

USING THE INVESTMENT METHODOLOGY DECISION MATRIX

We share the following matrix that illustrates our point, which we first learned from Roger Gibson, author of *Asset Allocation*. This matrix classifies investors according to what they believe will be effective in adding value. Identify which quadrant you currently fit into. Our goal in this chapter is to move you into the quadrant that insures the highest probability of consistent success in meeting your clients' expectations.

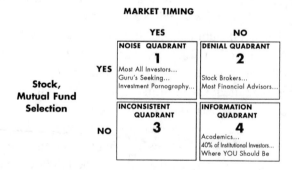

Figure 4-1:   Investment Decision Matrix

Quadrant one is composed of investors who believe that both market timing and fundamental analysis are effective. They believe that they, or others, will uncover stocks or mutual funds that are mispriced and then exploit the mispricing. They want to believe that financial gurus exist who can accurately predict when the market will turn up or down. People also believe that a knowledgeable advisor can pick investments by utilizing research to determine the right individual security or mutual fund. Most of the public is in this quadrant and the media plays to this thinking. The reality is that these methods mostly fail to deliver even market returns.

Quadrant two includes most of the financial services industry. These firms have had the experience to know that they can't predict broad market swings. They also recognize the risk of wrong predictions usually means losing clients. However, because they have access to hundreds of market analysts, they believe they can uncover the one investment option that isn't fairly priced; and thereby, extract value for the investor. It is the "American Dream" revisited to believe that, by going to the right schools, getting the right degrees, working at the right companies, being bright enough and hard working enough, you will be able to uncover mispriced securities which the rest of the market has not recognized. Unfortunately, as un-American as it seems, this methodology appears on average to add no value after cost for investors.

Quadrant three is the tactical allocation quadrant. An investor in this quadrant would have to believe that, even though individual securities and mutual funds are efficient, somehow they, and only they, can see broad mispricing in major sectors of the market. They believe they can exploit this undervalued sector by purchasing it, then waiting for the market to finally recognize its mistake and fully value the sector. To us, it seems fairly arrogant to believe that markets are efficient and that only you can see a broad market mispricing which, someday in the not too distant future, everyone else will catch on to, leaving you with a profit. No prudent investors can be found here.

Quadrant four is where most of the academic community resides. This is where you will find the informational investors. These men and women dispassionately research what works and what does not work. Academic studies indicate that the average risk premium return from active management is negative rather than positive after cost.

The reality is that we're all tempted to sell what people want. And, people want to believe in gurus, market timing, stock selection, and mutual funds—quadrant one. However, there is no evidence that gurus exist.

Let's say you don't believe that markets are efficient. What are the three likely outcomes if, as in quadrant one, you promise to outperform the market?

The best possible outcome is that you will outperform the market. And, if you do, your clients will be happy that you do meet their expectations, but will expect an even greater margin next year. What's the likelihood that next year you will outperform the market by a bigger margin? Last year, 86% of the U.S. large-cap mutual fund money managers didn't keep up with the passive strategy of the Standard & Poor's 500. In the last 10 years, 84% of mutual fund managers didn't keep up.

If you don't outperform the market, a second possible outcome is that you could equal the market. Your clients will be disappointed. Even if you consistently equal the market, you're going to lose your clients. Their expectations are that you were going to beat it; you told them you could.

The third outcome is that you underperform the market. Of course, you're likely to be fired quickly. What's the likelihood that you will underperform the market? The likelihood is well over 50% that you're going to underperform the market after cost. Academic evidence suggests that markets are efficient and it's costly to try to add value. Why do you want to promise that you can outperform the market? It's a loser's game!

If you want to design a consistently successful business, you have no choice but to follow the strategy of quadrant four.

Become an informational advisor. Design your business to recognize that you can't add value by being caught up in the noise. Even if you do not believe markets are efficient, the only prudent way to create substantial value for your clients and equity for yourself is to run your business as if markets were efficient.

The academic evidence suggests that three out of the four quadrants don't add value on average. Indeed, all evidence clearly illustrates to us that markets are extremely efficient. The more you review the academic research, the more convinced you will become also.

The only way you can guarantee consistent experience is to promise what you can deliver. The only thing you can deliver with any degree of certainty is market returns. Where you add value is not by beating the market, but providing peace of mind and keeping investors from making costly mistakes.

We tell our advisors that one of the most liberating experiences is when they move from noise investing to information investing. Once they understand that markets are efficient, they have tremendous peace of mind that they can communicate it to their clients. Their clients start looking at publications and other financial reporting media differently. They begin to recognize the noise and no longer look for investment advice in the media. If they do read the publications or watch television, it is for entertainment only.

By the time you finish reading the next section of this book, you will have a firm grasp on how markets work and you will understand why Wall Street wants noise investors. Noise investors do generate value; they create liquidity for informational investors.

THE EMOTIONAL CURVE OF INVESTING

Now let's look at what happens when clients' emotions are added onto the investment noise that is ever present.

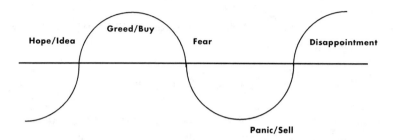

Figure 4-2: The Emotional Curve

The noise investor hears about a hot new mutual fund from a friend or business associate. He gets mildly excited, but holds back until he talks with his broker or financial planner. He flips through the paper, hoping that the mutual fund is going to go up and that a distinct trend will become evident. Let's say the fund does continue to go up and his hope turns to real excitement. It feels as if he's made a secret discovery! Greed strikes. What does he do next?

At this point, many investors call their brokers or no-load providers and purchase the fund. But, as is often the case with hot tips, as soon as the investor purchases the mutual fund, it goes down. Most investors have developed the belief that they can cause any security to go down by just purchasing it. Now what is his emotion?

Often, it is a combination of fear and hope. What is he hoping for? That the fund will go back up. How far up? He would be happy if it just went back up to where it was when he bought it. He could break even and wouldn't have to tell anyone about his secret misadventure. He would vow never to do it again! But the fund continues to go down. What does he do now?

Panic—most investors sell at this point. What happens next? Some new information comes out and the mutual fund hits an all-time high! Now, that's an emotional roller coaster ride that is familiar to every one of your investors.

If an investor continues, based on emotion, to buy high and sell low over a long period of time, he can do significant damage to himself and his family. Tell your prospects and clients this will be their experience, if they are noise investors. Your job is to protect them from themselves and keep them from making these costly mistakes.

Besides the emotional roller coaster syndrome, noise investors become caught up in compartmentalizing different investments. They tend to focus on investments in isolation, but academic studies tell us they should do just the opposite. Each investment should be evaluated as to its singular contribution to the portfolio's total return. Risk is not best evaluated on an asset-by-asset basis, which is the common practice of noise investors.

Most investors feel they are diversifying by being in more than one mutual fund. What they don't realize is that they are *ineffectively* diversified if they are in only one area of the market, such as U.S. large-company stocks. A portfolio containing only one type of investment is unbalanced, having no dissimilar investments that could help carry the whole portfolio through tough times.

An informational advisor focuses on the overall investment strategy and portfolio, rather than viewing a specific investment in isolation. Academic studies tell us that each investment should be evaluated as to its contribution to a portfolio's total return.

The question you should be asking is, "How do I become informationally grounded?" We believe you need to help your investors have a consistent experience, one that delivers consistent returns.

Most financial advisers are looking for the one marketing technique that will have clients beating down their doors. When they realize that the miracle technique doesn't exist, they start looking for the miracle product that will do it. But clients aren't attracted to products or marketing techniques; what they're attracted to is a person who can solve financial problems.

The key is to focus on a specific specialty—whether it be asset management, estate planning, insurance or taxes—

instead of trying to solve all problems for everyone. Along with being focused, you must be very good at what you do for a specific target market. The more you understand a market, the more valuable expertise you can provide to clients.

BECOMING CLIENT-DRIVEN

Problem solving is not just listening to clients and then telling them what they want to hear. It is understanding clients' needs, objectives, and values; and then advising them what you would do if you were in their shoes.

Put the clients' interests first. Financial services marketing has primarily been product-driven, instead of client-driven. Client-driven focus turns the traditional relationship between user and provider of financial services and products upside-down. It ensures that everyone is working for the benefit of the advisor's clients. The biggest difference in a client-driven focus is that the advisor serves as an educator, as opposed to a salesperson.

The advisor has no product per se to sell, but brings experience and education to the client. A client-driven focus, therefore, allows you to be objective and to use your experience and knowledge to develop the best investment solutions. Since the financial advisor is not motivated by a commission structure, he is free to meet the needs of the investor. Commission-driven marketing can create an inverse relationship between the size of the commission and the quality of the investment solution.

We aren't downplaying that brokers do a great job of meeting the needs of speculators. They can provide all sorts of ways to take a roll of the dice. The problem is that too many people continue to confuse speculation with investing. With speculation, you want somebody with a crystal ball. It may not work very well, but as long as you're guessing about the future, you might as well stack the odds in your favor as high as possible. It's still pretty much a losing game, but it appeals to greed.

There is an entire sector set up to serve the need to speculate. It's still a very small part of the overall financial service industry that is set up to actually serve the investor.

A typical investment delivery system is like a car dealership. When you go to a Ford dealership, you know the salesman is there to sell you one of his cars. You expect him to do everything in his power to sell you a Ford. He's not expected to be objective. He doesn't work at developing a long-term relationship because he knows it is unlikely that the next car you buy will be another Ford.

This same delivery system has carried over to the investment business. The major brokerage houses advertise to try to convince you that they are the best at doing this or that. But ultimately, they have become like the superstore car dealers carrying all lines. People now perceive that they don't get objective advice from a commission-based purveyor and that's why we're seeing the fee-only financial advisor business exploding.

Successful fee-only advisors have mastered the ability to develop a long-term relationship that was unnecessary when the compensation was transaction-based. Understand that your livelihood depends upon your investors keeping their assets under your management for an extended period of time. That will only happen when your clients know that you are truly working for them. That is why it is crucial to make certain that your business is client-driven.

Most financial advisors have been taught to uncover their clients' desires by asking questions designed to place clients into an investment hierarchy system and then match a product to that desire. The advisors are not trying to understand their clients' actual needs, only what clients think they want. However, Modern Portfolio Theory teaches that it is the portfolio as a whole that counts, not the results of individual investments.

When you follow a client-driven approach, you have to know which mix of asset classes stands the best probability of helping the client meet her objectives. If you follow the old product-driven approach, you may be placing your client in risky investments, where the market does not reward your client. To be client-driven, you must know this information and be able to distinguish between what people say they want and what really works.

Of course, clients will question you when the best performing asset class significantly outperforms the portfolio's total return. To help you better frame the benefits of diversification so that your client will understand your focus on their needs, we consulted with our Chief Investment Officer, Meir Statman, a professor of finance at Santa Clara University and a national expert in behavioral finance.

Imagine that it is time to renew the insurance policy on your home and you have to pay another $800 for the coming year. This reminds you that a year ago, you paid $800 to the insurance company and that money is now gone forever; you received nothing but a canceled check. Are you so upset and frustrated that you are going to cancel your insurance policy? Of course not, because you know that the fact that you did not collect on your insurance policy means that no one burglarized your home, nor was it destroyed by some disaster. Insurance helps you reduce the risks of owning a home.

Diversification is like insurance. It helps reduce the risk of the overall portfolio because assets in the portfolio have dissimilar returns. When a fire consumes a house, the return on the house is a big negative number. But this is also the time when the insurance company pays and the return on the insurance policy is a big positive number.

The relationship between the returns on the house and on the insurance policy is perfectly dissimilar. The correlation between the two is perfectly negative, a minus one. You always get paid when you sustain a loss on the house, and you never get paid when you do not sustain a loss.

The relationship between the returns on the various assets in the portfolio is not perfectly dissimilar but dissimilar enough, surely, to unnerve us from time to time. In a year when returns on large U.S. stocks are very high, returns on

Japanese stocks might be negative. In a year when returns on large U.S. stocks are low, returns on bonds might be high.

The return on your portfolio in every period is always somewhere in the middle—always better than the worst performing asset class and always trailing the best performing asset class. You never shoot the lights out, but you never go bust. This is what dissimilar returns, diversification, and reduction in risk are all about.

A noise advisor might claim that diversification is nothing but a guarantee of mediocrity. Why hold a diversified portfolio of many asset classes where your return will always be in the middle of the pack when you can forecast the winning asset and place your portfolio entirely in that asset? One year, you will be all in large U.S. stocks and another, you will be all in Japanese stocks. To follow that line of reasoning—why pay for insurance every year when you can forecast whether a fire would break out this year or not?

You are wise when you do not try to forecast whether a fire would break out this year and you are equally wise when you do not try to forecast when asset classes will outperform others. The sorry records of those, such as Granville, Prechter and Garzarelli, who have tried to forecast which assets would excel are by now well-known. But anecdotes are not enough; we need to examine the data systematically, as all scientists do.

Michael Solt and Meir Statman analyzed the weekly forecasts of more than 140 writers of investment newsletters for the period from 1963 to 1985 in a *Financial Analyst Journal* article. They found there is a zero correlation between the bullishness and bearishness of newsletter writers and subsequent stock returns; you would do as well by tossing a coin. Statman is currently updating this study through the present, and can tell you that newsletter writers have not improved their forecasting ability one bit.

Diversification is the best way to manage risk and long-term returns. You can choose to take more risk for higher long-term returns; but the risk you take with a diversified portfolio is a wise, systematic risk that is likely to be compensated with higher long-term returns. Meir and I have written about a chase after illusions in our paper, "Performance Games," which was published in the winter 1997 edition of the *Journal of Portfolio Management*. We describe the games that actively managed mutual funds play with their investments, their benchmarks, and their customers. We also describe the cognitive errors that lead investors to fall for these games and confuse illusions for reality. You may contact us if you would like to receive a copy. It will provide you with several stories you can share with your clients.

A typical stockbroker might push products designed to fit almost every financial situation. This type of stockbroker has a credenza lined with prospectuses and financial sales literature. When a new prospect walks in the door and wants an investment that can provide growth, this broker picks a growth and income mutual fund off the shelf. When the prospect rejects it in search of a tax advantage, the broker simply reaches back to the shelf to select a variable annuity product. If the investor now says he wants tax-free income, the broker obliges by producing municipal bond sales literature. This broker is really just a facilitator. He will not only do a disservice to the investors, but will never create equity in his business.

One of our clients, a physician, had $7 million saved for his retirement when we first met. One million dollars was invested with five different brokerage accounts and the rest was in Treasury bills. He told us he needed to invest for growth and income, as he was now contemplating retirement. This prospect had already interviewed nearly 30 different financial advisors who had all said they could provide whatever he wanted. Needless to say, he was very jaded by the time he came to see us.

We didn't automatically reach into our credenza for a product; we asked him a lot of questions about his total investment picture. We then educated him about our investment philosophy and the way we manage money through the investment consulting process. He insisted on inappropriate investments and had initially rejected our recommendations. We were prepared to walk away from his business. We told him we would not participate in what we believed over time would be costly mistakes. No account was important enough to have us forget that we were in the business of helping clients become informational investors.

He decided to work with us. When we asked him why, he said, "You're the only advisor who didn't reflect back my words and try to tell me what you thought I wanted to hear." Investors want financial advisors who are confident with their advice and are ready to stand behind it.

Advisors are going to have to learn this new information, and distinguish between what people say they want and what really works. If you focus on delivering the best advice for solving a client's specific problems, you will have a loyal client for life who will refer everyone he knows. You will have effectively differentiated yourself from all the other advisors—he can trust you! And he will be right.

You can tell your clients that, regarding financial gurus, there is both good and bad news. The bad news is that gurus do not exist. The good news is that they do not need them. Capital markets work. Every publicly traded company has as one of its primary goals to maximize shareholder value. Some will be successful. Others will not. On average, their return will be the cost of capital. Assisting your clients in capturing the market return will increase substantially the probability of their success. Enlightened self-interest works.

Next, we will show you how you can successfully meet your clients' needs through incorporating our five key concepts of asset class investing and our interpretation of how Modern Portfolio Theory should be applied.

CHAPTER FIVE

FIVE KEY CONCEPTS TO INVESTMENT SUCCESS

In working with thousands of investors in all walks of life, from individuals just getting started to the CEOs of some of the largest corporations in the country, we have identified several fundamental needs facing all investors. As an advisor, you need to understand these needs first before trying to provide any client solutions. We will begin by identifying the five fundamental needs that all investor have.

Next, we will show you how you can successfully meet these needs through the five key concepts of asset-class investing from Modern Portfolio Theory. Incorporating these concepts into your investment solution will allow you to meet your clients' financial needs and build stronger client-advisor relationships.

Risk Aversion

Investors are risk-averse. Some might argue that a better phrase might be "risk ignorant." Only a few investors truly understand the concept of risk. If they did, the number of investors who have been disappointed in how their investments have worked would be cut in half. Most investors who are risk ignorant often take inappropriate risk, which results in the huge number of lawsuits and arbitration hearings. Billions of dollars are still sitting in bank savings accounts, yielding approximately the inflation rate, due to this aversion to risk.

Most investors recognize that they are taking some risk, but do not know how to quantify the amount. Your job is to help them understand the risk exposure that they should be taking. Most investors do not even understand that by investing in Treasury bills, which we often refer to as risk free investments, they are exposing themselves to some risk. When you calculate the investor's Treasury bill net return after tax and inflation, he is often assured of little or no return at all. Prudent investors want to know how best to safeguard their life savings. By helping them understand the risk return trade-off and embracing the level with which they feel comfortable, you can not only help them make informed decisions, but also help them have the highest probability of maximizing their return at the level of risk they are comfortable with.

What is risk? Risk is nothing more than the uncertainty of future rates of return. Risk is created by the volatility of the marketplace. Volatility measures the rate and range of the up and down movements of the price of a security. Will Rogers used to say "don't tell me about the return *on* my money until you tell me about the return *of* my money." The less certain you are that an investment's actual return will be close to its expected return, the more risk that investment carries. Historical risk of an investment can be statistically measured using standard deviations. A key component of any investment plan is understanding and measuring risk. Investment risk can be measured using standard deviation to signify volatility in terms of past performance.

Standard deviations describe how far from the mean the performance has been, either higher or lower. If the distribution of returns is normal, one standard deviation added to or subtracted from the mean will encompass about 68% of the occurrences; two standard deviations cover approximately 95%. For example, in the following chart, the average arithmetic annual return from 1926 to 1996 for the S&P 500 was 10.71%. The standard deviation for the S&P 500 for that period was 20.31. We would expect that returns would fall between 10.4 to 31.0% approximately two-thirds (68%) of the time, if we utilize the Standard & Poor's 500 Index's historical standard deviation of 20.3. The higher the standard deviation of return, the higher the risk involved with the investment.

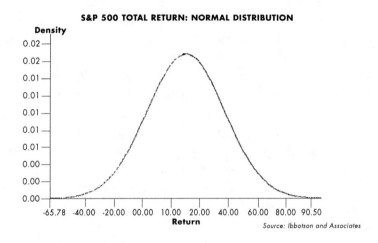

Figure 5-1:   Standard Deviation as a Measure of Risk

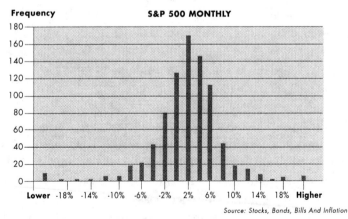

Figure 5-2:   S&P 500 Monthly 1926 - 1996

We have illustrated what the distribution of returns would have been if the returns were a normal bell shape distribution. The actual monthly distributions for the Standard & Poor's 500 Index from 1926 to 1996 were not quite as neat.

While the distribution is not perfectly normal, the standard deviation measure helps to explain what the distribution will likely be. The greater the range of returns — the greater the risk — the larger the standard deviation. Generally, the current price of a security reflects the expected total return of an investment and its perceived risk. The lower the risk, the lower the return expected. Risk can be classified into two broad categories: loss of principal and loss of purchasing power. The risk of losing principal comes from investing in securities whose value fluctuates either due to systematic risk or non-systematic risk. Systematic risk is that risk which is common to the whole economy and cannot be diversified away. A measure of extra return, or risk premium, is demanded by investors to bear this market risk.

Nonsystematic risks, or diversifiable risks, are those specific risks associated with an individual company that is independent of market risk. Nonsystematic risk can be diversified away. The market does not reward you for risks that can be diversified away. Unfortunately, most investors do not understand how to eliminate nonsystematic risk.

The risk of losing purchasing power is generally derived from investing in assets whose expected rates of return are too low to counter the erosion of their principal value by taxes and inflation.

Each of your investors has her own risk tolerance level. It is the trade-off between the risk that they are willing to take to receive a specified expected rate of return and their financial condition, objectives, and needs. You should not have your clients take more risk than they are comfortable with. Doing so is the surest road to financial failure for both your client and yourself. If there is a downturn and you have taken more risk than the client is comfortable with, your client will close the account and probably promise never to work with you again. If you designed your client's portfolio with his risk tolerance in mind before the downturn, you will be able to help your client ride it out to investment success.

Return Enhancement

If your clients are like most investors, what they want is candy (i.e. huge returns), but what they need is a balanced meal (a well-diversified portfolio) so they can survive the long run. This is the essence of the selection process most investors go through when they read the financial press or consult their stockbroker or financial advisor. They are looking for the best way to enhance their returns without a realistic consideration of risk. It is incumbent on you to develop a framework of return with an acceptable level of risk for each of your clients.

Investors want to believe that there is an investment guru who can point out the investments that have high expected rates of return with little, or better yet, no risk. They think, "If only I search a little harder, I can find the right oracle." The media plays to this pursuit. Most investors do not think of themselves as sufficiently knowledgeable, so they are tempted to grasp at the newest prophecy by the latest superstar investment guru. Our society reinforces hero worship. There has to be a winner. There has to be an easy way.

To be successful you need to help your investors understand that fulfillment of this search for the "investment holy grail" is not through finding a guru who will show you the light, but in achieving an understanding of how markets work and applying this knowledge effectively. You need to help your investors understand the concepts behind investing instead of focusing on the last few years of a mutual fund's performance.

Our definition of a sophisticated investor is anyone who has invested money at least once, lost it, and didn't like the empty feeling they were left with. Most investors certainly meet that definition. If they have been investing for more than five years they are very likely to have some horror stories to tell. Think of your own investment experiences. The challenge you face in managing your client expectations is to resist getting caught up in the numerous magazines and investment newsletters that play to our emotions and offer contradictory advice. One of the reasons why many investors fail is because decisions are often based on misleading information.

Expected return is generally understood to mean the statistically achievable return (based on historical data and future probability assumptions) over a sufficiently long time horizon. Expected returns are theoretical returns; they are not guaranteed future performance. However, calculating expected rates of return provides you with a guide to determine whether that investment should be made. Secondly, it allows for a tracking of realized performance as contrasted with the expected performance. This allows you to stay on track and know you're on track.

For security analysis, the expected return of a portfolio is the weighted average of all the expected returns of the investments that comprise the portfolio. The expected rate of return is what the prudent investor attempts to maximize at his selected level of risk. The success of the strategy is dependent upon the assumptions that were made to calculate the expected return.

Desire to Meet a Future Financial Objective

We all have financial goals we're working towards. It could be having enough money to send children or grandchildren to college, having financial independence, or providing for a comfortable retirement. Often these goals change through the years. Your clients' goals will be determined by the dollar amount they have to invest and the amount of time they have to get there.

For most investors the number one goal is having a secure retirement. They want to be able to live comfortable without outliving their money. Investors of all ages share this concern. Can you think of anything more frightening than to be 85 years old and in perfect health with no money? Or worse, having to return to work?

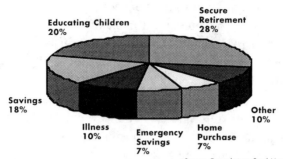

Figure 5-3:   Areas of Concern

Investors indicated that securing their retirement was their number one goal, with educating their children a close second.

Dependable Income Stream

To reach financial independence and retirement goals, your clients will likely have to develop a dependable income stream either now or sometime in the future. Many investors depend on a single asset class like a savings account which often guarantees that they'll never reach financial independence. The challenge is not only to get a higher rate of return, but also at a level of risk that is reasonable and will allow you to stay invested for the long-term.

What is your "real rate of return?" The income stream your clients need today is not the income stream that they will need tomorrow. Just think, if you were planning your retirement in 1976, you might have budgeted your income needs based on houses that cost $35,000, cars under $5,000, and gas at less than 30 cents a gallon. What was a very comfortable retirement income in 1976 would be a struggle today, unless the income grew to provide for the significant increases in cost of living. Over the last 20 years inflation would have eroded by two-thirds your income. Think how this would have affected your family's lifestyle. Their quality of life would have been greatly reduced. Most investors know they need to provide for inflation, but have no idea how to accomplish it.

Liquidity

What if your clients had an emergency? Without having investment liquidity, they will not be able to respond. Liquidity is the ability to realize the value of your investments by selling. Liquidity solves these problems and reduces the barriers investors face to get started in a proper and prudent investment program. An effective rule of thumb is that your clients should have six months of living expenses in cash equivalencies.

Start with a Clean Sheet of Paper

Once you have reviewed your clients' financial needs, you are in a position to design an investment program to help meet them. Recently, one of the most popular concepts, in business management circles is process management—which is often referred to as "reengineering." This is nothing new. Knowing your process, you know where you are, where you want to go, and how you are going to get there, without getting caught up in the distractions.

In building your clients' investment program, you can use many of these reengineering techniques to get started. The first step is to start with a clean sheet of paper. For the moment, set aside your biases. We are very fortunate that a tremendous body of knowledge has been built by the academic community that's been empirically tested.

The Five Key Concepts to Investment Success

Investing can at times seem overwhelming, but the academic research can be broken down into our Five Key Concepts to Investment Success. If you examine your own life, it is the simpler things that consistently work. Successful investing is no different. However it is easy to have our attention drawn to the wrong issues. These wrong issues can derail our journey.

CONCEPT 1

UTILIZE DIVERSIFICATION EFFECTIVELY TO REDUCE RISK.

Most of us understand the concept of diversification: "Don't put all your eggs in one basket." However, no matter how sophisticated we are, it's easy to get caught in this trap. Many investors have a large part of their investment capital in their employer's stock even though they understand that they are probably taking too much risk. They justify their holdings due to the large capital gains tax that they would have to pay if they withdrew funds—or they imagine that the company is just about to take off. Often it is the only investment they know anything about and this creates a false sense of comfort.

Our firm's corporate headquarters being in Silicon Valley provides us with a very high percentage of clients who watched their companies go public and themselves become millionaires. Too many do not understand the risk they are taking by maintaining their position, rather than diversifying. They could continue to reach their families' financial goals after tax, if they would only diversify. Unfortunately, some learn of the risk unique to their company only after the stock has plummeted and they are no longer on track to achieve their financial goals.

Quite often, investment portfolios that are diversified in more than one stock are ineffectively diversified, and usually concentrated in only one area of the market, such as U.S. large-company stocks. This sets the investor up for both an emotional and a financial roller coaster ride. With only one type of investment, there will be no other investments that will help balance the portfolio through tough times.

The overall risk in a portfolio is *not* the average risk of each of the investments; it can actually be less if your investments do not move together. Simply by including investments in your portfolio that don't move in concert, you can reduce the specific risk of individual investments. When investments are combined that move differently in time, in proportion, and/or in direction, you have the basis for effective diversification. "Dissimilar price movement diversification" protects you from having all your investments go down at the same time, thereby reducing risk.

Examine your current portfolio recommendations and try to determine which investments you recommend today that do not move in tandem. As you go through this book, we will illustrate many different combinations of investments that exhibit this dissimilar price movement concept. For example, large-company and small-company stocks do not tend to move at the same rate or direction.

CONCEPT 2

DISSIMILAR PRICE MOVEMENT DIVERSIFICATION
ENHANCES RETURN.

A mathematical fact: If you have two investment portfolios that have the same average or arithmetic return, the one with the lower volatility will have the greater compound or geometric rate of return over time. Let's assume that we have two mutual funds with different investment goals, which you have owned for two years. Both of them have an average arithmetic annual rate of return of 10%. How would you determine which fund had better performance?

You would expect that the ending value of each mutual fund would be the same, but nothing could be further from the truth. Unless they have the same risk or volatility, that will not happen. If one of the mutual funds took much more risk and was therefore more volatile, their ending values would be significantly different. Mutual fund A is much less volatile than mutual fund B and, as a result, has a greater compound rate of return and a higher value at the end of two years. The risk of a portfolio can be less than the average risk of the component investments. To the extent that assets do not move in concert with each other, their specific risks can be diversified away. If two portfolios have the same average return, the one with the lower volatility will have the greater compound rate of return over time. Mutual fund A has the least volatility (less up and down movement). As a result, it has a higher long-term geometric rate of return and wealth is enhanced over time.

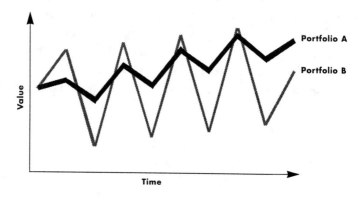

Figure 5-4: Two Portfolios with the Same Average Rate of Return

The best use of this key concept for investment success is the combination of investments within a portfolio that move dissimilarly, thus reducing the volatility of the portfolio. This is particularly important when your client is withdrawing income. The lower volatility will provide both a more stable income stream and increased terminal wealth. Look at your recommended investments that make up your model portfolios. Does the most volatile investment have the higher compounded return? Probably not.

CONCEPT 3

INSTITUTIONAL ASSET CLASS MUTUAL FUNDS

Many financial advisors who understand the first three concepts attempt to use traditional retail mutual funds to implement them. This use of actively managed funds is like trying to fix a sink with a screwdriver when you really need a pipe wrench. You need the right tools.

Initially, institutional asset class mutual funds were not available to advisors. Often the minimum investment for these mutual funds was in the millions of dollars, effectively removing them from reach for most advisors. When we first started offering our investment strategies, we were forced to use the retail mutual funds available to the general public. We found significant structural problems with these retail mutual funds. We didn't have any choices when we first got started. But along the way we discovered better tools. You will too.

Institutional asset class mutual funds are mutual funds which represent whole market segments of securities with similar risk characteristics. They can be used as tools to achieve effective dissimilar price movement diversification. In the past, they have only been available to large institutional investors.

The four major attributes that institutional asset class mutual funds possess are: lower operating expenses, lower turnover resulting in lower taxes, lower trading costs, and consistently maintained market segments.

Lower Operating Expenses

Institutional asset class mutual funds are true no-load mutual funds. A true no-load fund has no sales commissions when you purchase or redeem shares. They have no back-end loads, redemption fees or 12b-1 marketing fees. However, all mutual funds have operational expenses that include management fees and administrative expenses. The average retail equity fund today has a total expense ratio of 1.64%. The expense ratio is the operating expenses expressed as a percentage of average net assets. Operating expenses include management, administrative, and custody fees. The average retail mutual fund operating expenses are almost three times greater than those available to institutions. It's the difference from buying retail versus wholesale. Other factors being equal, lower cost leads to higher rates of return over time.

Lower Turnover Resulting in Lower Taxes

The average retail mutual fund had approximately a 86% turnover rate in 1996. This indicates that 86% of the mutual fund assets were traded in 1996. If you've invested $100,000, approximately $86,000 will have been bought and sold in the underlying securities for the year. This is important because each time you trade, there is a transaction cost involved— whether it's a commission and/or the "bid/ask" spread—which can easily amount to much more than the total operating expenses that are disclosed in the prospectus.

Why do retail mutual funds have such high turnover? For a few reasons: First, we've already stated that they're under tremendous pressure to perform. Second, the only way that a mutual fund manager can add value "perceived in the market" is to attempt to guess market turning points or the individual securities that are going to outperform the market. Just attempting these two feats creates substantial turnover. And by the law of probability, a few of them will succeed, but most will not. In addition, a portion of the retail public is chasing performance. They tend to move in and out of retail mutual funds, forcing the manager to buy and sell more often than he would like.

When mutual fund managers succeed, they are highlighted in the financial press and money comes racing in. Imagine that you are a mutual fund manager and you were just written up in *The Wall Street Journal* as the top performing mutual fund for the year. Not only are your parents proud, but you are likely to receive a significant increase of new investments immediately from the public. They want to participate in your newfound success. Who pays the cost of investing these funds? The existing shareholders bear the burden of investing new money, not the new investors. If you have a mutual fund with $500 million now and $100 million comes in, that's a 20% increase in assets. The new shareholders are going to buy at today's net asset values (NAV). You, the fund manager, now have to buy securities for your new investors with their $100 million. The trading costs of investing that amount of money will be significant. You may have some market impact and drive up the prices of the very stock you are placing this addition $100 million in. The market impact would likely be very significant if your mutual fund, for example, invests in small company stocks.

So, if you take a long-term perspective and stay in a fund that has "hot money" coming in, you're going to bear the cost. What happens when the performance is poor? Well, the fund may be featured again on the cover of *The Wall Street Journal*. The active mutual fund manager's parents are no longer proud: $100 million or more leaves. Who pays that cost? The exiting shareholders are able to redeem at NAV, so the cost of selling out that portfolio is borne by the remaining shareholders. Institutional investors won't put up with it and they will not invest in publicly available funds. That's why they've created this separation between themselves and the public. You should, too.

You have control over the first two attributes—operating expenses and turnover by the mutual funds that you selected. Institutional investors significantly increased their returns by lowering costs and turnover by demanding a separate group of mutual funds for institutions. You can now get access to these funds.

Access only solved half your problem. Your clients, unlike most institutions, are subject to tax. You need to determine how effective institutional asset class mutual funds would be in a taxable environment. Each time the mutual fund manager sells a security, assuming that you have a profit, your client has a capital gains distribution. Mutual funds are required to distribute 98% of their taxable income each year, including realized capital gains, to stay tax-exempt at the mutual fund level. Since no mutual fund manager wants to have his performance reduced by paying corporate income taxes, they distribute all income. You will receive dividends for both ordinary income composed of interest and stock dividends and capital gain distributions from profitable sales by your mutual fund. If your mutual fund has a turnover of 80% per year, on average you will realize 80% of the capital gain and these gains will be taxable each year. On the other hand, if you use institutional asset class funds, the average turnover is approximately 16%—on average 84% of the taxable gains are deferred until you want to recognize them.

Two recent academic studies indicate that mutual fund capital gains and dividends will reduce after-tax returns for shareholders, and that asset class mutual funds can protect against those tax losses. These two studies, one from Stanford University and the other published in the *Journal of Portfolio Management*, demonstrate that tax efficiency is an important factor to consider in equity mutual fund selection. Numerous mutual funds, in their quest for top performance, may reduce their shareholders' potential after-tax returns by producing high taxable distributions, such as capital gains resulting from frequent buying and selling of appreciated securities in a fund. Dividends, taxed as ordinary income, may also reduce potential after-tax returns.

In a study commissioned by Charles Schwab and conducted by John B. Shoven, professor of Economics at Stanford University and Joel M. Dickson, a Stanford Ph.D. candidate, taxable distributions were found to have an impact on the rates of return of many well-known retail equity mutual funds. The study measured the performance of 62 equity funds for the 30-year period from 1963 through the end of 1992. It found that the high-tax investor who reinvested only after-tax distributions would end up with accumulated wealth per dollar invested equal to less than half (45%) of the funds' published performances. An investor in the middle-tax bracket would see only 55% of the performance published by the funds.

Another study, by Robert H. Jeffrey and Robert D. Arnott, published in the *Journal of Portfolio Management*, concluded that extremely low portfolio turnover can be a factor in improving a fund's potential after-tax performance. Asset class funds typically have very low portfolio turnover, which translates into less frequent trading and, therefore, may result in lower capital gains. Low turnover also may benefit shareholders by holding down trading cost.

Jeffrey and Arnott compared the performance of large, actively managed equity mutual funds with a passively managed equity index fund from 1982 to 1991. They found that only 21% (15 of the 72 equity funds) outperformed the index fund on a pre-tax basis during that period. Only five (five of the 72 funds) outperformed an index fund after factoring in taxes. The Jeffrey and Arnott study raises the important point that despite high turnover and capital gains distributions, some funds can produce higher after-tax returns than funds with low portfolio turnover and no capital gains distributions. This was demonstrated by the five funds in the Jeffrey study that outpaced the after-tax returns of an index fund over the nine years examined. Jeffrey and Arnott note, however, that it may be difficult to predict which funds will exhibit that performance. "While it is tempting to assume that these exceptions are evidence that 'it can be done' (i.e., that funds producing superior after-tax returns can be identified 10 years in advance), the reality is that the chances of success are slim at best."

The Jeffrey and Arnott study concluded that "Passive indexing is a very difficult strategy to beat on an after-tax basis and, therefore, active taxable strategies should always be benchmarked against the after-tax performance of an indexed alternative."

Lower Trading Costs

Trading costs can be much more significant than operating expenses and harder to determine. Let's just examine one trade that a mutual fund might execute over the counter on NASDAQ. If the stock was currently at $10 ask and $9.50 bid, what would be the cost of buying and selling the stock assuming no price change? You'd buy it for your client at the ask for $10 and sell it at the bid for $9.50—a $0.50 cost. This represents a 5% cost of trading on your client's purchase price of $10. If their portfolio turned over 80% during the year, they would have a cost of 80% of 5%, or a total hidden cost due to turnover of 4%—a hidden cost that can derail your client's investment program.

Trading costs can far exceed management fees. Trading costs are composed of agency cost (commissions and/or bid/ask spread) and market impact. While trading costs are greater for small stocks than for larger stocks, they are very significant for both. Trading cost increases significantly as you invest in smaller company stocks. To calculate this effect we need to define a range of sizes. We started with the New York Stock Exchange (NYSE). As of the end of 1996, there were 1,920 companies on the NYSE (see table note). In the table below, we have divided the companies into 10 equal groups (deciles) based on market size. Market size is based on market capitalization, which is equal to the market price of that issue multiplied by the number of shares outstanding. Each decile holds 192 stocks, ranked by their market size. We have included the American Stock Exchange and NASDAQ issues in the last two columns below, allocated on their market size.

NUMBER OF COMPANIES

Market Capitalization Deciles	Size ($MM)	NYSE Largest Company	NYSE	AMEX	Nat'l NASDAQ
1	162,790	General Electric Company	192	1	18
2	7,096	Federated Dept. Store	192	2	30
3	3,273	Dow Jones & Co. Inc.	192	6	55
4	1,938	BJ Services Co.	192	7	83
5	1,175	Federal Signal Corp.	192	5	116
6	784	Heilig Meyeers Co.	192	12	175
7	524	Zilog Inc.	192	20	240
8	352	Marcus Corp.	192	31	430
9	201	Coopers Cos Inc.	192	92	787
10	95	Harborside Healthcare	192	391	1895

Figure 5-5:   Number of Companies

General Electric Company was the largest company listed on the NYSE and had a market capitalization of over $162 billion on December 31, 1996. The largest company in the 10th decile was Harborside Healthcare with a market size of only $95 million. What a difference. These differences in size play a significant factor in cost. The smaller the market size, the higher the potential trading costs and the smaller the daily trading volume.

DAILY TRADING VOLUME PER ISSUE

Size Deciles	Average Price	Percent Spread	Shares	Dollars
1	$53.92	.53%	904,445	$47,294,212
2	42.70	.60	506,539	19,300,213
3	38.19	.71	336,778	10,772,236
4	33.12	.98	211,360	5,354,680
5	27.32	1.25	164,897	3,697,177
6	25.79	1.26	117,658	2,645,244
7	22.87	1.61	88,745	1,636,101
8	19.16	2.21	60,099	846,424
9	14.84	2.99	37,894	415,914
10	$ 8.35	6.19%	17,462	$ 119,259

Figure 5-6:   Daily Trading Per Issue

The smaller the market capitalization, the higher the potential trading costs and the smaller the daily trading volume. The bid/ask spread as a percentage of price is a conservative estimate of actual trading costs. This estimate is over 11 times as great for the smallest decile as for the largest decile (6.19% versus 0.53%). An investor purchasing at the ask and selling at the bid would pay trading costs of 0.53% for the largest stocks and 6.19% for the smallest stocks, if the trades do not move the market. A large order that is a significant part of the daily trading volume is likely to move the market against the investor, adding additional cost. Forty-seven million dollars represents the daily trading volume of a single decile 1 stock or more than the combined volume of about 400 decile 10 stocks. The trading costs are even higher when you invest internationally.

Consistently Maintained Market Segment

Most investment advisors now agree that the largest determinant of performance is asset allocation. Effective asset allocation can only be accomplished if the building blocks that are utilized maintain consistent market segments. If you are using traditional retail mutual funds, the manager may change his exposure over time, significantly changing the effectiveness of your allocation.

In the graphs below, we have to compare two popular funds, Fidelity Magellan and Vanguard's S&P 500 Index from August 1981 through March 1997. In examining the exposure distribution, it becomes very apparent that the portion of Fidelity Magellan's return that is explained by the corresponding benchmark return over time changed substantially as contrasted with the Vanguard S&P 500 Index.

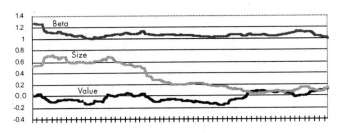

Jan-82 Jan-83 Jan-84 Jan-85 Jan-86 Jan-87 Jan-88 Jan-89 Jan-90 Jan-91 Jan-92 Jan-93 Jan-94 Jan-95 Jan-96 Jan-97

Figure 5-7:   Fidelity Magellan Estimated Three-Factor Model Loadings

This significant change, as contrasted with the modest

change inside the Vanguard Fund, would make its inclusion in an asset allocation difficult at best, if you were trying to control the asset allocation for your client. If you want to maintain a consistent allocation, then only mutual funds that have relative constant exposure should be considered. Institutional asset class funds are, by their very design, consistent.

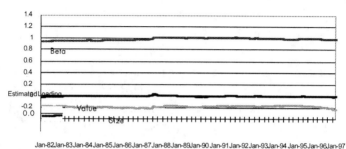

Figure 5-8: Vanguard Index 500 Estimated Three-Factor Model Loadings

CONCEPT 4

GLOBAL DIVERSIFICATION.

We've all read about the concept of a "global village"— that we're getting closer and closer together. Technology is creating a new paradigm where businesses around the world are tied together just as markets are now tied together. Then why should you include international institutional asset class mutual funds in your clients' portfolios?

American markets have gone straight up for the last 10 years. It's been a great market for the U.S. side but international has been weak, particularly the Japanese market. Many investors have been disappointed with their allocations. Advisors are being asked, "Why don't you just change the allocation or get out of international completely?"

We've had such a great experience in the U.S. market recently that we all want to invest based on that experience:

That's the "rearview mirror" method of investing. We're tempted to invest only in U.S. companies, but many things in life are counterintuitive, and one is the international market.

What investors think advisors are doing by investing in international is trying to get higher rates of returns. They're not the reason you should have your clients invest international. Individual stocks of companies around the world with similar risk have the same expected rate of return; however, they don't get there in the same manner or at the same time. There are tremendous dissimilar price movements in international and U.S. asset classes.

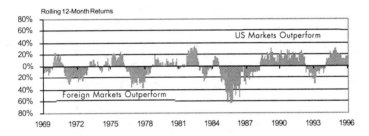

Figure 5-9:   US and Foreign Markets Perform Differently 1/69-12/96

Markets Don't Move Together

What becomes obvious from the graph above is the consistent experience that world markets don't move together, but over long periods of time the U.S. and international markets average about the same. For the most recent 10-year period, the U.S. equity market measured by the Standard & Poor's 500 Index did significantly better. In one 12-month period, however, the international equity market as illustrated by the Morgan Stanley Capital International Europe and Australasia, Far East Equity (EAFE) Index did 30% better than the U.S. market. Other than that period, though, the U.S. market has been the stronger performer. We have to look back to the five-year period beginning June 1986 to find the last time the international market came out the winner.

Over time, both performances tend to balance out. For the past 29 years, the S&P 500 and the EAFE Index have had annualized returns of 11.5% and 12.5%, respectively.

Cognitive Bias

So why do investors question what we know works? Behaviorists call it cognitive bias: the belief that whatever we are most familiar with will continue—for example, the sun coming up in the same spot every day. Since 1989, the U.S. markets have been so strong, the tendency is to question why we would ever include international markets. Answer: The very nature of dissimilarities in price movement and lack of predictability in timing markets is why we need to include both U.S. and international stocks.

The question then becomes what is the most advantageous allocation of international and American stocks? Currently, more than 60% of the world's markets, as measured by market capitalization, is overseas. All other things being equal, we should invest based on the market capitalization, which is the amount overseas. Rather than being subjective, we should let markets tell us what to do.

Our job as financial advisors is to help investors move from being "noise" investors to "information" investors. As noise investors, they get caught up in the emotion of the day. They are encouraged by the media to expect what is currently fabulous to continue, but the reality is that that will not happen. The financial services industry takes the best information from the academic community to understand how markets really work and how professionals can apply it for the benefit of clients. That's why advisors continue to include the international markets in their clients' portfolios.

It's easier, however, to sell what people want, and people want to believe that what they are experiencing will continue. It would be easier for financial professionals to raise money if they just sold U.S. recent winners and dumped the international allocation, but what we need to do ethically is not what is easy, but what is right, and that is what truly benefits our clients.

Market Repricing

Companies that have the same risk, no matter whether

they're in the United States or the United Kingdom, are going to have the same expected rates of return over time. That's because markets reprice according to new information. In the short run, though, local economic conditions affect returns and we experience dissimilar price movement, which is what Modern Portfolio Theory investing takes into consideration.

CONCEPT 5

DESIGN PORTFOLIOS THAT ARE EFFICIENT.

How do we decide which investments to utilize and in what combination? Since 1972, major institutions have been using a money management concept known as Modern Portfolio Theory. It was developed at the University of Chicago by Harry Markowitz and Merton Miller and later expanded by Stanford professor William Sharpe, Markowitz, Miller, and Sharpe won the Nobel Prize for Economics in 1990 for their contribution to investment methodology.

The five-step process of developing a strategic portfolio using Modern Portfolio Theory is mathematical in nature and can appear daunting. It is important to note that math is nothing more than an expression of logic and as you examine the process, you can readily see the common sense approach that they have taken—which is counter-intuitive to conventional and over-commercialized investment thinking.

Markowitz has stated that for every level of risk, there is some optimum combination of investments that will give you the highest rate of return. These combinations of portfolio exhibiting this optimal risk/reward trade-off form the efficient frontier line. The efficient frontier is determined by calculating the expected rate of return, standard deviation and correlation coefficient for each institutional asset class mutual fund and utilizing this information to identify the portfolio at the highest expected return for each incremental level of risk. By plotting each combination or portfolio representing a given level of risk and expected return, we are able to describe mathematically a series of points or "efficient portfolios." This line forms the efficient frontier. It is important to note that while a portfolio may be efficient it is not necessarily prudent.

Most investor portfolios fall significantly below the efficient frontier. Portfolios such as the S&P 500 that is often used as a proxy for the market fall below the line when several asset classes are compared. Investors can have the same rates of return with an asset class portfolio with much less risk or higher rates of return for the same level of risk. The chart below illustrates the efficient frontier relative to the "market." Rational and prudent investors will restrict their choice of portfolios to those which appear on the efficient frontier and to the specific portfolios that represent their own risk tolerance level.

Figure 5-10: The Efficient Frontier

The concepts of Modern Portfolio Theory are not widely understood and are often misapplied or used when convenient. But they represent a new investment paradigm shift as important as the telescope was to Galileo. Before you can move to a new paradigm, you have to examine the commonly held set of assumptions that lead to false beliefs. Many investors are making the most important financial decisions of their lives based on incorrect assumptions. They need your help.

CHAPTER SIX
———————————

BUILDING YOUR MODEL INVESTMENT PORTFOLIO

N ow that you have access to institutional asset class mutual funds, which ones should you utilize for your clients' portfolios? A good starting point is an examination of the historical performance of each investment category. This will allow you to get a better understanding of how each asset class has performed over long periods. This is not to say that the past indicates future performance; however, it does indicate reasonable relationships between various asset classes.

Time series information on domestic asset classes is readily available for you to review starting with 1926 through 1996. This time period includes The Great Depression, World War II, The Korean War, The Vietnam War, and numerous other major world crises. How did the investment markets perform? In the graph below, you can see that, historically, equities have far outperformed fixed income-asset classes. If you had invested one dollar in the Standard & Poor's 500 Index at the beginning of 1926, it would have been worth $1,366 (assuming reinvestment of dividends) by the end of 1996, while an investment in small-company stocks would have been worth almost $3,863.

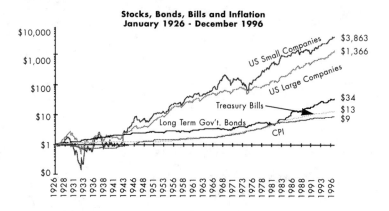

Figure 6-1:   Stocks, Bonds,, Bills and Inflation

Fixed-income investment asset classes had trouble keeping pace with inflation. That same dollar invested in 20-year U.S. government bonds would have been worth $34, and $13 if you had invested in 30-day U.S. Treasury Bills. Investments over this period required an increase in value of $9 simply to maintain purchasing power. The inflation rate is the absolute minimum goal for most investors. Most, if not all, of your clients need to do significantly better to provide for their tax liabilities and their families' quality of life.

The following table illustrates that not only have equities outperformed fixed-income asset classes, they also easily outpaced inflation. Shown below is a series of time periods. Over each of the periods, the S&P 500 Index increased more than both long-term U.S. government bonds and inflation. In most periods, the long-term U.S. government bond market barely exceeded inflation. Even in the years during which government bonds substantially beat the inflation rate, the S&P 500 beat both.

Number of Years	Time Period	S&P 500	LT Gov't Bonds	Inflation (CPI)
71	1926-96	10.7%	5.1%	3.1%
50	1947-96	12.6%	5.4%	4.1%
40	1957-96	11.2%	6.5%	4.5%
30	1967-96	11.8%	7.8%	5.4%
20	1977-96	14.6%	9.6%	5.2%
10	1987-96	15.3%	9.5%	3.7%
5	1992-96	15.2%	9.3%	2.9%

Figure 6-2:   **Nominal Annualized Total Returns**

The next table takes a look at the inflation-adjusted returns of 15-year time periods. Stocks dominated bonds in all periods. This time, however, both U.S. government and corporate issues are examined. In each period, equities beat fixed income by varying degrees. Interestingly, even in the period ending in 1980, when all three assets had negative returns after adjusting for inflation, the equities lost the least. In fact, the stock market, which has often been stereotyped as too risky, ironically had only one negative 15-year period, while Treasuries and corporates both had two.

15-Year Periods Ending In....

	1996	1995	1994	1993	1990	1980	1970	1960
S&P 500 Index	13.2%	10.7%	9.8%	10.3%	7.7%	-0.5%	5.6%	10.1%
LT Corp. Bonds	9.9%	9.2%	6.5%	5.9%	3.6%	-3.9%	0.6%	-1.9%
30 Day Treasuries	2.9%	3.2%	2.9%	2.6%	2.2%	-0.6%	1.0%	-2.0%

Figure 6-3:   Real (Inflation Adjusted) Annualized Returns

Time Horizon

Modern portfolio theory states that investments in equities will produce higher expected returns than investments in fixed income, given the higher risks inherent in equity markets. These risks are primarily due to the cyclical swings of the stock market. These cyclical swings are of greatest concern to your clients who will have to liquidate their investments in the near future. In light of most of your clients' long-term perspectives, it is prudent to attempt to achieve a higher rate of return by investing a large portion of your portfolio's assets in equities.

The minimum time horizon for you to invest any of your clients' portfolios in equities should be no less than five years. For any portfolio with less than a five-year horizon, the portfolio should be comprised predominantly of fixed-income investments. This five-year minimum investment period is critical. The investment process must be viewed as a long-term plan for achieving the desired results. This is because one-year volatility can be significant for certain asset classes. However, the range of probable returns over a five-year period is greatly reduced. Since fixed investments tend to be less volatile than equities, they should be used to reduce the overall level of risk to your comfort level.

Fixed Income

Many advisors purchase bonds and bond mutual funds as part of their clients' comprehensive investment portfolios. Long-term vehicles, such as U.S. Treasury bonds, are thought to be attractive because of their safety and higher yields. They are considered "safe" due to the high credit quality of these bonds, which are backed by the full faith and credit of the U.S. government. However, long-term bonds have many different types of risk that must be considered, such as reinvestment risk, call risk, purchasing power risk, liquidity risk, and interest rate risk.

A bond represents a loan to an issuer, such as the U.S. government, usually in return for periodic fixed-interest payments. These payments continue until the bond is redeemed at maturity (or earlier if called by the issuer). At the time of maturity, the face value of the bond is returned to the investor. Bonds with maturities of less than five years are considered short-term, those with maturities between five and 12 years are intermediate-term, and bonds with maturities longer than 12 years are long-term.

The major risk your clients face in bonds is interest rate risk. Prices of bonds move in the opposite direction of interest rates, thus, when interest rates rise, prices of bonds fall and vice versa. For example, consider a newly issued 20-year Treasury bond with a 6% coupon rate purchased 12 months ago. If in the last year, interest rates had increased by 2%, new 20-year treasury bonds would be offered with 8% coupons. The 6% bonds would be significantly less than the newly issued 8% bonds, due to the higher coupon rate. This illustrates how rising interest rates force bond prices down. Alternatively, interest rates may fall and force bond prices up. The inverse relationship between interest rates and bond values is a risk that you must evaluate for your client.

The chart below illustrates the historical rates of total return for 20-year Treasury bonds over six decades. During the 1980s, long-term bond investors enjoyed their best decade in history, with gains averaging 12.7% per year. Unfortunately, many investors continue to only consider the most recent period when analyzing investment options. We call it rear-view mirror investment. It is like trying to drive a car while only looking where you have been through the rear-view mirror. It is critical to analyze all statistical evidence available in financial decision-making. You never want to dismiss data without very good reason.

Consider the decade of the 1950s, the worst decade for long-term bond investors, with an average annual loss of -0.1% if you reinvested the interest income and substantially lower if you did not. This practical example of the interest rate risk of long-term bonds illustrates what can happen when interest rates rise. The volatility of long-term bonds, particularly over long time periods, approaches the volatility of common stocks. Clearly, long-term U.S. Treasury bonds don't have the price stability which many fixed-income investors are seeking.

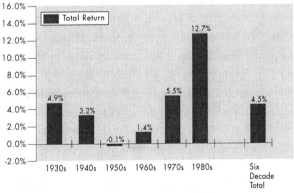

Long-Term Treasury Bond Returns Through Six Decades

Figure 6-4: Long-Term Treasury Bond Returns

When the marketplace values a bond, the length of time to maturity is critically important. The longer the term to maturity, the longer the expected stream of interest payments to the bondholder. The market price of any bond represents the present value of this stream of interest payments discounted at the currently offered interest rates. As interest rates fluctuate, the present value of this stream of interest payments constantly changes. The longer stream of interest payments, which long-term bonds have versus short-term bonds, creates higher price volatility for the long-term bonds.

The higher risk of long-term bonds is acceptable, provided we are sufficiently compensated with higher rates of return for the additional risk. Eugene Fama has studied the rates of return of long-term bonds from 1964 to 1996. Fama has shown that long-term bonds historically have had wide variances in their rates of total return without sufficiently compensating investors with higher expected returns. He found that bonds with maturities beyond five years actually have had lower total returns than those with maturities of less than five years and higher standard deviations.

The predominant investors in the long-term bond markets are institutions, including corporate pension plans and life insurance companies. These investors are interested in funding long-term debt obligations such as fixed annuity payments or other fixed corporate responsibilities. They are not concerned with volatility of principal or with the effects of inflation since their obligations are a fixed amount. You are concerned with inflation and volatility. Your clients live in a variable rate world and have a limit to the amount of volatility they feel comfortable taking.

In terms of variability of total return, long-term bonds look more like stocks than like shorter-term fixed-income vehicles such as Treasury bills. And yet, over long time periods, their respective total returns have consistently lagged those of equities. A look at the following graph will help illustrate the higher standard deviations and lower total returns of bonds with maturities beyond five years.

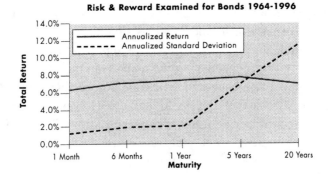

Figure 6-5:   Risk versus Reward

Your purpose in holding for your clients some fixed-investment asset classes should be to lower the risk of the overall portfolio. Replacing the traditional long-term bond holding with a combination of common stocks and short-term fixed income vehicles will maintain your clients' portfolios' expected rates of return, while decreasing volatility.

Studies show that the efficient market hypothesis holds true not only for stocks, but for bonds as well. There appears to be no ability to predict future changes in interest rates. Interest rate changes, as well as equity price changes, are immediately priced into the market. The best estimate of the future price of any fixed instrument is the price of a similar instrument today. There appear to be, on average, no money managers who are able to predict interest rate movements in an attempt to provide superior returns over the corresponding asset class.

In building your clients' portfolios, you need to recognize the role fixed investments play. The fixed investments are in your asset class portfolio simply to mitigate risk. For that reason, it makes no sense to have longer maturity instruments, unless you have a specific time horizon liability and you will be funding it with a matching debt instrument. The risk of inherent greater volatility with long-term bonds without the reward for that risk results in our recommendation that you avoid all debt instruments

81

with maturities beyond five years. In addition, to maintain a high-quality portfolio, we recommend you hold only government or high-quality debt instruments of AAA rating.

Institutional asset class funds attempt to add value without predicting future changes in the market. In the case of a bond fund, there will be no interest rate forecasting beyond the implicit forecast of the yield curve. However, alternative strategies still can be used to enhance returns. Research concludes that the current yield curve is the best estimate of future yield curves. This estimate enables asset class mutual fund managers to calculate the expected horizon returns and determine optimal maturity and holding periods.

The current shape of the yield curve will determine the choice of maturity. In the chart below, the fixed-income institutional asset class mutual fund has a constraint of a maximum maturity of two years and a maximum average maturity of one year. The manager will extend maturities within the constraints when there is an anticipated reward for doing so. This will result when the yield curve is steep.

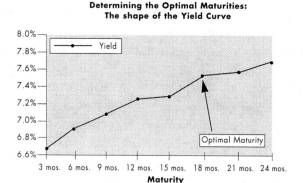

Determining the Optimal Maturities:
The shape of the Yield Curve

Figure 6-6:   Optimal Maturities

The money manager will stay with short maturities in his selection of debt instruments when longer maturities do not provide additional returns. With an inverted yield curve, as illustrated below, the money manager invested in cash equivalents.

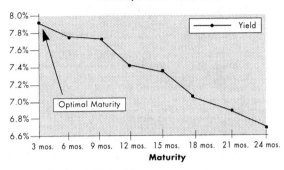

Figure 6-7: Optimal Maturities

Using the current yield curve as an estimate of future yield curves, the money manager can construct a matrix of expected returns. He can then determine the optimal maturity and holding period. In this example, the highest expected annualized return is 9.73% for a strategy of buying a fixed instrument with a maturity of 18 months and selling it in three months, when the maturity is 15 months.

Maturity (months) at Time of Sale

21	8.65							
18	8.32	7.98						
15	8.79	8.85	9.73					
12	8.50	8.45	8.68	7.64				
9	8.39	8.32	8.44	7.80	7.95			
6	8.22	8.13	8.17	7.65	7.65	7.35		
3	8.07	7.98	7.98	7.54	7.51	7.29	7.22	
0	7.90	7.79	7.76	7.37	7.30	7.08	6.94	6.66
	24	21	18	15	12	9	6	3

Maturity (months) at Time of Purchase

Figure 6-8: Finding the Optimal Maturity and Holding Period

This investment strategy is known as the "matrix pricing strategy," developed by leading theoreticians in the area and the basis of several investment funds. It is simply riding the yield curve. In studies, as well as applications, it appears to add 50 to 100 basis points over comparable index funds

annually over extended periods. For our clients, we currently utilize three fixed income asset classes—a money market,
a two-year high-quality corporate, and a two-year government bond mutual fund.

Tax-Free Securities

We did not mention tax-free securities in our recommended fixed portion of your clients' asset class portfolios.
All things being equal, most individual investors would prefer to have tax-free income versus taxable income. But all
things are not equal. Let's examine how the taxable fixed-
income market works and then contrast it with the tax-
exempt. The steady income and minimal risk attract most
people who invest in fixed-income asset classes. However,
due to the extreme volatility of interest rates since the mid-
1970s, fixed-income investors have been subject to increasing risk. As interest rates have risen, the market value of
those investments has fallen due to the lower yield. Investors
have preferred the new bonds that have higher interest rates.
In a rising interest rate market, you have to resign yourself
to accepting the lower interest rate of a long-term instrument
or selling the instrument at a discount.

There are four types of risks faced in the fixed-investment market:

- Interest rate risk — where the price of the bond changes
  due to interest rate fluctuations;
- Credit risk — risk that the issuer of your instrument will
  run into financial adversity;
- Call risk — risk that the issuer of your debt obligation
  will exercise the right to repay the debt prior to maturity,
  an event which could cut short your high rate of return; and
- Inflation risk — risk that your purchasing power will be
  seriously eroded by inflation.

How does each risk lead us to our decision not to recommend tax-exempt securities?

Interest rate risk will be approximately the same for instruments of similar maturities. The credit risk of many municipal

agencies, however, will not be the same. Their credit risk has significantly increased, given the budgetary problems at both the state and many local levels. Compare these risks with U.S. government securities, which have no credit risk.

What about call risk? In the municipal bond market, the issuing agencies often have a call provision for early redemption. This substantially reduces your upside potential in a bond. When interest rates go down, your bond will appreciate in value. However, the issuer is more likely to call or redeem your bond. He will pay for it with proceeds of new bonds sold at the lower interest rate. This often reduces his cost significantly, but limits your capital gains. If interest rates go up, you're stuck with a bond that has eroded in value and is no longer at a competitive yield. U.S. government bonds and short-term corporate bonds have very limited, if any, call risk.

The inflation risk is significant with all fixed investments. One should not invest in fixed investments to keep up with inflation. Fixed instruments should be used to build stability into the portfolio. Their percentage of the whole portfolio is a function of your willingness to take risk. Fixed investments protect the downside risk of your account. In addition, fixed investments provide funds to rebalance or reoptimize your portfolio into additional growth investments when a significant down market occurs.

In addition to their increased risk, tax-exempt securities have much greater trading costs. These additional costs negate using any enhanced strategy such as "matrix pricing strategy." The increased turnover such a strategy would bring would create a negative added-value. When we examine the differences between the taxable and tax-free investments, it is in most investors' best interests to maintain the taxable investments in their asset class portfolio. If market conditions change to favor tax-free investments, repositioning to appropriate funds for your clients should be considered. While paying taxes has never been a favorite pastime of any client, often it can make sense to do so, even with the current tax structure.

Equity Investments

Deciding which equity investments you should include in your clients' asset class portfolios to provide the needed growth opportunity requires some study. You know that the market is highly efficient, that there appears to be no ability to do any market timing—so we need to stay fully invested. There also appears to be no ability to select individual securities and expect to beat the market. What should we do?

Annualized Returns (%)

Time	1	2	3	4	NYSE Decile 5	6	7	8	9	10
1928-30	**-1.84**	-5.18	-13.32	-13.20	-8.30	-17.98	-18.12	-25.59	**-27.17**	-25.13
1931-33	**-8.71**	-3.26	0.74	1.50	-6.27	0.10	0.08	5.87	1.77	**15.93**
1934-36	**23.86**	28.26	24.38	33.66	36.99	37.33	41.90	46.92	**57.33**	55.65
1937-39	**-3.99**	-7.06	-6.48	-9.28	-8.68	-7.58	-9.80	-15.73	**-18.54**	-22.40
1940-42	**-2.16**	1.54	1.44	2.52	1.35	3.14	1.36	5.27	5.79	5.43
1943-45	**23.30**	35.33	35.65	44.04	49.62	45.30	58.55	64.45	75.03	**93.59**
1946-48	**1.30**	-1.01	-2.01	-4.09	-2.54	-4.36	-6.86	-7.43	-6.78	**-8.02**
1949-51	22.95	**26.66**	23.79	24.16	**22.05**	24.85	24.34	26.31	23.29	26.18
1952-54	**9.63**	19.54	**20.69**	18.84	19.64	20.42	19.30	16.59	17.98	16.61
1955-57	**7.48**	7.33	3.61	4.46	5.08	2.13	2.09	3.16	2.33	**1.88**
1958-60	**16.28**	19.34	22.69	22.95	21.76	21.38	23.76	23.00	**25.25**	23.71
1961-63	**11.42**	10.43	9.31	9.02	6.54	6.55	9.70	9.69	7.73	**6.50**
1964-66	**4.31**	8.83	12.74	11.41	12.34	14.90	12.50	12.98	12.75	**16.57**
1967-69	**7.24**	7.82	12.52	12.64	17.12	18.10	16.61	23.34	22.80	**31.38**
1970-72	**13.13**	9.76	10.42	7.64	7.31	7.14	5.59	1.88	**-0.50**	0.27
1973-75	-6.47	**-5.30**	-6.79	-5.57	-9.84	-11.00	-10.54	-9.99	**-11.10**	-9.84
1976-78	**5.86**	8.68	14.21	17.16	21.34	24.62	27.00	28.53	29.57	**37.51**
1979-81	**12.90**	20.77	22.11	23.78	23.47	**26.40**	25.00	24.24	25.70	25.42
1982-84	15.35	14.49	15.57	15.31	16.07	**17.36**	17.02	16.44	15.57	**12.01**
1985-87	16.92	**19.22**	15.62	15.92	13.17	10.65	10.97	8.67	5.70	**2.33**
1988-90	**14.81**	11.69	11.94	11.65	7.09	6.12	8.05	4.98	-0.20	**-4.98**
1991-93	**13.35**	20.64	24.93	21.59	31.30	28.31	28.80	24.89	29.60	35.09
1994-96	**20.72**	16.22	15.35	16.40	14.26	14.92	16.06	**13.30**	16.55	14.17

Figure 6-9: Deciles 1-10

Earlier in the chapter, we illustrated how the U.S. equity market could be divided into deciles. Let's examine how each of these deciles has performed. In the table above, the equity market is again divided into deciles 1 through 10. On the left-hand column are three-year rolling time periods from 1928 to 1996. The figures in bold are either the highest returning decile of the whole group or the lowest returning one. The first row, 1928 to 1930, in the first decile had a negative 1.84%, but the tenth decile had a negative 27.17%. So, the first decile was the best and the tenth was the worst, even though for this period, all deciles were negative.

In the next three-year period, 1931 to 1933, the first decile had a negative 8.71%, but the tenth had a positive 15.93%, so they flip-flopped. Now the tenth is doing the best and the first is doing the worst. If you just scan this chart, you can see that the figures in bold are at one end or the other of the table for the most part—which means you're getting the most dissimilar price movement action, good or bad, either in your large-company stocks or in your very small-company stocks. This highlights how these groups behave differently.

Large Cap vs. Small Cap

We recommend that your investors currently place their domestic equity asset class stocks in the largest U.S. capitalized companies and U.S. small stocks in the ninth and tenth deciles. These asset classes have proven to have the most impact on the entire U.S. market's performance. Academic research shows the largest and smallest companies' stocks have low correlation with each other. Building a portfolio containing asset classes with low correlation to each other results in greater long-term performance for the investor while reducing risk through diversification.

To implement these recommendations, you should consider for your clients investing in index funds that attempt to replicate the Standard & Poor's 500 and the Russell 2000 Index. Institutional investors have, through recent enhancement, been able to add significant value through different strategies with new asset class funds.

The cost of trading in deciles 9 and 10 are significant. A mutual fund manager who wants to place any significant amount of capital in this area will find that the trading cost is not just the bid/ask spread, but also the market impact of his orders. Even index funds run into this problem and often underperform their indexes by a wide margin due to this increased cost. If you were managing a pure index fund, you would have to buy stocks at the ask and sell them at the bid. Your parameters state that you have to have the index dead on. Whatever the index does, you want to do. You are trying to follow the index as closely as possible in terms of that pricing. Now, what happens here under this strategy? What happens is that if you want to buy a block of 300,000 shares of a decile 9 stock and it is trading at $10, that's $3 million. Remember that decile 9 stock average daily trading volume is approximately $416,000. You're not going to be able to buy it at the ask price; you will move the market. For an active mutual fund manager, this is much worse; he is usually placing much larger bets in concentrated issues and trading much more often. This can easily work out to an underperformance of the market of 5% or more.

A few institutional asset class funds have successfully implemented a strategy that significantly improves trading costs, so as to capture the small-company stock effect. This is accomplished by utilization of a discount block trading strategy and a willingness to be slightly overweighted or underweighted on any particular stock in the index. In the chart below, we can see a typical block trade, which illustrates that the sellers of block trades are willing to absorb a discount bid.

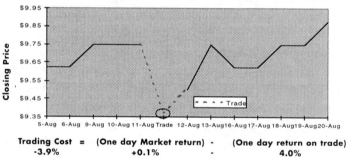

An Example of a 9-10 Trade

Trading Cost =	(One day Market return) -	(One day return on trade)
-3.9%	+0.1%	4.0%

Figure 6-10: Trade Example

In this example, a major shareholder wanted to sell 351,000 shares or 3.2% of the company. The company's market capitalization on this date was $106 million. The average daily trading volume for the previous month had been 15,600 shares. Prior to the trade, the last sale had been 9 5/8, with the current bid 9 5/8 and the ask 9 3/4. The shareholder sold his shares to the institutional asset class mutual fund manager not at the ask price of 9 3/4, not at the bid price of 9 5/8, but for 9 3/8, a trade value of $3.3 million. The trading cost was -3.9%. The trading cost is calculated by the bid/ask spread. The bid was 9 5/8 and the ask price to the institutional asset class fund provider was 9 3/8. The trading cost was therefore (9 3/8 - 9 5/8) - 3.9%. Why would the shareholder sell at this discount? Liquidity. If he had just placed the order on the market due to the relative trade size, he would have driven the market price down significantly.

Utilizing a discount block trading strategy can allow an institutional asset class mutual fund to realize the small-company stock effect without the significant trading costs. The negative 3.9% cost represents a positive 3.9% return to the investors in the fund. It is through these enhancements that institutional asset class mutual fund managers can achieve a comparative advantage for their clients without trying to predict the market. These advantage are now available for you to offer your clients.

Our knowledge of how financial markets work is constantly improving. So far, we have discussed two equity risks that your investors are rewarded for taking: market risk and size risk. We have successfully put this new research to work by investing in large- and small-company stocks around the world.

In the model portfolio you will develop, you will need to invest in asset classes that have both of these risk factors. But there is a third risk factor that your investor can be compensated for taking. We will show you how to use this risk factor to possibly add more then 300 basis points to your portfolio performance, with no increase in measurable risk.

It was Eugene Fama—then working with a fellow University of Chicago professor, Kenneth French—who uncovered this third risk factor. Fama and French determined portfolio performance was really attributable to three factors, rather than one single factor. What they discovered was that it was not simply a matter of how much an investor had in the market alone, but also the amount he invested in large and small companies and the third risk factor (percentage placed in high book-to-market ratio stocks) that determined investment returns. By gaining an understanding of these various concepts, you can better design your portfolio than by focusing on a single factor. Market risk, company size, and the book-to-market ratio (BtM) collectively explain 95% of the variability of returns an investor can expect.

Market Risk

Market risk is the risk experienced by investing in the equity market as a whole. Investors demand a higher rate of return than the risk-free rate of return for compensation for the increased risk of holding equities. Greater returns are demanded to compensate for the extra risk.

Size Risk Factor

Small-company stocks have significantly greater risk than large-company stocks. Small companies are small because they have limited resources. They are less able to weather downturns in the market. Investors demand a higher rate of return for the risk of investing in smaller companies. The market prices each security in accordance with its risk factor.

Book-To-Market

Fama and French concluded that the third risk factor could best be identified by companies with a high book value relative to their current market value. These companies were viewed as being out of favor; the company may be in distress. The book-to-market (BtM) ratio relates the value of a given company using generally accepted accounting principles with the market value assigned by the stock market. BtM is a ratio comparing the book value per share of a common stock with its market price.

They found that investors react very differently to companies that have either high BtM or low BtM. Just by knowing which one to include in your portfolio can allow you to beat the market. High BtM companies are unpopular with investors. Investors demand a higher expected rate of return to compensate them for the perceived higher risk factor. At the end of 1996, Kmart was currently a high book-to-market stock, whereas Wal-Mart was a high market price relative to its book value. Wal-Mart is the more popular of the two. Kmart is viewed by the market as a riskier investment.

Investors understand that low BtM companies like Wal-Mart, on average, will continue to do well. While companies in distress, high BtM companies like Kmart, on average, will continue to do poorly. Investors want to be compensated for this risk. They are not looking for a turnaround situation, because on average that does not happen. They want to be compensated for the likelihood that high BtM companies will not improve significantly.

In order for your clients to take advantage of this ground-breaking research, you need to accept the idea that you will earn higher rates of return owning portfolios of stocks of companies that do poorly. This is counter-intuitive to most investors. We have always known that we want to own nothing but the best companies. Thousands of analysts do nothing but try to identify these great companies for you. If only you could build a portfolio of nothing but excellent companies, wouldn't you be assured of investment success? No!

Michele Clayton in the *Financial Analyst Journal* of June 1987 raised this same question. In this article based upon the best selling book *In Search of Excellence* by Peters and Waterman, Clayton sets out to track the performance of both the excellent companies described in the book and the companies in their peer group who are truly unexcellent in their financial performance ratios. First, she examines several traditional fundamental analysts' business ratios. Without exception, on average, the excellent companies have much higher standards than the unexcellent companies have. In the chart below, we show her findings.

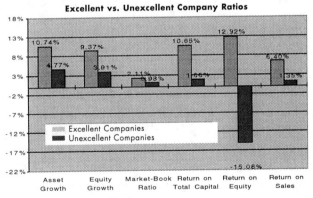

Figure 6-11: Company Ratios

91

The chart below shows the cumulative return that investors would have received if they had invested $100 in two portfolios, one of all the excellent companies and the other in all the unexcellent companies. Contrary to your intuition and most investment advice, the unexcellent companies significantly outperformed the excellent companies. This performance can be explained by the high BtM risk factor.

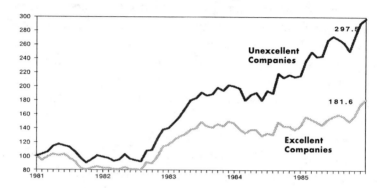

Figure 6-12: Cumulative Returns

HIGH BOOK TO MARKET

To achieve an optimally diversified asset class portfolio, you must take each of these three risk factors into consideration. Let's examine how a high BtM asset class can be constructed.

Previously, we divided the NYSE stocks into deciles based on their respective market capitalization. This time, we will divide the NYSE stocks by their book-to-market ratio. In the chart below, the 1,650 companies on the NYSE are divided into 10 equal groups based on their respective book-to-market ratio. The American Stock Exchange and National Market OTC issues are put into the NYSE decile groupings. Excluded from the chart are those companies that did not have available book value data such as American Depository Receipts, closed-end issues, and negative book value firms. This resulted in fewer companies than when the study was completed based on market capitalization.

92

Stocks in Decile 1 through 3 were considered low BtM stocks or growth stocks. Stocks in decile 8 through 10 were considered high BtM stocks or value stocks. Berg Electronics Corporation would have been the lowest BtM ratio of all companies on the NYSE of .012 on December 31, 1996. This means that its book value was only 1.2% of current market capitalization. It was clearly a growth stock. Potlatch Corp. would represent the opposite end of the spectrum. Its book value was 98.7% of market capitalization. It was a value stock. The Standard & Poor's 500 Index would have an approximate book-to-market ratio of 0.40. This relatively low BtM ratio would be expected. The S&P 500 Index is market weighted. Those companies that have higher market capitalization will be more heavily weighted in the composition of the index. The largest market valuation companies will tend to be growth stocks.

	Book-to-Market Deciles	Btm (Decile Lowest)	NYSE Name	Number of Companies		
				NYSE	AMEX	NMS NASDAQ
Growth	1	.012	Berg Electrs Corp.	165	66	533
	2	.172	Cardina Health Inc.	165	24	323
	3	.252	SBC Comm. Inc.	165	29	290
	4	.319	Fluor Corp.	165	39	249
	5	.387	Fisher Scientific Inc.	165	32	244
	6	.456	Barnes Group Inc.	165	34	301
	7	.533	Helmerich & Payne Inc.	165	52	318
Value	8	.633	Personell Group Amer	165	47	344
	9	.764	CTS Corp.	165	71	395
	10	.987	Potlatch Corp.	165	116	542

Book-to-Market distribution by exchange includes fewer names than size distribution by exchange due to exclusion of highly regulated utilities and negative bookvalue firms.

Figure 6-13: Growth and Value Deciles

In the bar chart below, Fama and French simulated the performance of both high BtM stocks and low BtM stocks for both large and small companies. Large-company stocks were defined as those stocks in deciles 1 through 5 based on market capitalization. Small-company stocks were defined as 6 through 10 based on market capitalization. The benchmark portfolio for large companies was the S&P's 500. The benchmark for small company stocks was the Center for Research in Securities Prices Index, decile 6 through 10.

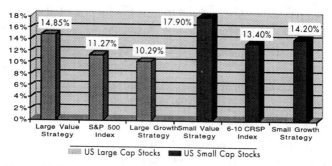

Figure 6-14: Growth and Value Comparison

Fama and French determined that risk, as measured by standard deviation, is roughly the same for stocks in their respective size category whatever BtM ratio. However, they found that the high BtM stocks produced a higher average annual return. High BtM stocks as a group produced greater than a 4% higher return with the same standard deviation as the low BtM stocks. The specific risk of owning one of the high BtM stocks is significant. However, owning all the high BtM stocks in a broad asset class is similar in risk to owning all the stocks in the market. Thus, we can expect higher returns at similar levels of market risk.

INTERNATIONAL HIGH BOOK TO MARKET ASSET CLASS

Does the three factor market work internationally? Another recent study by Carlo Capaul and Ian Rowley, conducted in conjunction with Stanford University's William Sharpe, both supported and supplemented Fama and French's findings. (Financial Analysts Journal, January/February 1993, pages 27-36.) Their research showed that an international high BtM stock portfolio not only outperformed the recognized global indexes, but also that the excess returns were greater on average than those found in the United States. These excess returns, combined with the low correlation of returns between countries, allow for lower risk.

Building an international asset class high BtM portfolio presents many challenges. First is the high cost of doing business overseas. However, that can be partly overcome through the wise use of institutional asset class funds. But how do your investors cope with the varying accounting rules in the rest of the world? The answer to this question is quite simple: We are interested in capturing the relative BtM risk factor in each country and do not have to compare accounting standards between countries. The same screening process we discussed for the U.S. is used for each country.

Fama and French went on to compare the relative performance of an international high BtM asset class portfolio to both Morgan Stanley's EAFE Index and a low BtM portfolio. The results were even more dramatic than in the U.S. The difference between high and low BtM portfolios was over 600 basis points. The difference between high BtM portfolios and the EAFE Index was over 500 basis points. This result is just too huge for you to ignore.

Historical Returns 1975-1996

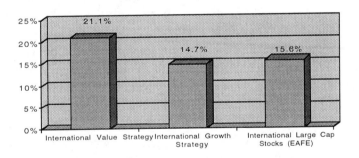

Figure 6-15: International Comparison

WHY THIS EXCESS PERFORMANCE?

High book-to-market indicates distress. The market sets a low market price relative to the company's book value and that results in a high BtM ratio to compensate for the risk.

There are at least two risks associated with the high BtM effect. One is "psychic risk" when dealing with "ugly" stocks, which don't perform—and you've got to take responsibility for what turns out to be "poor judgment." Ugly stocks are companies in distress. People in investment committees have trouble explaining to their boards of directors why they're holding such ugly stocks. Suppose you purchase Kmart. Kmart does okay. Well, that's fine. No big deal. Now suppose Kmart does poorly during that quarter. You bought Kmart because it's a high book-to-market stock. It does poorly. Now your portfolio is in trouble and you've got to explain your strategy to your board of directors. They're going to look over your shoulder and say, "How could you be such a fool to buy Kmart? Everybody knew Kmart was in trouble." That's a psychic risk—that you'll be in the hot seat.

Investors who don't have to be accountable to a board of directors, who don't have anybody looking over their shoulders, don't have to deal with psychic risk. It is their money and no one is pointing a finger at them to magnify their regret. They don't have any more psychic risk with Kmart than they do with Wal-Mart. Basically, there's nobody looking over their shoulders creating psychic risk.

The second risk of the high BtM effect is based on Merton Miller's work regarding the cost of capital. High BtM stocks have poor earning prospects. Companies with poor earning prospects have a higher cost of capital than companies with great earning prospects. Companies that are doing poorly pay a higher rate to borrow money than companies that are doing well. In the equity market, this translates into a higher expected rate of return on capital for investors providing that equity capital.

EMERGING MARKETS

Emerging markets, as an asset class, have rapidly become important components of any global portfolio. However, they also bring in different risks unique to their markets. Political instability, currency devaluation, and regulatory risk are much greater than developed countries. The lack of reliable data represents the largest problem of investing in the emerging markets. Many emerging markets have relatively low accounting standards, with very poor disclosure.

However, by adding an emerging markets asset class to your clients' holdings, you can create another layer of diversification in their portfolios. This will aid in reducing the overall risk of their portfolios. Historically, a combination of developed and emerging markets has actually been less volatile than a portfolio of only developed markets. Our research indicates that a very small position in these emerging markets, typically 5% of your equity portion, can increase return of the portfolio without increasing the overall portfolio volatility. In fact, because of the low correlation between these markets and other assets held, the overall portfolio volatility is reduced.

Our emerging markets asset class contains securities only from countries that meet stringent selection criteria. They must have a well organized market that provides ample liquidity to their shares. They must have a good legal system that protects property rights and upholds contractual obligations. It is also important to keep in mind that while these markets may be defined as emerging, the companies whose stocks are being purchased are well-established companies in these countries. Typical holdings are national banks, land developers, and phone companies of various countries. Current country selections in our emerging markets asset class include Indonesia, Turkey, Argentina, the Philippines, Portugal, Israel, Mexico, Brazil, Thailand, and Chile.

Building the Asset Class Portfolio - One Asset Class at a Time

The average financial advisor does not utilize many of these institutional asset class mutual funds for their clients. As with investors, most financial advisors unfortunately get caught up in the focus on the noise that seems to grab the headlines, which sets them up for failure. They think they are acting on material information. The reality is there is so much noise around that they do not have a chance of differentiating this noise from what is information. They utilize active management and do not stay invested for the long term. They have not developed a consistent message to assist their investors with becoming information investors. They are tempted to sell to their clients' "wants" versus their "needs."

Let's compare what the average investor might have experienced from 1976 through 1996, and compare the results if they had utilized the asset class lessons in this book. The first step is to decide what the allocation should be between equity and bond mutual funds. We have chosen the traditional institutional portfolio allocations for illustrations.

60% Equity - 40% Bonds

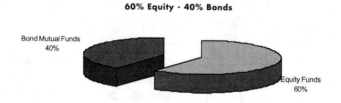

Figure 6-16: The 60%-40% Investor

Step 1. The 60%-40% Investor

The most often recommended portfolio allocation from investment professionals has been 60% in the equity market and 40% in the bond market. If we assumed that your client began with $100,000 in January 1976 invested in a combined portfolio of 60% in the average return of all equity and 40% of all bond mutual funds on the Morningstar Ondisc database, then he would have earned the following average rate of return on his investments through the end of 1996:

Portfolios	Years	Geometric Mean %	Standard Deviation %	Growth of a $1
60% Equity - 40% Bond Mutual Funds	21	12.56	9.29	11.99

Figure 6-17

For every dollar invested in 1976, the 60% - 40% allocation would have grown to $11.99. This will be the benchmark we will use to compare what you learned would have improved your returns prudently. However, this benchmark return overstates what investors would have earned for three reasons:

First, most investors would not have been able to stay invested for that period of time without second-guessing whether they were in the best mutual fund and/or whether they should be in the stock market. They would have likely changed several times over this 21-year period, chasing performance. Many times they would have been out of the market. This would have reduced their return significantly.

Second, income taxes would have significantly reduced their return. This would result from the high turnover of most retail mutual funds and the switching between funds they would have done over the years. This would have resulted in realized capital gains, which would have been taxed.

Last, the average return of all equity and bond mutual funds is overstated, due to survivor bias. The average is of all funds that are still in existence at the end of 1996. Many funds that performed poorly were merged into more successful mutual funds or terminated.

Even though a benchmark using the average rate of return of mutual funds significantly overstates the performance of what an average investor would have realized, it will provide an effective starting point to see how the asset class strategy can add value to your portfolio.

Step 2. The Indexed Portfolio

If you had done nothing more than use the most basic of asset class mutual funds, the S&P 500 and The Shearson Lehman

Government and Corporate Index, you would have accomplished approximately the same return at the same level of risk.

60% S & P 500 - 40% S/L Inter. Bonds

S/L Intermediate
Bonds
40%

S&P 500
60%

Figure 6-18: The Indexed Portfolio

Portfolios	Years	Geometric Mean %	Standard Deviation %	Growth of a $1
60% Equity - 40% Bond Mutual Funds	21	12.56	9.29	11.99
60% S & P 500 - 40% S/L Intermed. Bonds	21	12.88	9.52	12.74

Figure 6-19

All this without the high hidden cost of active management and freeing up time to spend with your family instead of trying to find the next hot mutual fund. However, we have learned of many tools that we can use as building blocks that will increase your expected return substantially without increasing risk. In the next few steps, we will add asset classes using simple percentage allocations. Even this simplistic approach adds significant value to your portfolio, as you will see.

Step 3. Substitute Short-Term Fixed Income

Substituting short-term fixed income for long-term fixed income significantly reduces risk while maintaining expected returns. In this example, we have replaced the Shearson Lehman Intermediate Government/Corporate Bond Index that has a weighted average maturity of 3 1/2 to 4 1/2 years with a 2-year fixed-income strategy that further reduces the average maturities for the portfolio. This lowers the risk. In addition, this new asset class has taken advantage of the matrix pricing strategy we discussed to increase expected returns.

Shorten Fixed Maturities

2 yr Fixed Income
40%

S&P 500
60%

Figure 6-20: Substitute Short-Term Fixed Income

Portfolios	Years	Geometric Mean %	Standard Deviation %	Growth of a $1
60% Equity - 40% Bond Mutual Funds	21	12.56	9.29	11.99
60% S & P 500 - 40% S/L Intermed. Bonds	21	12.88	9.52	12.74
Shorten Fixed Maturities	21	12.88	8.71	12.73

Figure 6-21

This reduction in risk (standard deviation) will allow you to introduce other riskier asset classes, such as international.

Step 4. Utilize Global Diversification

Foreign markets and domestic markets do not move in tandem. You can add international investments that will increase the effective diversification. In this example, we divided the 60% allocation in equity between the S&P 500 Index and the EAFE index.

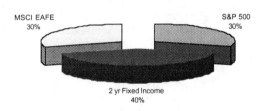

Add Global Diversification

MSCI EAFE
30%

S&P 500
30%

2 yr Fixed Income
40%

Figure 6-22: Utilize Global Diversification

Portfolios	Years	Geometric Mean %	Standard Deviation %	Growth of a $1
60% Equity - 40% Bond Mutual Funds	21	12.56	9.29	11.99
60% S & P 500 - 40% S/L Intermed. Bonds	21	12.88	9.52	12.74
Shorten Fixed Maturities	21	12.88	8.71	12.73
Add Global Diversification	21	13.10	8.82	13.27

Figure 6-23

Step 5. Introduce the Size Effect

The second risk factor that Fama and French used to explain market returns was the size factor. They found that investors demanded to be compensated with higher returns for investing in these riskier asset classes around the world. In this example, we have reduced each of the large equity asset classes by a half and reallocated that in small asset classes around the world.

Introduce the Size Effect

Int'l Small Companies 15%

US Small Companies 15%

S&P 500 15%

MSCI EAFE 15%

2 yr Fixed Income 40%

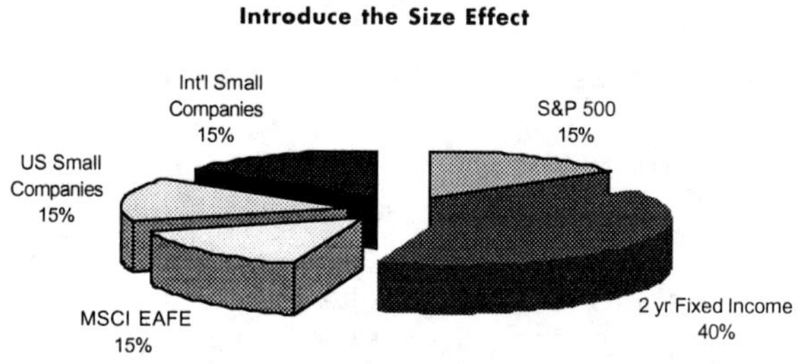

Figure 6-24: Introduce the Size Effect

Portfolios	Years	Geometric Mean %	Standard Deviation %	Growth of a $1
60% Equity - 40% Bond Mutual Funds	21	12.56	9.29	11.99
60% S & P 500 - 40% S/L Intermed. Bonds	21	12.88	9.52	12.74
Shorten Fixed Maturities	21	12.88	8.71	12.73
Add Global Diversification	21	13.10	8.82	13.27
Introduce the Size Effect	21	14.74	8.79	17.93

Figure 6-25

It is interesting to note that the introduction of this risky asset class reduces the portfolio risk while increasing returns.

Step 6. Introduce the High Book to Market Effect

The third risk factor that Fama and French used to explain market returns was the relative book-to-market (BtM) ratio. They found that this risk factor was rewarded most significantly outside the U.S. The replacement of the S&P 500 index and EAFE index with a high BtM asset class increased returns significantly while reducing risk.

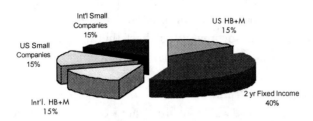

Utilize the High BtM Factor

Int'l Small Companies 15%

US HB+M 15%

US Small Companies 15%

2 yr Fixed Income 40%

Int'l. HB+M 15%

Figure 6-26: Introduce the High Book to Market Effect

Portfolios	Years	Geometric Mean %	Standard Deviation %	Growth of a $1
60% Equity - 40% Bond Mutual Funds	21	12.56	9.29	11.99
60% S & P 500 - 40% S/L Intermed. Bonds	21	12.88	9.52	12.74
Shorten Fixed Maturities	21	12.88	8.71	12.73
Add Global Diversification	21	13.10	8.82	13.27
Introduce the Size Effect	21	14.74	8.79	17.93
Utilize the High BtM Risk Factor	21	15.93	8.76	22.30

Figure 6-27

Implementing asset class investing allows your investors to beat the market returns of the average investor significantly. Using our benchmark average investor portfolio, we were able to increase the growth of a dollar over the 21 years from $11.99 to $22.30. This represents more than a 86% increase in the ending value of the portfolio over our benchmark. Most investors did not typically make returns anywhere near this benchmark.

GETTING A QUICK START ON YOUR OWN
ASSET CLASS PORTFOLIO

Step One: Identify how much money your clients can leave untouched for five years in an investment portfolio except for emergencies or income needs. This amount is the dollar amount they should get started with. You should recommend that they invest all the capital with you so that you can ensure that their investment program is consistent. Many investors mistakenly believe they are safer working with several advisors, as a further extension of diversification. This practice is wasteful and unfortunately, at best this introduces additional cost. At worst they end up making foolish and costly mistakes with noise investment advisors.

Step Two: Decide the risk your clients are willing to take. In the appendix, we have illustrated each of the five model portfolios we built. Examine the negative years. Most investors are not concerned with standard deviations, but with the absolute loss of capital. The worst financial recession since World War II was during the 1973-1974 time frame. Look to see which portfolio would have been able to weather the storm, knowing that the five-year periods were all positive. No one can predict that the next two years will not be as bad as the 1973-1974 period. You should help your investor decide on what risk they are willing to take, based on the assumption that the next two years will be the same as the 1973-1974 period.

Step Three: Consider using one of the model portfolios that most closely aligns with the risk your investors want to take as their target investment allocation.

Step Four: Select the asset class mutual funds that best incorporate the concepts that we have discussed on a cost effective basis.

Step Five: Use an account at one of the custodians that provide low cost execution. It is unlikely that one mutual fund family will have all the asset class mutual funds that you will need for your portfolio. Custodians, such as discount brokers, will make rebalancing much easier to complete.

Step Six: Rebalance or reoptimize at least annually. By systematically rebalancing to the original model portfolio at least annually, you will gradually sell those asset classes that have gone up while buying those that currently have lower returns. This discipline eliminates the negative results of emotional trading and helps maintain the portfolio's risk profile.

A great debate has taken place in the industry about exactly which portfolios are most efficient. In the past, we have focused on four model portfolios—defensive, conservative, moderate, and aggressive—and have seldom deviated from these. This has allowed us an extremely consistent marketing, sales, and operation program in order to grow our business and our advisors' businesses substantially. Recently, we have made huge technological improvements in our portfolio management systems, which have allowed us to explore more flexible portfolio construction. This more flexible portfolio construction is being considered only in light of always serving the investor first, not with any consideration towards marketing. As you design your own business plan, you should always focus on doing what's right by your investors in regard to their needs versus what they may want.

Our Investment Committee has determined that there is a range of portfolios around the efficient frontier that meet a high degree of confidence in similar expected rates of return and risk. To better facilitate this, we have made a number of changes. The first was to increase the number of our model portfolios to five. The fifth portfolio is an all-equity portfolio. Below, we have illustrated five model portfolios and their historical range of returns before any fees.

Global Defensive

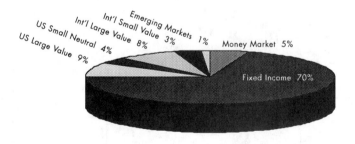

Global Defensive

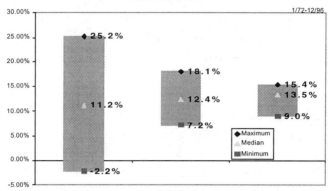

These are historical results and not guarantees of future performance.

Global Conservative

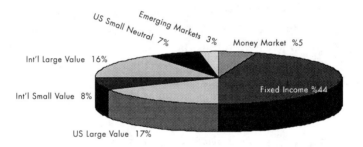

Global Conservative

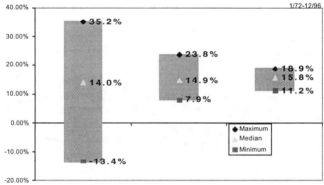

These are historical results and not guarantees of future performance.

Global Moderate

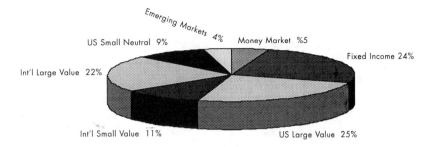

Global Moderate

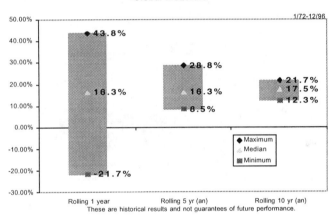

These are historical results and not guarantees of future performance.

Global Aggressive

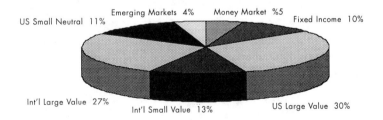

107

Global Aggressive

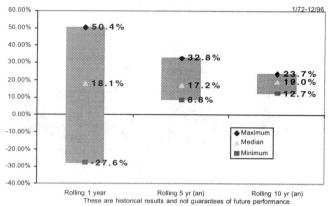

Rolling 1 year   Rolling 5 yr (an)   Rolling 10 yr (an)
These are historical results and not guarantees of future performance.

Global Equity

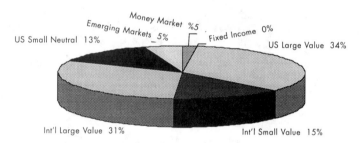

Global Equity

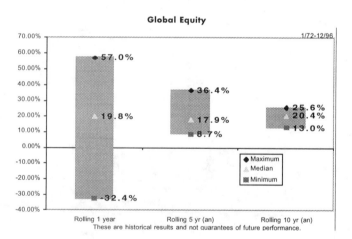

Rolling 1 year   Rolling 5 yr (an)   Rolling 10 yr (an)
These are historical results and not guarantees of future performance.

Figure 6-28:

108

In addition, we now give our advisors more flexibility in determining the appropriate combination of asset classes in each portfolio. For example, currently we have a stated policy of 50% international and 50% domestic. Most of us would agree that it's arguable that 51% should be in domestic and 49% international. How far does this range of confidence go? Our Investment Committee has established a range of confidence from which advisors working with our firm can deviate from the model portfolios for economic and behavioral issues of their clients as follows: International versus domestic—recommended portfolio, 50/50% allocation—can overweight international 60%, but not less than 30%. Large versus small stocks—current recommended portfolio, 70/30% allocation—can overweight large cap 80%, but not less than 50%. The emerging market recommended percentage allocation would be 5% of the equity component. Advisors would have the ability to have any allocation between 6% and 0% of the equity.

Market neutral versus value. Currently on the large positions, we go 100% value, utilizing the high book to market strategy and in the small positions, we stay with the market neutral, the Decile 9-10 asset class. In our portfolio mix, we allow advisors, after considering their clients' economic and behavioral issues, to be anywhere between 100% market neutral to 100% value in both large and small.

In the appendix, we've reproduced our Internet screen and the resulting spreadsheet that the program produces allows our advisors to customize their clients' portfolios. To the extent that you deviate from model portfolios, it is important that you build the systems that support all the key elements of your business plan.

Relative Performance of the Model Portfolios

Let's compare how the five model portfolios that include fixed income would have performed relative to all balanced retail mutual funds that were in existence from 1975 to 1996. It is easy to see how asset class investing can let you prudently beat the market.

	Fund Name	Total Return (Annlzd) 15 Yr	Standard Deviation 10 Yr
1	Global Equity	19.00	14.25
2	Global Aggressive	17.64	12.38
3	CGM Mutual	16.69	16.91
4	Global Moderate	16.15	10.25
5	Fidelity Puritan	15.84	11.04
6	Merrill Lynch Capital A	15.37	11.67
7	State Farm Balanced	15.36	11.31
8	Vanguard/Wellington	15.31	11.72
9	Dodge & Cox Balanced	15.22	11.05
10	MFS Total Return A	14.81	10.07
11	Phoenix Income & Growth A	14.67	8.60
12	American Balanced	14.51	9.70
13	United Continental Income A	14.48	11.54
14	IDS Mutual A	14.44	10.26
15	Franklin Income I	14.36	8.03
16	George Putnam of Boston A	14.30	11.15
17	Vanguard/Welleslley Income	14.21	7.73
18	Delaware A	14.19	15.15
19	Global Conservative	14.10	7.50
20	Sentinel Balanced A	13.90	9.24
21	T. Rowe Price Balanced	13.75	10.66
22	United Retirement shares A	13.52	11.77
23	EV Traditional Investors	13.15	9.81
24	Alliance Balanced Shares A	13.15	11.93
25	Federated Stock & Bond A	13.07	7.50
26	Keystone Balance (K-1)	13.03	10.34
27	Kemper Total Return A	12.95	14.60
28	New England Balanced A	12.93	14.67
29	Founders Balanced	12.77	10.06
30	Stein Roe Balanced	12.75	10.41
31	Pax World	12.65	9.63
32	Composite Bond & Stock A	12.61	9.05
33	Pioneer Income A	11.58	6.70
34	Global Defensive	11.46	4.36

Figure 6-29:

It is very hard to stay on track with the tremendous amount of noise present. Often things are not as they appear. In fact, every year this list will look better and better as funds that are not successful cease to exist and are dropped from the databases.

In 1996, for example, 242 of the 4,555 stock funds tracked by Lipper Analytical Services of Summit, N.J., were merged or liquidated. These disappearances could have a significant effect on reported performance. Consider the annual performance that Lipper reported in 1986. At that time, Lipper reported there were 568 diversified U.S. stock funds that had an average rate of return of 13.39% for the year 1986. Today, Lipper reports that the average return for 1986 was 14.65%.

How did this substantial improvement in the data series come about? The new number is based on the performance of only the 434 funds from the 1986 group that are still in business today. Numbers can be misleading.

One of the challenges you will have is that most investors don't want to pay any taxes. With the publicity of tax-managed mutual funds, it's important for you to understand how to help your clients with their tax liability. Let's explore that together in the next chapter.

T he types of investment tools that most financial advisors use in a managed account are primarily retail mutual funds that are inherently tax inefficient. The ideal tax-efficient mutual fund is a fund that would make no taxable distributions whatsoever. Its pre-tax and after-tax return would be identical.

Let's take a look at how a fund like this might work. Let's assume that we have a mutual fund that has a dividend rate of 2% with capital appreciation of 8%, so a total return each year of 10%. We assume the current federal income tax is 39.6% and the capital gains tax is 28%. No state income tax is assumed.

In our example we will compare three types of mutual funds, the traditional tax-inefficient fund, the capital gains tax-efficient fund, and the totally tax-efficient fund.

THE TRADITIONAL TAX-INEFFICIENT FUND

The traditional tax-inefficient fund distributes all its ordinary dividend income each year, and also realizes and distributes all the capital gains annually. We call this a tax-inefficient fund, but this really is the traditional mutual fund. While most mutual funds certainly distribute all ordinary income, many do not distribute all capital gains. Because most retail funds have relatively high turnover, they tend to distribute a very large amount of their capital gains.

In addition, traditional funds are cognizant of the disadvantages of having large built-up capital gains. In most cases, we are seeing about 80% of capital gains realized annually. In this example, to keep it simple, we are going to assume a distribution of 100% of the capital gains.

THE CAPITAL GAINS TAX-EFFICIENT FUND

The second type of fund is the capital gains tax-efficient fund. Here, all ordinary income is distributed annually and is taxable. However, they are able to avoid the capital gains being realized currently.

Lastly, the totally tax-efficient fund makes no taxable distributions. They are able to avoid not only the capital gains, but also the ordinary distributions.

In the accompanying chart, we compare the returns on each fund on an after-tax basis. The differences are extremely significant over time and will represent substantial dollars.

Chart 7-1 (Chart showing three bars — tax-inefficient fund with 6.97, capital gains tax- efficient fund 9.21, and tax-efficient fund 10%)

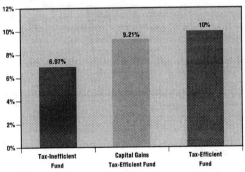

Figure 7-1: Compound Rates of Return After Taxes on Distributions of Hypothetical Funds

THE TOTALLY TAX-EFFICIENT FUND

Let's isolate a tax-efficient fund. One of the most tax-efficient strategies today is an asset class mutual fund. The largest mutual fund utilizing this strategy is the Vanguard Index 500. Since its inception in September 1976, its total rate of return has been 14.2% annually. The only way an investor would actual receive this return is if he paid no tax along the way. By avoiding income tax, $1,000 invested at the inception would have grown to $14,882.

Unfortunately, unless you are a tax-exempt investor, you have to pay taxes and you never see the true total return. If somehow you could be taxed only on the ordinary income component, you would have averaged a rate of return of 12.58%. The $1,000 invested would have netted $11,133 after taxes—over 25% less.

And, since most of us have to pay both ordinary income and capital gains taxes currently, at the assumed tax rate in our example, the $1,000 would have netted only $9,820. This lowers the rate of return to 11.89%. This is serious erosion of capital for one of the most tax efficient mutual funds available today.

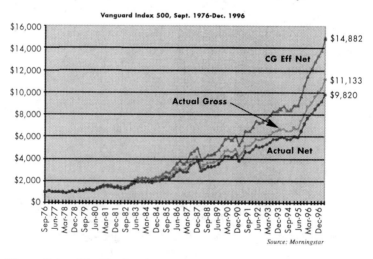

Source: Morningstar

Figure 7-2:   The Tax Impact on Mutual Funds

We could help our investors dramatically by implementing a more tax-efficient strategy. How would we go about doing this? First, in the capital gains tax-efficient portfolio, we would simply hold winners. By not selling them, we would not realize the capital gains. We would sell losers to offset any realized gains from stocks being taken away from us in mergers and acquisitions. Also, we would recognize and carry forward the large losses through selling these losers. The simple strategy for a capital gains tax-efficient fund would be to sell whenever there was a material loss and realize the loss as quickly as possible.

If we were attempting to have a fully tax-efficient fund, we would have to somehow create deductible expenses that would offset the ordinary income distributions of the dividends. One suggestion we heard jokingly is to increase fees, but we don't think the clients dislike taxes that much. A more effective way of accomplishing this would be leverage. Unfortunately, in the S&P 500, you would need about 50% leverage to be able to shelter the ordinary income. We would have to margin the securities by 50% and that borrowing cost would create the deductible expense to offset the ordinary income resulting in no taxable income. To reduce the amount of leverage required, we could buy and hold only low or no dividend yielding stocks. That just doesn't make sense.

Today, there are a number of tax-managed mutual funds being aggressively marketed. They are attempting to become capital gains tax-efficient. None, at this point in time, have actually tried to be totally tax-efficient. The longest running fund today that is tax-efficient is the Schwab 1000. It has been able to avoid capital gains distributions since its inception in April 1991, but has made the income distributions. A number of other ones have come forward, particularly Vanguard.

Why haven't we seen more of the capital gains funds? First, when you minimize capital gains distributions, you create a substantial deferred capital gains problem. You have a potential meltdown. Techniques used to defer these small capital gains in the near term are likely to result in huge capital gains distributions sometime later. By using the strategy of deferring capital gains distributions, the mutual fund has a substantially growing inventory of low cost basis stocks. If the mutual fund has a net redemption, it is going to be forced to realize these gains and these distributions potentially could be extremely large. Most investors or advisors do not understand the impact of this. Unpleasant surprises may possibly result in lawsuits.

If we look at a selected group of the funds today in the accompanying table, we can see that the potential capital gains exposure, which is defined as capital appreciation as a percentage of a mutual fund's total assets, is growing substantially. For one particular fund, Stagecoach Corporate Stock (an S&P 500 index fund) started in January 1984, 53% of its current net asset value upon liquidation would be taxed as a capital gain. There is no reason a taxable investor would knowingly want to buy into this fund with all the other choices.

Selected Mutual Funds, through January 1997

Tax Managed Funds	Inception Date	Fund PCGE
Schwab 1000	4/91	33%
Vanguard Tax-Mgd Cap Apprec	9/94	16%
Vanguard Tax-Mgd Grth & Inc	9/94	14%
Index Funds		
DFA U.S. Large Company	12/90	27%
Fidelity U.S. Equity Index	2/88	25%
SEI Index S&P 500 Index A	8/85	29%
Stagecoach Corporate Stock A	1/84	53%
Vanguard Index 500	8/76	24%

Source: Morningstar

Figure 7-3:   Potential Capital Gains Exposure (PCGE)

In building the total tax-efficient fund, we encounter problems. Minimizing income distributions is only accomplished by increasing risk dramatically through the use of leverage or specializing in low dividend yield stocks. Most of these result in very undesirable portfolio characteristics; low dividends and poor diversification are detrimental to the overall investment strategy.

There is a tremendous contrast between tax-efficiency and investment strategy. Most of us find this troublesome. Investment strategies that work are typically not the most tax-efficient. If we compared small caps with large caps, almost all of us would agree that the expected rate of return is greater with small caps due to the higher risk and that a portion should be held. However, the more we allocate to the small-cap sector, the more it becomes tax-inefficient, because in a small-cap portfolio, you sell winners, stocks that have grown, and you hold losers, stocks that are smaller. By contract, large caps are relatively tax-efficient. You sell losers, stocks that are smaller, and you hold winners, those stocks that have grown.

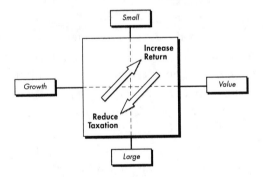

Figure 7-4:   The Contrast Between Tax Efficiency and Investment Strategy

In another investment strategy, value versus growth (high BtM versus low BtM), most of us would agree that the expected rate of return is greater for value. In value stocks, we sell winners, stocks with lower book-to-market, and hold losers, stocks with higher book-to-market. This is less tax-inefficient. In growth stocks, we sell losers and hold winners, which is more tax-efficient.

Most of us still remember investing in the 1970s and 1980s, when we last mixed up the priority between economics and tax motivations. What we find is the after-tax risk premiums associated with having the small bias and value bias are significant enough to warrant tilting your portfolio toward both, even though they are less tax-efficient than large cap and growth. We should focus on investing first and then ask what we can do with the existing investment structures that add the most after tax.

What are the practical implications? First, we can segregate client funds to the extent possible. We should put the fixed-income and the small-cap and value strategies with the higher tax liabilities into the tax-exempt funded accounts. In the taxable accounts, we should use the large-cap market portfolio strategies.

However, tax-efficiency alone should not determine investment strategies. The extra costs of generating these tax efficiencies, such as trading and increased management fees, often eliminate their benefits. The risk premiums captured using leading edge research—even though tax-inefficient—will often be large enough to make them dominant on an after-tax basis.

What can we conclude? There is an inherent conflict that advisors need to recognize between investment strategies and tax-efficiency. Unfortunately, you can't have the best of both. Mutual funds today are not naturally tax-efficient. However, individual securities do not allow us to accomplish the broad asset class diversification that we desire. The cost of implementing global and small-cap strategies with individual securities for most of our investors does not make sense. It is cost prohibitive when we start investing international. In addition, the specific risk inherent with individual securities negates most, if not all, of the tax benefits associated.

Today's existing tax-managed mutual funds emphasize minimizing capital gains distributions, but present substantial long-term peril to advisors who do not manage their clients' expectations. Generally, minimizing income distributions is largely ignored.

There are no simple solutions. Institutional asset class mutual funds provide a partial solution in that they are relatively tax-efficient. An alternative that advisors should consider for their clients who have relatively high tax sensitivity is variable annuities.

VARIABLE ANNUITIES

Today's variable annuity is more popular than ever. Why? Because the variable annuity could be the answer to not only the tax issues we have addressed, but the shortfall retirement problems of longer life expectancies and longer retirement periods. This comes at a time when corporations and government are getting out of the retirement business. All of these trends are leading to drastic reductions in expected pension benefits.

The variable annuity market is exploding. In 1994, it totaled more than $160 billion and is expected to reach twice that by the end of 1996, with over $500 billion in fixed low rate annuities. Income and gains from variable annuity investments build up tax-deferred over years, until the investor begins withdrawing money out after retirement. An investor does not get a tax deduction for money placed in a variable annuity, but there are no annual limits on contributions, as in company-sponsored retirement plans or Individual Retirement Accounts (IRAs). When an investor takes money out of a variable annuity after retirement, he or she will then be taxed at ordinary income tax rates, not at the capital gains rates that apply to investments withdrawn from mutual funds.

The advisor must be careful in selecting a variable annuity. Most variable annuities still have high sales charges, high

costs, and only offer actively managed mutual fund investment programs. When you step back and look at all the factors, you can begin to see why the financial press has been
writing negative articles about variable annuities. The concept
of variable annuities, however, is solid, and the solution it presents is simple and academically sound.

The arrival of no-load, low cost variable annuities and
variable annuities that offer institutional asset class diversification has begun to change the negative press, and with
good reason.

What are variable annuities?

They're contracts between an insurance company and an
investor (known as an annuity buyer) purchased either with a
single payment or a series of payments during the accumula-
tion period. With a variable annuity, the value of the account
will fluctuate with changes in the market value of the underlying securities owned. The investment performance will
determine the amount of money available at the time of withdrawal. Unlike fixed annuities, variable annuities are not
guaranteed as to principal and/or interest, but have the potential for higher returns.

Inside the variable annuity

Variable annuities are long-term investments, and the
ideal long-term investment is one with a reliable compound
return and not a lot of ups and downs over the years. Mutual
fund managers tend to focus on stock selection and/or market
timing. But these are costly to implement, with an extremely
low probability of success, and have actually proven ineffective in adding value.

In addition to lowering fees and eliminating commissions,
some variable annuity companies are now offering institutional asset classes inside the annuity wrapper. These annuities
include all the major groupings of equity securities in combination that we have discussed. Combining asset classes in this
way can both increase return and reduce risk within a tax-
deferred environment.

120

But still a problem remains—the cost of variable annuity operations is often greater than the tax benefits. For example, it does not make sense to use an S&P 500 index mutual fund inside a variable annuity. The cost of even a low cost annuity wrapper negates most if not all the benefits of this relatively tax-efficient mutual fund. However, if you use value strategies in your portfolios, the results will be different. Value strategies have a much higher expected return. However, they eventually realize much more of their gain as taxable. This is why the value strategies make so much sense in the variable annuity.

The bottom line is that because a value strategy is "buying the dogs and selling the winners," it creates realized capital gains which are best held within a variable annuity wrap because the gains can be deferred. Therefore, you can remove the negative effects of taxation by deferring all taxes for a period of time (10 years, for example), while you enjoy the same premium within your variable annuity—and the negative aspect of the value strategy, tax inefficiency, is erased.

But which variable annuities offer this? How can an advisor of a variable annuity company that subscribes to Modern Portfolio Theory offset the negative effects of taxation in value investing—and do it all with low costs and no sales charges?

There have been many articles published about variable annuities and asset class investing. But little has been written about the benefits of combining a no-cost, low fee variable annuity with a state-of-the-art asset class investing program. The logic is compelling. Investing in a variable annuity that has no sales charges and is comprised of no-load institutional asset class mutual funds will automatically save your client money. A variable annuity that is not a market-driven product but is, rather, a consumer-oriented long-term investment, offers the best currently available investment vehicle for accumulating substantial wealth in equities on a tax-deferred basis.

121

First, the owner of the annuity doesn't pay taxes on annuity interest until the funds are paid out when he or she retires. Second, unlike a mutual fund, the annuity does not pay out income or distribute any capital gains, so the investor accumulates units which grow tax-deferred, making the compound effect even more dramatic. Third, unlike fixed-rate annuities, where an insurance company determines how to invest funds, a variable annuity allows the investor to choose his or her own investments, such as mutual funds. And that's why it's important to enhance returns inside the wrapper of the variable annuity. It's also important how you choose a variable annuity. There's still a huge universe of thousands of no-load mutual funds. The solution is to become a knowledgeable advisor who understands asset class investing and who understands how a variable annuity could be the answer to many of your clients' retirement problems. This is also why the variable annuity story is so compelling.

Unfortunately, the public is unaware of the benefits of variable annuities. Most articles written about variable annuities are negative, discounting their value by pointing out three major problems:

The cost of variable annuity operations is often greater than the tax benefits.

No variable annuity has ever been created with the consumer uppermost in mind.

Variable annuities are managed by either a mutual fund company or by an insurance company and the majority of mutual fund managers fail to match the S&P 500 stock index.

The solution is to find variable annuities that answer all three problems. There are variable annuities with no front-end or back-end sales charges and with low maintenance fees that are consumer driven and have an investment strategy that could match or beat the various indices.

If you have knowledge of and access to this type of variable annuity, this will give you a considerable edge in building a business, and customers will be compelled to bring their

Total Insurance Expense <= .85%

Product Name	Subaccounts	Insurance Expense	Portfolio Fees	International Options	Death Benefit	Insurance Company	Duff & Phelps Rating	Fixed Account	Phone Number
No Load									
RWB/DFA Variable Annuity	7	0.65%	.40-1.00%	Yes	6yr Step	Providian	AA+	Yes	800-366-7266
Galaxy	4	0.55%	.70-1.40%	No	Principal	America Skandia	AA-	Yes	800-541-3087
Providian Advisor's Edge	17	0.65%	.40-1.50%	Yes	6yr Step	Providian	AA+	Yes	800-797-9177
Scudder Horizon	6	0.70%	.50-1.08%	Yes	Principal	Charter National	N/A	Yes	800-242-4402
T. Rowe No-Load	5	0.55%	.70-1.05%	Yes	5yr Step	Security Benefit	AA-	Yes	800-469-6587
Touchstone	7	0.80%	.50-1.25%	No	Principal	Western-Southerns	AAA	Yes	800-669-2796
Value Advantage Plus	21	0.45%	.80-1.47%	Yes	Principal	Fortis	N/A	No	800-827-5877
Vanguard Variable Annuity Plan	7	0.55%	.23-.34%	Yes	Principal	Providian	AA+	No	800-462-2391
The Schwab Variable Annuity	21	0.85%	.35-1.75%	Yes	Principal	Great-West Life	AAA	Yes	800-838-0650

Figure 7-5:   Variable Annuities

business to you. There are no simple solutions. An alternative that advisors should consider for their clients who have relatively high tax sensitivity is a variable annuity.

CHAPTER EIGHT

THE INVESTMENT MANAGEMENT PROCESS

The key to building a hugely successful asset management business is to develop great relationships with your clients. It will give you a significant competitive advantage and will maximize your creation of equity. This is not to imply that all your clients need to be your best friends.

Every financial advisor we have ever asked to describe their relationship with their clients has responded, "Great." Most mean they have great rapport. They are often "close friends" with all their clients. While this generally makes business more enjoyable, it can also backfire and blur the lines between your business and your personal life.

Friendship is not the highest value that your clients look for in an advisor. Clients want professionals whom they can trust and who truly impress them. You have to build trust and systematically impress your clients at every moment of truth you have with them. A moment of truth is any contact you have with your clients when you have the opportunity to delight them.

In the book, *Cultivating the Affluent*, Russ Alan Prince and Karen Maru File report that they found the most satisfied, affluent investors had averaged 14 total contacts (in-person, mail, and telephone) with their advisors in a six-month period. Those who were very dissatisfied had averaged only 8.6 contacts over the same period. Many financial advisors from the transactional side of the business could never provide that level of service to each of their clients. They have been taught to sell and move on. They have very few clients, but a lot of customers. This leads them to maximize their own income in the short run, often to the detriment of their clients' long-term success, and creates little or no equity in their business.

Some financial advisors are really only selling their client list when they think they are selling their business. Unfortunately for most, that is all they have to sell. A client list is truly not very valuable. Your clients do not have to stay with the new owner. However, if you have the systems in place to build and maintain great relationships on purpose, the clients will stay with the business no matter who is advising. The clients will be better served and you will have the flexibility to leverage your business by bringing in more client service personnel. Your business would sell for a premium.

The investment consulting process we have utilized is based on a series of scheduled meetings designed to build trust and impress your clients from the very first meeting. Your key strategy is to leave nothing to chance.

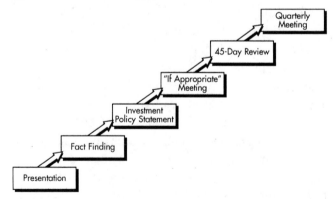

Figure 8-1: **Investment Management Consulting Process**

THE PRESENTATION

Your goal at the first meeting is to qualify your prosp
You need to determine whether they are a candidate for your
services. If so, you must establish trust immediately so the
prospect will want to proceed to the next step with you.

The presentation can be in a one-on-one setting or conducted in an investment workshop format. The process is
effective in both formats. If you decide to follow the workshop approach, team up with a good speaker who has the same
target market, and share expenses and promotion. It's easy to
find CPAs or attorneys who share your target market. By
teaming up, you not only benefit from having another good
presenter; you gain credibility from each other. Additionally,
your co-presenter can increase the number of attendees.

Your presentation should start with determining the values,
goals and concerns of your prospect(s). You will be judged by the
quality of questions you ask. One of our top sales consultants, Bill
Bachrach, discusses in his book, *Value-Based Selling*, the art of
building high-trust client relationships on purpose by initiating a
brief exchange about the importance of money in your clients'
lives. We strongly recommend that you incorporate a discussion of
"What is important about money to you?" in the first five minutes
of meeting with a new prospect. Used effectively, this exchange
will allow you to determine the prospects' values, tap into their
positive emotions, and rapidly gain their trust.

Many financial advisors are taught to sell their prospects
something first, then make them a client. Unfortunately, you
only have one time to make a great first impression. If you take
the traditional approach, you immediately position yourself as a
salesman. While there is nothing wrong with being a salesman,
by focusing on their values, you will become their trusted financial advisor. In questioning your prospects about the importance
of money, your job is to uncover their value-based emotions so
that they can make the connection between making smart financial decisions with you and fulfilling their life values.

Start with the question, "What is important about money to you?" and let your prospect respond. Let's say he answers, "Security". After writing the first response on your yellow pad or your fact-finder form, then ask, "What is important about security to you?" Continue uncovering his values until you think you have heard his final answer. (If your presentation is to a group at a seminar, have the audience respond to the questions as a group while you write their answers on a whiteboard.) Then you can ask the confirming question: "Is there anything more important to you than (the last value mentioned)?" If the prospect says yes, ask what is more important and continue with the questioning format. If the prospect answers no, you are ready to ask for a precommitment.

The precommitment begins to establish the basis for your relationship. Tell the prospect, "Suppose we can create a strategy that will help you make smart financial choices. I'm talking about the choices you could make to achieve (insert each of his value responses). If that were the case, would you and I have a basis for working together?"

If the prospect's answer to the precommitment is yes, you have established an agreement in principle to move ahead. If the answer is no, you need to find out why. Think about it—if your prospect tells you he will not want to work with you even though you can develop a plan that will achieve all his values, there is a problem. You will have found out in the first five minutes whether or not you have a potential client.

While Bachrach's techniques seem remarkably simple, you will need practice. When you can use these techniques effectively, you will see a significant improvement in your success. Call Bill's office at (800)347-3707 to find out more about how you can become proficient in these techniques. It is one of the highest payoff investments our firm ever made.

Once you have your prospects' precommitment, the balance of your presentation should provide the key concepts of your investment strategy. We like to begin by presenting the difference between noise investors and information investors using the decision matrix we discussed in chapter four. Then, depending upon the prospect's need for more information (not ours), we would walk him through the five key concepts of Modern Portfolio Theory we discussed in chapter five. If he still had questions, we would illustrate the building block format of how our methodology would be implemented as discussed in chapter six. Lastly, we show them how implementation of our strategy would have a higher probability of addressing his needs, objectives, and values.

We then discuss drafting a personalized Investment Policy Statement (IPS) for him. This is the time to set up the next appointment. Explain that the goal of the next meeting will be a fact-finding interview to gather accurate information about your prospect in order to design an IPS tailored to his specific needs.

Don't rush your prospect. Modify the speed of your presentation to correspond with the recipient's rate of understanding. Money management is too complex to explain quickly. If you see his eyes glaze over, slow down. You can make a presentation in 15 minutes, but some prospects need more time to assimilate the information. Don't allow the prospect to become performance driven. Chasing performance numbers can counter the logic behind money management. Empirical evidence clearly shows that attempts to beat the market by buying performance result in inferior returns.

At the close of the presentation, walk your prospect through the actual process of working with you. Explain that the reason most of us are uncomfortable when making any major decision is that we do not have faith in the integrity of the process. Clearly articulate each step of your investment process. The next meeting will be the fact-finding meeting. Then, you will schedule a meeting to review the complimentary personal IPS. It will illustrate where they are now, where they want to go, and how to achieve their goals based on their risk tolerance. We like to tell them that, even if they wanted to invest at the IPS meeting, we would not let them.

We are looking for a life-long relationship. We ask the prospect to take the written IPS home to review and see if he has any questions. The next meeting is what we call the "if appropriate" meeting. At this meeting, you review their questions and, "if appropriate," begin working together. Then schedule quarterly meetings to review your progress.

When presenting to a group, invite the audience to set up a personal meeting with you, with the offer of the complimentary personal IPS. You still need to walk them through your investment management consulting process in closing your group presentation.

THE FACT-FINDING INTERVIEW

Your goals for the second meeting with a prospect should be to define his or her needs, objectives and values, and to determine his or her current financial position. Be sure to make it clear to the prospect that you are collecting the information necessary to write an IPS tailored to his or her specific needs.

Both for your potential client's benefit and your own, you should never try to sell a specific investment plan or instrument until you understand that particular person's needs, objectives and values.

We like to send the prospect a letter as a reminder for this meeting. In the letter, we request that they bring all the financial information they have readily available as it relates to asset management. This would typically include their last two years' income tax forms, recent financial statements, bank statements, mutual fund statements, brokerage statements, life insurance policies, employee benefit statements, any wills, and/or trusts. We also ask them to bring any additional information that they believe would be helpful in better understanding their financial situation.

In our QuickStart workshops for advisors, we are often asked how to get prospects to provide this information at the first meeting—particularly if they are combining the presentation and fact-finding meetings. These are the only two meetings that we ever recommend combining. The way to get them to bring the information is quite simple—just ask. Tell them you value both their time and yours. To make the most productive use of both, and to develop a professional IPS, you need to know their financial situations. Without this information you cannot do a high-quality job. You should never lower your standards.

If a prospect feels uncomfortable bringing his financial information to the fact-finding meeting because he is unsure if he is going to work with you, tell him to bring it in his briefcase. Then, after your preliminary discussion, if he does not agree that there is a basis for exploring doing business together, you will stop the meeting there. You will not ask him to open his briefcase. On an extremely rare occasion, you may have a prospect that still does not want to share his financial situation. Since you cannot properly determine if you can add value without this information, do not continue to work with him. More likely than not, he will prove to be a difficult client.

After reviewing with the prospect all the information necessary to complete the IPS, schedule the next meeting. Describe again at the end of each meeting the investment management process and where he currently is in the process.

The IPS Meeting

Present your prospect's Investment Policy Statement and summarize your recommendations. You may wish to emphasize certain features of your program that are most relevant by going into greater detail. At this point, you should discourage immediate action; instead, suggest that your prospect take the material home for review. Set up a fourth meeting where you can answer any questions and, if appropriate, set up accounts. Money management can be designed to be simple, yet both personal and comprehensive, in delivering the best for your client.

On occasion, you will have a client who wants to invest immediately after the IPS presentation. We have found that by

not taking the account until he has a chance to review everything, we have built better long-term relationships. We
believe this happens for two reasons: first, throughout the
investment management consulting process, the client is at
ease knowing that he is not going to have to make a financial
decision until the "if appropriate" meeting. This allows him
to stay focused on the process of working with you to solve
his financial needs. Lastly, it continues your differentiation
strategy of being his trusted advisor.

We feel that the IPS is such a critically important first step
that, without exception, we have prepared one with each of
our clients. An IPS defines in written form the investor's
financial objectives, the amount of funds available for investment, the investment methodology, the strategy that will be
used to reach those objectives, and it helps to identify risk tolerance levels.

It ensures that both the client and advisor are in sync on
the long-term goals and objectives and serves as a guideline
for the client to benchmark his progress each quarter. The
written IPS helps to maintain a sound long-term plan, when
short-term market declines cause your clients to doubt your
investment strategy.

Your clients are normal investors. They will get caught up
in the emotion of the day. It's only through long-term planning that they are going to be successful and not fall back into
old habits. In the heat of a market downturn, it is critical to
have a strategy in place ahead of time.

Creating an IPS embodies the essence of the financial
planning process: assessing where you are now, where you
want to go, and developing a strategy to get there. Having
and using this policy statement compels your clients to
become more disciplined and systematic, increasing the
probability of satisfying their investment goals. In addition,
if your clients are trustees, the development and use of a
written IPS will go a long way toward ensuring they will
meet their fiduciary responsibilities.

132

ESTABLISHING YOUR CLIENT'S INVESTMENT POLICY STATEMENT

In every IPS you create for your clients, you should include the following six areas of discussion:

1. State their long-term needs, objectives, and values clearly and concisely.

Long-term goals can be anything from early retirement to purchasing a new home. One of the most common goals among our clients is to become financially independent. What that often means to our clients is that their investment portfolios will provide them with the income necessary to increase and maintain their quality of life. This is as important for our clients who are still working as those already retired.

Include your client's values from the "what is important about money to you?" discussion. This will continue to personalize their IPS and help remind them of why they have begun this journey with you as you review the IPS in future quarterly meetings.

2. Define the level of risk the client is willing to accept.

Along the road to reaching their financial goals, there are going to be bumps caused by a downturn in various markets. It is important for your clients to understand the amount of risk they're willing to tolerate during the investment period. In designing a portfolio, you must determine the absolute loss your clients can sustain in any one-year period without terminating their investment program. As we know, no one can predict market movements and they have to be in a position to weather any storm.

The best way to determine the level of risk in a portfolio is to look at its performance during 1973-1974. These years experienced the worst financial recession since World War II. No one can predict the future; the next two years might be similar to 1973 and 1974. There is a 5% probability that in the next 20 years, we will experience a similar downturn. You probably remember waiting in line for gas. The S&P 500 Index lost 37.2% and small-company stocks lost 56.5%. An investment in the largest mutual fund today, Fidelity

Magellan, would have been painful for most investors. The value of an investment of $200,000 made on January 1, 1973 would have declined to $86,000 by December 31, 1974. Most investors would have a hard time maintaining a long-term perspective and staying with the program during such a loss.

Show an analysis of how your client's portfolio would have performed during 1973-1974. In the appendix you will find simulated model returns for each year from 1972 to 1996 to assist you in this process. Choose the portfolio which your client would have been comfortable with. If your client would have closed their account because of that downturn, they are taking too much risk and should consider a lower risk model portfolio. Investments tend to be cyclical and no one can predict their performance in the short-term. The best performing year for both the S&P 500 Index and small-company stocks was 1975, when they earned 37.2% and 65.7%, respectively.

3. Establish the expected time horizon for your client's investments.

Each investor has to determine the investment period in which his capital will be placed. The investment process must be viewed as a long-term plan for achieving the desired results. The minimum expected investment period must be at least five years for any portfolio containing equity securities. Any portfolio with less than a five-year time horizon should be comprised predominantly of fixed investments. A five-year minimum investment period is critical. As seen in the appendix, one-year volatility can be significant for many equity asset classes. However, over a five-year period, the range of returns is greatly reduced.

4. Determine the rate-of-return objective and select the asset classes.

Even sophisticated investors tend to focus on their rate-of-return objectives rather than risk. The rate of return is going to be a direct result of your client's willingness to take risk and a search for the long-term nature of his objectives.

We have identified the specific return/risk profiles of each optimized model portfolio. You can use these ranges of returns for each risk level as the framework to determine your client's return expectation for your portfolio, as well as its component asset classes.

Asset Class	Expected Return	Standard Deviation
Money Market	4.90%	3.30%
Fixed Income	6.70%	3.90%
US Large	13.60%	20.30%
US Small	19.40%	38.50%
Int'l Large	13.60%	20.30%
Int'l Small	19.40%	38.50%
Emerging Markets	16.00%	29.00%

Figure 8-2:   Expected Returns

The range should be consistent with the weighted average expected rate of return of the portfolio asset classes over the last 20 years. Don't just look at the last five years, since that is likely to be an unusual period. You should also examine some difficult market periods, like the 1973-1974 time frame, to see if your client can stay the course.

List all the different asset classes that you might want to consider in your client's portfolio. You may be surprised by the differences between what you've been using in the past and what you should be utilizing. The table below illustrates what fund families advisors are currently using.

Vanguard Group	10.6%	Stein Roe Funds	3.3%
DFA Funds	9.5%	Strong Funds	3.3%
Alliance Capital	4.1%	Warburg Pincus	3.3%
Fidelity Group	3.8%	Montgomery Funds	3.1%
Neuberger & Berman	3.8%	Dreyfus Group	3.0%
Franklin Templeton	3.7%	Oakmark Funds	3.0%
MFS	3.5%	Berger Group	2.8%
Putnam Funds	3.5%	Kemper Funds	2.8%
Janus Funds	3.3%	Cohen & Steers	2.6%
Keystone Funds	3.3%	Federated Funds	2.6%
PBGH Funds	3.3%	T. Rowe Price Funds	2.5%

Source: Prince & Associates

Figure 8-3A: Fund Families Consistently Employed by Independent RIAs

5. Document the investment methodology to be utilized.

There are three basic investment methodologies: security selection, market timing, and asset class investing. The only proven methodology for the prudent investor to use is asset class investing. Whichever you recommend, you should clearly state your reasons in the IPS.

For fiduciaries you will want to refer to the *Restatement of the Law Third,* published by the American Law Institute. It is commonly referred to as the Prudent Investor Rule. It clearly points out why active strategies will expose the fiduciary to additional risk over passive strategies. It does not state that you can not use active strategies, just that you should have in writing a reasonable basis to justify the additional cost and risk. You may want to include text on a few key discussion points that the book addresses because these are the standards that your clients acting as fiduciaries are going to be held accountable to.

Every financial advisor should have a copy. Call your local bookstore to order ISBN: 0314842462. The list price is $63.50.

6. Establish a strategic implementation plan.

Creating an investment road map is an essential step for investors in successfully managing their own expectations. To be successful, you must take full responsibility for your clients' investment portfolio decisions. The written policy statement will enable you to better define your clients' investment expectations and put you in a position to decide how best to implement your asset class portfolio.

Establish the means for making periodic adjustments to the portfolio as needed. We re-optimize our clients' portfolios quarterly. The IPS creates a benchmark to measure investment portfolio performance. If needs and objectives have been clearly defined, it becomes much easier to determine how the portfolio is performing relative to these.

THE "IF APPROPRIATE" MEETING

By the fourth meeting, the prospect ideally becomes a client. In preparation for the meeting, you should have all the paperwork completed based on the assumption that he is going to move ahead. Begin the meeting by discussing the agenda to review the investment management process; review and answer any questions regarding the IPS; and discuss if it is appropriate to move ahead with the investment program.

Ask your prospect if there are any other items that should be added to the agenda. If he has any objections at this time, he will likely voice them now. Fight the urge to address the objections immediately and simply add them to the end of the agenda. In most cases, you will be able to address these as part of the IPS review.

Proceed with your agenda and if the IPS is satisfactory, then ask the prospect to acknowledge the beginning of your relationship by signing the paperwork you have prepared.

As advisors, we are often concerned about the fees that we charge and spend a great deal of time rationalizing them to our prospects in this meeting. We spent a lot of time showing how our fees were competitive, whether or not our prospects question them. A new advisor taught us the error of our ways. He asked me to sit in and critique him on an IPS presentation he was making to prospects. Prior to joining our firm, he was a very successful tennis player, reaching a ranking of 28th in the world. He knew how to deal with pressure. He was doing a good job during the presentation of the IPS; however, there was room for some refinements. As I began writing notes that I wanted to review with him, the advisor kept watching out of the corner of his eye.

He began to sweat as he continued to make his presentation. When he came to the fees, he simply pointed out that they were very reasonable and then continued. Immediately, I began writing notes of how he should have gone into detail of how competitive our fees are in comparison with other financial services providers or the prospect doing it on his own.

At the end of the presentation, the advisor asked the prospect if we where going in the right direction. The prospect reflected for a moment and then stated that he liked the program very much, particularly the reasonable fees. I immediately crossed out the need to rationalize the fees with every prospect. Often it is the new advisors, who do not come with preconceived notions of how business should be done, who are the most successful.

Set the stage for the next meeting in 45 days. At this meeting you will review with the client a notebook which you will have sent him containing a copy of all the paperwork, including the IPS, and with tabs for various communications. It is designed to be used for the next five years, which will help the client to think beyond just the next quarter. We advise clients that they will be receiving a lot of material from the custodian that they should bring to our meetings so that we can help them organize it within the five years of tabs in their notebook. We are thinking of tabbing the notebook for 10 years. Why not start your clients thinking even longer term?

This is a good time to remind your clients about all the noise they will hear which may create confusion. We like to tell the story about car buyers being the largest readers of car advertisements. Not, as you would expect, before they buy, but after. They are attempting to rationalize their purchase. Tell your new clients when they start looking at the financial magazines for positive reinforcement, they will be disappointed. They will end up with buyer's remorse if they count on the media to reinforce their prudent investment decision to become an information investor. They need to start viewing the media more as entertainment. They are in the business of selling magazines.

THE FORTY-FIVE DAY MEETING

The focus of this meeting is to help your new client get organized with the workbook you sent them. Show them how to read the various statements and then, where to file them in the notebook. After this, quarterly meetings should be scheduled as a matter of course.

During one of our 45-day meetings, a client asked when reviewing a monthly brokerage statement how often she could expect the line that shows change in account value to look good. We thought it was a good question. If we were going to manage our clients' expectations prior to managing their money, we should know the answer to that question.

You must help your clients have reasonable expectations for the short-term. Viewing the last 71 years of stock market performance will help you better to explain to your clients what they might expect. During the period from January 1926 through December 1996, an investor would have had to earn a 3.1% average return per year just to keep pace with inflation. On average, it would take $9 today to buy the same goods that one dollar bought in 1926. Most investors certainly wish to set a minimum goal of maintaining purchasing power.

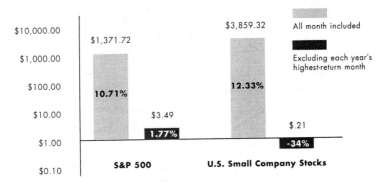

Figure 8-3:   Growth of $1, January 1926 through December 1996

Stock market investing has been effective over the long-term for maintaining purchasing power. The S&P 500 Index grew at an average rate of 10.71% per year from 1926 to 1996. One dollar invested in stocks in the S&P 500 would have grown to $1,371.72 over this time period. Even after considering income taxes and the spending of dividend income, common stock investment kept pace with inflation.

139

However, higher expected total returns are the reason that we invest in equities.

The S&P 500 Index return includes a risk premium over the Treasury bill for the additional risk which investors assume in the stock market. This risk premium is not a constant each month or quarter. To answer our client's question of how each monthly statement's change in account value was going to look, we took the best performing month for S&P 500 during each calendar year from the performance statistics. We found that the return would have dropped to a meager 1.77%. Our client's account would have grown to only $3.49—a great deal less than $1,371.72 if he or she had stayed fully invested. Over 90% of the gain recorded each year has been concentrated into a single 30-day period of time. Therefore, on average, there was only one really good month for our client each year.

It seems that not only large-company stocks experience this "one good month" scenario. Small-company stocks have enjoyed better long-term performance than the large company stocks, due to their increased risk. As indicated in the chart below, the small stocks have grown at an average annual rate of 12.33% over this 71-year period. Although these stocks are more volatile by nature than the large-company stocks, the rewards have justified the higher risk. One dollar invested in small-company stocks at the beginning of 1926 would have grown to $3,859.32 by the end of 1996. Missing the best performing month in each calendar year would reduce the total return to a negative .34%. The account would have fallen from $1.00 to a mere $.21 versus $3,859.32 if the client had stayed fully invested.

We can expect this relationship to continue, with only one of four quarterly reviews each calendar year resulting in significant positive returns on average. The other three will be flat or possibly down. While this seems pretty unexciting, it is important to make your clients aware that it is only through a patient, long-term perspective that they will realize their financial goals. Share these numbers with your clients and they will remind you of it each quarter asking you whether this quarter is one of the good ones. They need to know what to expect or they will be distracted by the noise.

THE QUARTERLY MEETING

These meetings become an opportunity to resell the investment process, as well as show how the investment process is working. Continue to educate your client not to chase performance numbers. Explain again how attempts to beat the market by buying performance result in costly mistakes. This can also be an opportunity to uncover new changes in his or her financial situation and make adjustments.

You will need to assist your clients in understanding the frustration they may experience with their diversified portfolios. Such portfolios will always under-perform the best-performing asset class. In years like 1996, clients will compare your performance numbers against the S&P 500. In negative years, they will question why they don't just buy certificates of deposits at their banks. They will experience the pain of regret. Regret must be understood and controlled or it could compel your clients to take an action that you would regret even more—such as jumping into actively managed funds and into market timing.

To understand regret, and the difference between regret and risk, consider the following story that our Chief Investment Officer, Meir Statman, uses with advisors to illustrate the risk of regret. There are two routes from your home to work; route A and route B. The two routes are equally long, equally scenic, equally congested, and equally prone to accident. In other words, the two routes have the same risk and the same expected returns. Imagine that you fell into the habit of using route A every day.

One morning, driving on route A as usual, someone rear-ends your car. How do you feel? Now change the story and imagine that one morning, for no particular reason, you decide to change your driving pattern and take route B. Someone rear-ends your car. How do you feel?

If you feel greater pain in the B scenario than in the A scenario, that is the pain of regret. The pain comes because when the accident happens in route A, it is hard for you to imagine what you could have done to avoid it. After all, you must drive to work, you cannot control bad drivers, and you always drive on route A. The accident is unfortunate, but you are not to blame.

However, when the accident happens on route B, you can easily imagine if you had just stuck with your routine, you would have not been in this accident. The blame is on you because you went out of your way to choose route B. Regret is the pain that comes when you can easily imagine, after the fact, that a different choice would have led you to a better outcome.

You must invest if you are to achieve your financial goals, and you must take the risks that come with investment. In the best of all worlds, there would never be the pain of regret associated with your clients' portfolios. This is because, by design, their portfolios are identical to their benchmarks. So your clients' portfolios should provide neither the pain of regret that comes from underperforming the benchmark nor the joy of pride that comes from outperforming the benchmark.

Unfortunately, we cannot ensure the best of all worlds. Hindsight bias is a common cognitive error that leads clients to believe that they "knew all along" what, in truth, they did not know. So they believe, at the end of 1996, that they knew all along that at the end of 1994, large U.S. stocks would be winners in 1995 and 1996 and that Japanese stocks would be dogs. Affected by hindsight bias, your clients would compare the 1995 and 1996 actual returns, not with their portfolios as benchmarks, but with portfolios that are entirely invested in large U.S. stocks and entirely out of Japanese stocks. They feel the pain of regret because they can imagine having portfolio returns equal to those of large U.S. stocks and they kick themselves for having a diversified portfolio.

Your investors will not be alone in their tendency and in their pain. Jonathan Clements writes on March 4, 1997 in *The Wall Street Journal*: "Let's admit it: Most of us haven't beaten the market in recent years. In fact, we haven't even come close. This is somewhat galling, especially for those of us who have been doing all those prudent things that the experts suggest. We built well-diversified portfolios, combing a smattering of large-company, small-company and foreign stocks.

Results? If you are like me, you have trailed the market by an impressive margin in the past few years. When we talk about the Market, of course, we are referring to the Dow Jones Industrial Average and the Standard & Poor's 500 Index. But keeping up with these indexes has been mighty tough. Lately, the easy money has been made in the easy stocks, these big blue-chip companies that are so comforting to own and that dominate the Dow Industrials and the S&P 500.

"It's not simply that the S&P 500 and Dow Industrial stocks have had strong returns. The fact is, they have outpaced virtually every other investment. If you put money into anything other than these blue-chip companies, you almost certainly hurt your returns."

The heading of Clements' article is "Even If you Trail the Market, Don't Give Up on Diversifying." This is good advice. Your clients will experience the pain of regret, so you need to properly prepare them in your quarterly meetings.

If you follow all the steps we've just outlined, you'll have a very effective sales process. You will have earned and maintained your clients' trust by truly impressing them at every step of the process on purpose. You will have begun the building of your hugely successful asset management business. However, there is even more that you can easily do to differentiate yourself from the competition.

BECOMING YOUR CLIENT'S PERSONAL CFO

We all have to compete along what we call a value-price matrix. Most independent financial advisors will choose to compete primarily just on value. This does not mean that they can totally ignore price, but few can compete with Fidelity, Schwab, or Vanguard on price. Advisors have to be competitive on price, but must also raise the bar substantially on value while being profitable. Here we can compete effectively if we provide to our clients what they perceive as high value on a cost-effective basis.

Many financial advisors attempt to answer part of the challenge to add value by offering financial planning. Clients do value financial planning services, but few, if any, planners can provide this service on a profitable basis. It is critical that any additional services that expand the scope of your business do so without distracting you or your staff from your unique selling proposition.

As a fee-based asset manager, you are paid for your investment management. If you offer financial planning in-house, taking your time to complete the planning process is inefficient and will limit your success. You need to be the business development officer of your firm, not the technician.

In most cases, financial plans are utilized as a delivery tool for higher margin business, not as a profitable service. We use to create financial plans for all our clients that were often over 100 pages dealing with every financial issue. The preparation of these plans required many hours of work, both with the client during fact-finding meetings and with our staff. We would run the plan over and over again until we finally agreed that it was right. By then, the client was overwhelmed by the sheer weight of the document. Often the financial plan was never implemented; it was just too much work for both of us without the benefit that each of us expected. Additionally, no matter how good our financial plans were, if the investments did not work, having a plan did not make any difference.

Now, in the initial presentations, financial advisors working with us begin positioning themselves as their client's personal chief financial officer (CFO). Instead of trying to solve all the client's financial issues prior to working with them on their investments, we have turned it around. The advisors act as a "coach/confidant" to their clients to first get their investment houses in order; then in quarterly meetings, deal with what they mutually agree are the highest priority financial planning issues. Each quarterly meeting is structured into 15-minute segments. They begin by asking the clients what has happened in their lives since the last meeting. They then review the performance of the account(s) relative to their expectations. Lastly, they discuss the mutually agreed-upon financial planning issue. We feel so strongly about this concept that we have trademarked Personal CFO™.

To create the information necessary to assist our financial advisors through the process, we contracted with Coopers & Lybrand to build a library of modular financial planning components which include general and specific issues that affluent investors are likely to encounter. Prior to having the quarterly meeting, the advisor logs on to our Intranet site *www.rwb.com* to access the Personal CFO™ library.

The advisor would first review the voice clips with the highlights of the financial planning issue reviewed by a partner at Coopers & Lybrand; and then, the voice clip that gives a roll-play example between an advisor and his client discussing the issue. Also on the site are action sheets reviewing the highlights of each issue and links to any third-party material that would provide more detailed information, if required.

Below are two examples: one is a general issue of estate planning; the second is a more specific issue regarding the 15% excise tax on distributions.

BUILDING BLOCKS OF ESTATE PLANNING

Immediate Action Required: Yes

Issue: There are certain building blocks that are considered fundamental to planning an estate. These building blocks will provide a sound financial base, if implemented correctly.

Discussion: There are several documents and strategies that are essential to estate planning. By themselves, these documents and strategies are important, but when combined, they can significantly strengthen an estate plan. Following is a blueprint of the building blocks that should be a part of every estate plan.

Family Living Trust - This trust will serve as the primary vehicle for the orderly and economical transfer of the assets in an estate. With some exceptions, all assets should be transferred to the living trust. These exceptions include retirement plans (e.g. 401(k) plans), IRAs, and insurance policies, which pass by operation of law. Assets not transferred to the living trust or passing by operation of law will be "poured over" into and administered under the terms of the trust upon death. If the value of assets held outside the living trust exceeds the state probate limit, the estate will be subject to probate. This often entails unnecessary additional costs and expenses, as well as delay in transfer of wealth to beneficiaries.

Will - this document allows for the estate to be distributed according to the decedent's wishes. It allows inclusion or exclusion of certain beneficiaries and control over the distribution of estate assets upon death. The basic provisions of a will are similar to a living trust. Wills used in conjunction with a living trust are much simpler. They generally consist of only "pour over" provisions. The "pour over" provisions are used to transfer assets not held in the living trust at death or passing by operation of law to the living trust. The living trust then serves as the vehicle for the transfer of wealth (see above).

Limited Power of Attorney - These powers limit the holder's authority to the transfer of assets into a living trust. This is extremely useful where a person becomes incapacitated and unable to handle his or her affairs. It allows assets outside the living trust to be transferred to and administered under the terms of the trust. Without this power of attorney, the courts will need to be petitioned to conduct the incapacitated individual's affairs.

Durable Powers of Attorney for Healthcare - Healthcare powers of attorney outline steps to be taken in the event the individual granting the power becomes incapacitated. The document removes the burden of making difficult medical decisions. For example, the person executing the durable power of attorney may explicitly request that life support not be used if, in his or her doctor's opinion, the individual will not recover.

Plan Structure - At the death of the first spouse, the will "pours over" assets into the living trust. The living will then directs the split of the trust assets. Generally, the deceased spouse's assets will be split among a credit shelter and a marital trust. The credit shelter trust will be funded with assets up to the remaining unified credit equivalent (generally $600,000) with the remaining assets going to the marital trust. The reason this is done is to take advantage of a credit that each individual is currently allowed of $192,800, which offsets combined gift and estate tax liability. In essence, the credit allows each individual to transfer up to $600,000 during his or her lifetime and/or at death without the imposition of gift or estate tax. In addition, transfers to a surviving spouse (marital trust) are not subject to estate tax.

Conclusion: One of the cornerstones of personal financial planning is an effective estate plan. In order to have an effective estate plan, there are fundamental parts or building blocks that must be in the foundation.

Action Items:

1. Review your current estate planning documents to ensure the items listed above are included. If you do not have any of the above, consider talking with your attorney to discuss their applicability to your situation.

2. Review and change your documents as necessary. You should review your estate planning documents anytime there is a major life event (i.e. birth, adoption, death, change of employment status) to determine whether the event warrants a change to your planning documents.

Additional Client Information: Coopers & Lybrand L.L.P. Monograph, "Wealth Preservation: Planning Your Estate"

Materials for Advisor: National Underwriter, "The Tools & Techniques of Estate Planning" 10th Edition

1996 SMALL BUSINESS JOB PROTECTION ACT (THE ACT) TEMPORARILY SUSPENDS 15% EXCISE TAX ON RETIREMENT ACCOUNT DISTRIBUTIONS

Immediate Action Required: Yes; during 1997, 1998, or 1999, depending on individual circumstances, a participant can take an excess distribution from their retirement plan without being subject to the 15% excise tax.

Issue: There are many taxpayers who could benefit from the suspension of the 15% excise tax. However, individuals should consider their own situations carefully and run the numbers to examine whether leaving money in a tax sheltered retirement account, considering the positive effect of compounding, is a better deal.

Discussion: Distributions from retirement accounts (e.g. pension and profit-sharing plans, 401(k) plans, IRAs, 403(b) plans) are subject to several different taxes:

1. Income tax - levied when distributions are received by the participant

2. Estate tax - levied at the participant's death

3. Excise tax - levied if the participant withdraws amounts too early, too late, too little, too great, or dies with too high a balance in such accounts

The Act suspends the 15% excise tax for taking excess distributions (annual withdrawal over $160,000 or a lump sum withdrawal greater than $800,000 in 1997) for the tax years 1997, 1998, and 1999. However, amounts withdrawn to avoid the 15% excise tax will still be included in a participant's income and subject to income tax.

NOTE: The Act does not suspend the excise tax for excess accumulations left in retirement accounts at death.

The first reaction for most participants would be to take distributions to minimize or eliminate the impact of the 15% excise tax in the future. For most participants, however, the benefit of deferring income tax coupled with compounding will far outweigh the benefits that might be gained by avoiding the 15% excise tax. In addition, if the participant has not attained age 59, he or she could also be subject to a penalty for early withdrawal, further reducing his or her benefits.

Conclusion: A careful analysis of a participant's objectives considering cash needs, marginal tax rates, beneficiary elections, age and investment rate of return is required to determine if a participant should take advantage of the suspension of the 15% excise tax and accel-

149

erated retirement plan withdrawals.

Action Item: Meet with your financial advisor and accountant to see whether taking an excess distribution during 1997, 1998, or 1999 will benefit you.

Additional Client Information: Coopers & Lybrand L.L.P. Monograph, "Investing to Grow Your Wealth"

Materials for Advisor: IRC 4980(A), 1996 Small Business Job Protection Act Section 1401(c)

One of the most frustrating issues facing financial advisors can be the inability to motivate clients to take action on important issues. Your client will have many demands on his time; often personal planning issues become the easiest to put off. As a Personal CFO™, you know that putting off proper planning will only lead to further confusion and possible loss. So what do you do? You act as the facilitator.

With the Personal CFO™ library, an advisor can set the stage for action. At the quarterly meeting, the investment advisor brings up the agreed-upon prioritized financial planning issue. The two-page write up is not intended to solve the issue, but rather to create a framework for discussion. Remember, as the advisor, you are looking to create value-added services to meet your client's needs. You are not expected to fully meet each of the needs all by yourself.

Most clients will react positively to your discussion of their planning needs, but often are unsure of going further due to the time commitment involved. This is where you act as the facilitator, suggesting that this is an important item and that you would be willing to contact the client's attorney and/or CPA, with his permission. We have found that the client will agree almost 100% of the time.

Now you have impressed your client by positioning yourself as a problem-solver. By using the resources of the third-party provider, you easily obtained information without tying up time. This planning item or others on the menu may be applicable to other clients. You acquire a pre-endorsed refer-ral to the client's other professional advisors. These services will allow you to elevate your practice above those of your competitors, as well as above your client's other senior advi-sors. Whether these advisors are lawyers, insurance agents, or CPAs, if you position yourself correctly, you can become the primary leader of the group.

Setting the meeting with the client's advisors is easy. All you need to mention is that your mutual client wanted you to call to review his financial planning issue. The advisor should be pleased since the process of review will result in billable hours. A complete review process of the client's situation should be conducted at this point. If the advisor is not sure of all the technical issues, access your third-party provider. Advisors using our Personal CFO™ pro-gram can submit technical questions concerning a menu item via e-mail. A senior Coopers & Lybrand specialist will provide answers to these questions within 48 hours.

Effectively addressing the client's planning issue rein-forces your value-added service in the mind of the client. You may significantly improve the financial situation of your client and you have created a successful professional working relationship with the client's other advisors.

Follow-up is an important element to successfully meet the needs of your client. Bring the planning process full circle. You initiated the issue and your client should expect progress or resolution on the issue typically at the next quarterly meet-ing. When first discussing the issue, get agreement both to move ahead and a commitment of when the action items are to be completed. Remember, you are acting as a coach; the client or his advisors will typically be responsible for the com-pletion of the agreed upon action items. You act as the facili-tator, but you hold your client accountable to have the action items complete on time. Don't move to a new issue until your client has completed the current issue.

In preparation for the quarterly meeting review of Personal CFO™ issues, it is important that you schedule time in your agenda to review the findings of your joint work with your client's other advisors. We suggest that you invite the other advisor(s) to the meeting, if appropriate. There are three important reasons to consider this:

1. You want to highlight your professional conduct in your area of expertise. Remember that you may want to formalize an alliance with your client's other advisors. It is important for the client's advisor(s) to see you in this setting with the mutual client. The advisor(s) will experience first-hand your ability to manage your client's investment expectations and to see how potential referrals to you will be handled.

2. You want to highlight the contribution that the client's advisor(s) has made to the planning process. Your client meeting presents an excellent opportunity for the other advisor(s) to show his or her added value to the client.

3. Finally, you will want to have a technical expert on hand to help answer any remaining issues the client may have.

Implementation of recommendations should significantly improve the financial well-being of your client. This is obviously the primary goal, but you have also begun the process of differentiating your firm from your competitors. You have set the foundation for a successful strategic alliance. Effective implementation of recommendations may provide framework for capturing future dollars to manage.

This program is powerful. By following this format, advisors can begin the process of repositioning themselves in the eyes of their clients. This repositioning is important to meet the challenge of growing competition in our industry. The financial service industry and in particular, fee-based asset management, is extremely competitive. This competition has begun to increase dramatically and we expect the trend to continue and accelerate over the next few years.

Most advisors have positioned their practice on their ability to pick the best funds or programs for their clients. This market positioning is becoming increasingly difficult to sustain in our industry. Like it or not, brokerage firms and other advisors also market their ability to pick the best funds and programs. Furthermore, the major wirehouses, such as Merrill Lynch, are intent on entering this market segment. Merrill Lynch is sponsoring ads claiming they have revolutionized the investment service industry by replacing commissions with fees in their compensation structure. The public will believe them, even though they are 10 years late. They have the marketing budget and capital to support this claim.

Change how your clients perceive you. Work on positioning your firm as a problem solver and the Personal CFO™ for clients. Take your business to a higher level. Clients have shown that they are willing to pay for value-added services. They are willing to refer advisors that they believe add additional expertise. By positioning yourself and your firm as problem-solvers, you will easily be able to elevate yourself above the fray.

The Personal CFO™ program is one of several programs that Reinhardt Werba Bowen Advisory Services has developed for associated advisors. We believe that we have a responsibility to provide value-added services beyond the normal offering of TAMPs. Whether you go it alone or work with a TAMP, you will need to address the value-price matrix.

To maintain your client base, you must continue to increase your clients' perception of where you fall on the value-to-price service matrix. This means you must consistently deliver value-added services beyond the simple equation of investment advice. Failure to deliver these expanded services will expose you to further price competition.

If your investors do not see increasing value from your services, they will look for less expensive alternatives. This is competition that can be expected to increase significantly over the next few years.

III

LAYING THE FOUNDATION OF YOUR
ASSET MANAGEMENT BUSINESS

W e've explored the opportunities in the asset management business. They are huge. We've learned how to add value for our investors by helping them avoid making costly mistakes and providing them with peace of mind. We accomplished this by using the investment management consulting process. Utilizing asset class investing, we can deliver market returns in each of our asset classes. We will always deliver our clients' expectations.

We are now ready to build our businesses. The first step is to establish and put in writing your plan. Chapters 9 through 19 are all critical components of your business plan. In each chapter, we point out what we believe works very successfully in the asset management business. Throughout each of these chapters, you'll hear us focusing on systems. Systems are the solution. They are what allow you to create huge value in your asset management business while serving your clients well.

CHAPTER NINE

BUILDING YOUR BUSINESS PLAN

W hen I ask advisors how business is going, most respond, "It's great." But when I ask them to quantify this success, the answer is "Who's got time to count?" Advisors are usually so busy keeping their businesses operating that they never have time to find out why they aren't achieving their capabilities. The best indicator of value creation is market value. Free markets work. Most advisors would have to be content selling their businesses for only a fraction of the potential value. That is, if they could sell their businesses at all.

Here's the problem. Most advisors and their practices are one and the same. The owner's personal presence is required to maintain the business. Without the owner/advisor, there is no business in fact. It is hard to build equity in a business like that, and difficult to sell it. When an advisor retires or leaves the business, he normally attempts to sell his customer list, explaining to clients that a colleague will now be handling their affairs. But more often than not, a client chooses someone else as the advisor's successor, and the attempt to sell a client list just doesn't work.

156

Advisors do not conceive of selling their financial advisory practices the same way another type of business owner would typically sell his business. But advisors can sell their businesses for what they're worth. How? By putting in systems that consistently work—and blueprinting those systems into a business plan.

BLUEPRINTING YOUR SYSTEMS

The business must become the product. A turnkey operation must be created that almost anyone could run, even if you never open any more offices. Why? It's the only way to ensure consistent experiences for clients, whether you're there or not.

Use your systems to create a meaningful competitive advantage by differentiating yourself from your competitors in your clients' eyes. In his book, The E Myth, Michael Gerber writes, "It's the systems that can give the consumers the perception of controlling their own experience." He goes on to say that what every great business sells is control. Control over clients' experiences when they buy from you. Control is the ability to give customers what they want the first time, and to replicate what they have received faithfully from that point on.

What is the difference between systems and blueprinting? A system consists of integrated components that work in an absolutely predictable fashion. Blueprinting is the documentation of those systems into a business plan. Once you have blueprinted your practice, the experiences you provide to clients can be duplicated time and time again.

Blueprinting consists of writing down procedures that work, and updating with each improvement. Go step by step, noting all the big picture details.

KEY COMPONENTS OF YOUR BUSINESS PLAN

The first step in building your plan is to visualize. In chapter 10, we will discuss how to create a picture in your mind of what your business will look like when you achieve the level of success that you want. It's important to realize that things have to be created twice—first in the mind and then in reality. To make sure the reality happens, though, you have to capture it.

Next, there's a reality check to find out where you are in the business cycle. Advisors will be at different starting points. You could be just beginning a business. Maybe you've just transferred from a big firm; you're a breakaway stockbroker who wants to create equity by leaving the "firm," so you're in effect creating your first business. You have to deal with the normal challenges a business faces at that stage, but there are also some abnormal things that can happen. We will identify the specific normal and necessary issues that come up at each stage of business development. We will also warn you of abnormal areas to be cautious of so that your business does not become dysfunctional.

Everyone reading this book should be envisioning their past experience as the old company. A very big mistake is wanting to modify "Old Co." In writing your business plan, you should be designing and visualizing your new company and laying the foundation for that new business. Take out a clean sheet of paper, because if you work off your past business plan, you're likely to be setting yourself up for failure.

One of the reasons you bought this book was the desire to create tremendous equity for yourself. Most advisors haven't yet created that equity. Trying to do that inside their existing firms is not the ticket. By moving forward and creating "New Co." you can have the business and quality of life you really want.

The most important resource you have is your employees. Nothing great has ever been completed by any single individual. It takes a collective effort to make great things happen. As you visualize your business, determine the kind of team you will need. Most of us focus on the in-house employees we're going to need, but that business model is changing fast. Many very successful advisors are now teamed up with turnkey asset management programs and have become "virtual" corporations. We have advisors with over $100 million working with us today who have only one employee. We have advisors with over $50 million who have no employees and work out of their homes. And we see people with dysfunctional businesses who have $100 million and 12 employees.

Think through what you want to accomplish. As we discussed before, there's an important difference between being interdependent and being independent. Decide which way you want to go. This is going to be a key element in deciding the number of employees you will have.

Once you decide to hire employees, it's critical that you have the right players on your team. It should go without saying that you hire attitude first and then skill, because skill can be taught, and attitude can't. Most of us, early in our careers, made many mistakes in hiring. We examine what it takes to make good decisions when hiring in Chapter 12. Your employees' interests must be well aligned with your interests. We lay out an effective plan of how to hire the team, build the team, and compensate the team.

When you know what your business is going to look like, where you are in the business cycle, and just who is on your business team, it's time to build a solid financial model. In building a financial model, start with the numbers you want to achieve over the next 12 months. We suggest that you undertake an overall five-year plan. Set aside your old prejudices. Be creative in your financial plan, but look at the numbers realistically in terms of what you're willing to hold yourself accountable to. One of the ways to create tremendous equity is demonstrating your skill at hitting the numbers.

Most financial advisors spend a disproportionate amount of time on marketing and sales. The problem is that most of us don't spend time on strategically develop a marketing plan. We're ready to communicate the benefits without having clearly laid out the groundwork that will differentiate us effectively in the market. We haven't clearly identified the target market we want to communicate to and ensured that our marketing plan complements our business plan. Once we've laid out our marketing plan, it's a matter of creating an environment conducive to sales.

Once we've generated the ability to create a stream of pre-qualified and pre-endorsed prospects through our marketing efforts, the tactical sales process begins. The marketing plan is the strategy. The tactical marketing plan is sales.

Operations is a critical defensive strategy that so many advisors ignore. With operations, if you make a mistake, you no longer impress your clients and you're likely to ultimately break their trust. A simple mistake such as sending out a report only a few cents off raises questions about your ability. After all, if you can't get reports right to the penny, what kind of job are you doing with your investment management? What other mistakes are you making? By turning this equation around, you can delight and hugely impress your clients. Operations could become your biggest profit center because highly satisfied clients will share their experiences with their associates. This is the great leveraging effect of having delighted clients.

One of the easiest ways of being derailed is to ignore compliance. Advisors often view the compliance department as the anti-sales group. But you can turn this around, too, and use it to your competitive advantage. By footnoting everything we do, disclosing any potential conflict, and going way overboard to meet our clients' needs and treat them fairly, we've created a huge advantage. Investors can see that we're on their side.

There's a global paradox; small companies have a huge advantage over large companies if they use technology wisely. However, technology can be a lot like a sailboat, giving you just two happy moments: when you buy it; and when you sell it. In between, there's a big hole in the water into which you pour time and money. The challenge is to leverage technology to successfully complement all the components of your business plan.

You can think of a business plan as a wheel and the components as spokes. If any one of the spokes is missing, your business is likely to become unbalanced and dysfunctional. The synergy of laying out your business plan and looking at all the spokes is much more powerful than concentrating on any one component. Most of us try to create our businesses

160

by focusing on only one issue such as marketing or investments, whatever our personal area of interest or expertise. We need to take time out to visualize the overall business we want to create. If we're careful to do exceptional maintenance on each of the spokes, we're sure to achieve good balance and success for our clients and ourselves.

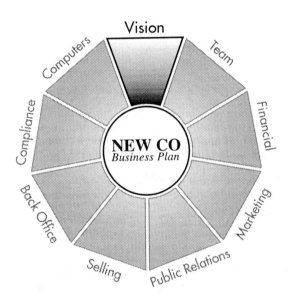

CHAPTER TEN

VISION PLANNING

I s what you are doing today what really matters to you in the long run? The problem is, we get caught up in too many activ- ities and we forget to focus on what's really important in our business and personal lives. What matters most gets buried under layers of pressing problems, immediate concerns, and to-do lists. The biggest challenge is that if you are going to get serious about building a hugely successful asset management business, you can- not afford to get lost in the day-to-day crises.

We believe the difference between truly successful people and those not so successful is that the successful create a vision of where they want to go, then set a course to get there. They create their ideas first in their minds and then they make them happen. It's the carpenter's rule, "measure twice, cut once." You make sure of what you want before you create the blueprint. You need to clear- ly define what you're trying to accomplish. But most business planning consists of nothing more than a statement of written objectives. This is too one-dimensional. But there is a way of plan- ning that is so powerful it can take your business over the top in a few short years. It's called vision planning.

Vision planning simply means visualizing the destination, reflecting both possibilities and dreams. It is superior over other types of strategic business planning because visual plans are easier to create, more inclusive, and a better springboard for proper action. It incorporates both sides of the brain, the creative side and the rational. To have a clear vision means you can start with a clear understanding of your destination. It means knowing where you are going so that you better understand where you are now and so that the steps you take are always in the right direction. Once you have a sense of your own personal vision, you have the essence of your own productivity. Your vision can direct your life. You know what direction to head toward because you've been there. You then can confidently set your long-term and short-term goals. You can plainly see the best use of your time, energy, and talents.

WHY VISUAL PLANNING WORKS

It is a simple and direct roadmap to where you want to go. Once you understand what you want, it's easy to create a strategy to get there.

It will stimulate intuition and emotions.

Seeing is believing. It creates a higher sense of commitment. If you can see it, you can commit to it.

Images awaken the imagination. Creativity is stimulated in making visual plans. Small ideas get bigger. Visual plans are worth a thousand stored-in-the-drawer plans.

Abstract ideas become more accessible. Good visual plans turn facts and impressions into purposes.

Images add potency to plans. Plans with pictures and images create belief, commitment, and results.

In working with our advisors, we found the following exercise has been one of the most worthwhile experiences at QuickStart. It helps our advisors seek a better balance of visual planning, daily planning, and yearly planning. What this exercise does is bridge both the possibilities and the probability of their goals. Once your vision is clear, you can go on to create a mission statement and incorporate planning strategies, which will give your plans structure. A mission statement has real value if it moves you towards your vision. Strategy is the best way to get there. The challenge is to create a vision of where you want to be five years from now.

Before You Begin:

It is best to have someone help you through this exercise. Find a quiet place in which to be introspective. Sit comfortably in a chair with your feet flat on the floor and relax. Close your eyes and imagine. Your imagination is vast. Don't just center on your business—imagine a program of quality for your whole life. Talk to your significant other, your employees and parents, enroll them in this vision. Let them become part of your plans. Personally, we have had some very strong observations after going through this series of questions.

In our QuickStart workshops we lead advisors through the following questions, pausing between each to let the advisors create their own vision plan.

QUESTIONS TO ASK YOURSELF

Imagine that you are waking up in your bed. It's today's date, but five years from now. As you wake up, is there anyone in bed with you? (That always gets a laugh, but it also can give you some powerful insights.)

Imagine yourself getting up and looking out the window. Are you in the same house you live in now?

What are you eating for breakfast?

What kind of car do you drive and what route do you take to work?

As you pull up to your office, what does it look like?

When you walk in, who greets you?

How do you feel?

What is displayed on your walls?

Your first meeting is with a client you've had for five

years. What does she say?

How do you feel about what you have done for her?

One of your employees walks in all excited. What does she share with you?

Walk yourself through the rest of the day. Don't just focus on business. Focus on the quality of your life. Where do you want to be? And a great question to ask is: How did you get there?

After we went through the series of questions, we saw a mission statement hanging on our lobby wall. It defined exactly what we wanted to do—help advisors build hugely successful asset management businesses.

Take Your Time

Make a commitment to work on your five-year plan over the next 90 days.

Do not to attempt to do your five-year plan by the end of next week. Take bite-sized pieces, moving forward to realize your vision.

Visual planning is the most powerful way to plan. We have found it takes abstract ideas and makes them assessable. Our belief is that if you can visualize what you want your life to be, you can make that vision a reality.

To reach the next level of success, you have to redesign your firm to achieve all you are capable of achieving. Since everyone reading this book will be at different starting points, it is important to recognize where you are on your corporate life cycle. By identifying where you are, you can learn what normal challenges are to be expected and how to deal with them and, at the same time recognize circumstances that are abnormal and likely to create setbacks. This will often make the difference between success and failure. It's critical that this information be communicated to your employees and partners so they feel a part of the team. This will empower everyone to help you take the steps necessary to be all that you can be.

CHAPTER ELEVEN
_____

WHERE ARE YOU IN YOUR BUSINESS CYCLE

When we started in the financial planning business, we would accept any client, under any terms, just to make the business happen. This is the Infancy Stage. All effort was put into trying to survive. Our survival instinct works against us focusing on what is important in building a hugely successful asset management business. You need to fight your impulses to get off track.

When you start experiencing rapid growth, survival is no longer a day-to-day issue. You move into the Pre-adolescent Stage. With this growth, we found that some clients were more profitable then others. With many new clients, we were actually losing money with the services we offered. The firm was really doing well outwardly. Unfortunately, we did not have the systems in place to handle this growth. We found ourselves just working harder while attempting to be everything to everyone. This lack of focus and effective systems is typical at this stage. Many asset management firms never get past this stage because they do not understand the need for systems.

166

It was then that we realized our professional practice hadn't really grown into a business. The partners of our firm really just shared jobs doing financial planning for our clients. While what we did was a great service for our clients, it was not the best we were capable of achieving. We took a step back in order to mature, to become a firm we could be genuinely proud of as having all the characteristics of a fully developed adult firm. In order to achieve this, we had to become more introspective and decide what business we truly wanted to be in.

We began our journey first to the Adolescent Stage. We would no longer be everything to everyone. We began focusing on developing the systems necessary to passionately deliver the "best" investment services to our clients. Growth has been nonstop ever since, through the collective efforts of everyone involved. It has not been without challenges. You will face many of the same challenges. Understanding where our company was on its corporate growth cycle and how to recognize what was normal in each stage of that cycle, helped each of the employees and the principals deal with the changes each stage brought. We were able to distinguish between problems that we should expect in our journey and problems that would likely derail us.

Today, we now manage over $1.5 billion and are growing at approximately $40 million a month as we begin our attainment of the Adult Stage. Each stage is outlined below to provide you with a road map to guide you logically on to the next stage of your business, toward your destination. It will help you to discuss with your employees, where you are and what to expect on your journey.

The Formulation Stage

In this stage, the organization is not yet born; it exists as an idea only. As an entrepreneur, you have an emotional commitment to an idea and believe in its functionality in regards to the market flux.

THE INFANCY STAGE

During the infancy stage of the life cycle, you develop the energy of a prophet; you become a zealot. You are focused on communicating your message and you're not particularly profit-oriented. It's normal to be excited. The excitement will propel your idea into reality.

During infancy, you're focused on producing results; you're action-oriented and opportunity driven. There are few systems in place, few set rules or policies. Performance is inconsistent and management is by crisis. There's little delegation; it's a one-man show. You are being constantly tested, and passing the tests is crucial to your survival. You are committed to the process. Negative cash flow is to be expected during this period so it's important for you to have sufficient capital. Hard work makes up for lack of capital. You make mistakes; that is to be expected.

Abnormal risks at this stage that can lead to a dysfunctional business: There may be chronic negative cash flow and you may feel unable to continue. Cash becomes paramount but may be slow in arriving. A loss of commitment can result. Delegation may be premature. You can't transfer responsibility until adequate systems are in place. Or you may rush to establish rules, systems, and procedures before you know what the best practices are. You may feel overwhelmed or alienated by too much external influence too early.

THE PRE-ADOLESCENT STAGE

Your business is really working. You have moved into a state of momentum. Opportunities seem endless. Rapid growth can breed arrogance and a lack of consistency or focus. A new danger emerges during such a go-go cycle: The company is now well established to the point that it can no longer be a one-man show. Leadership, style, and philosophy must now be designed into systems. In most cases, it doesn't work for the owner to attempt to decentralize merely by delegating authority and responsibility.

A distinction must be made between making decisions and implementing decisions. When the task is to implement a decision that has already been made, and the authority given is only tactical in nature, that is delegation. When the task is to initiate decisions—that is, for others to decide on issues and make the decisions—that requires decentralization. But in this go-go stage of your organization, you cannot afford to decentralize yet. To the extent that you decentralize, there is a loss of control. This is a time for delegation.

THE ADOLESCENT STAGE

During the adolescent stage, the organization is growing up—like a teenager trying to establish a separate identity. The first stage of adolescence is the correct delegation of authority; in fact, it now becomes critical to delegate. Your team should be in place. You want to move from the stage of absolute monarchy—where you made all the decisions, to the constitutional monarchy, where everyone (including you, the former ruler) is willing to abide by the constitution and by the systems and processes agreed upon. Everyone must walk the talk. There's a fundamental change occurring in leadership; you've got to move from being an entrepreneur to becoming a professional manager. There's some displacement. Everyone in the company must switch from "working harder" to "working smarter."

There will be some conflict between the administrative types and the entrepreneurial types. During this stage, it is easy to temporarily lose sight of your vision because of the unsettling changes taking place. Some systems at this stage mistakenly reward wrong behavior. A warning signal is a yo-yo delegation of authority. Policies are made but not followed, so new policies are anxiously made. Individuals may tend to receive bonuses for individual production while the overall performance of the team suffers. Power shifts back and forth nervously while nothing really happens. This results in a rapid decline in mutual trust and respect. These are the warning signals of a company on the verge of falling off the cliff. Communication is critical at this stage.

THE ADULTHOOD STAGE

You have survived the inevitable growing pains and you've designed workable systems with accountability; it's time to further empower team members. Expansion of areas of responsibility and the sharing of critical business information and financial data are particularly powerful. Each person on your team will comprehend the reason for what he or she is doing. Share the company's vision. If we do A, then we will achieve B, which will move us to C. Team members, when empowered by financial information that makes sense to them, feel like they're truly business people making a difference to the company, not just replaceable hired hands.

In our organization, we teach employees about our business plan and how to read a financial statement, so they all understand how the company makes money. Being able to differentiate between various components of financial statements results in all employees—the secretary, the mail room clerk, every employee of the firm—knowing just what impact they personally have on that statement. The reason for this is we want everyone to be able to walk the talk. Each team member truly becomes an entrepreneur, actively participating in furthering the profitability of the company. All operations must be transparent, not mysterious. Team members, empowered by knowledge, assume full responsibility for their decisions and the resulting numbers.

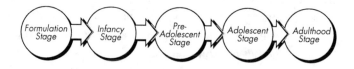

Figure 11-1: Corporate Growth Phases

In the Adulthood Stage you reach the optimal point in the life cycle curve, where you are able to focus on functional systems and organizational structure. You have achieved a shared vision created from the input of every member of the organization. The company has become result-oriented. At this stage, the organization should concentrate on truly satisfying its clients. That should be the driving force behind the organization—its focus and its mission: to help investors achieve their financial goals. The organization makes solid business plans and follows through with those plans, with a resulting predictability of outcome that may well exceed expectations.

Each stage of your corporate growth cycle has its own set of problems, opportunities, and patterns—and because each stage is unique, it's important to recognize what's normal. When you are aware of the stage your company is in at any given time, you can take the appropriate steps to move through the process faster. By being aware of each stage beforehand, you then have a road map that can direct you logically on to the next stage of your business, toward building a more successful business.

Update your business plan every six months at scheduled times and also review it at monthly accountability meetings. Everyone in the company thereby becomes aware of variances from the plan, not only on the financial side but in the operational and marketing areas as well.

If you establish the right systems, document your findings, and blueprint your practice, you will achieve what few advisors even dream about a hugely successful asset management business that consistently impresses clients and reinforces a high degree of trust. You will have the option of running your successful business yourself, hiring a general manager, or selling your business for a huge premium. The difference between your firm and others is that you will be able to produce substantially greater results with significantly less effort.

CHAPTER TWELVE

CREATING YOUR BUSINESS TEAM

How do you assemble a business team if you don't already have a great one? You want to create a team that will build a hugely successful asset management business. To do that, you not only have to develop the team, you have to keep the team members focused, committed, and working together with passion. Following is a model that has helped us build a billion-dollar asset management team.

Start with a strategic planning session led by an outside facilitator. Don't act as the facilitator yourself. The reason is that you want your team to believe you are open minded and unbiased. It helps if you are. You don't have to follow everything the facilitator suggests, but you do need to consider the team's input. The key questions you want to address at this session are; what kind of business do we want to create? Where do we want to be in the future?

You need to set up systematic reviews of your business. In this case, we review our business plan every six months. This maintains momentum, strengthens our vision, emphasizes suc-

maintains momentum, strengthens our vision, emphasizes success, and helps us stay on track.

You want a performance-based measurement system. To achieve this, define the three most important aspects of your business that you want to measure. Typically, for an asset management business, these are assets under management, gross revenue, and net income.

Design a performance-based compensation system that is tied to these three key measures. Every six months, each individual in our firm examines his or her own individual goals, in line with corporate goals and team goals. Every six months, individuals also assess their own performance. That performance is directly tied to the profit sharing plan.

Create systematic celebrations of winning—small and frequent. Every major management survey reports that one of the least important rewards is dollars. Use your imagination to find ways to make people feel part of the team's success.

Champion your team philosophy. As a CEO, you need to have a stump speech that lasts no more than three minutes. Communicate your message at every opportunity. Your speech should include what a great company your's is, how your company is acting as a change agent for the industry, and how you are actually helping your investors. For example, we talk about how our company is a pioneer in applying the latest in academic research to help our clients ensure their financial futures.

Second, include where we are going as a company. Our goal is to help as many individuals as we cost-effectively can.

Third, we have the kind of people we need to achieve our goal. Our team is made up of passionate people who are highly skilled, motivated, and entrepreneurial. We are armed with the information necessary to win.

Fourth, We emphasize the benefits that will come to those who help the company get there—and not just financially. There's a sense of pride and mission in being part of an organization that's creating success.

Support a culture of learning and creativity. You cannot demand creativity, but you can support and encourage it. You should be a learning organization that furthers the knowledge and skills of your team members.

And don't forget about furthering yourself. Develop a sounding board with people who are capable of coaching you and keeping you on track.

THE SYSTEM IS THE SOLUTION

Systematically, what we do to reinforce this model is to create a process. On a weekly basis, we have a team leader meeting where the key people in our organization get together for a formal two-hour meeting. The goal of the meeting is to arm the team with information necessary to achieve our business plan. We have agreed on a process for dealing with each agenda item and we do not allow information processing in this meeting. We're looking to share information so that everyone leaves informed. If there's a need to process information, subgroups are set up to brainstorm these issues during the week. At the team leader meeting, however, we stay on track. We manage time with vigor. We always end the meeting on time or before. We record further meeting agreements, action items, results, assignments and accomplishments.

Every meeting ends with a review of the action items. They are read out loud to make sure there's agreement. We summarize the meeting, gain closure, set the agenda for the next meeting, and conduct a meeting assessment to discuss what we can do to improve the process next time. By the end of the day, the action items are sent electronically to all participants.

TEAM LEADERS

The first thing each team leader does is create a status report which identifies who's on the team, the team's mission, six-month goals, and what the team will be accountable for.

The second team item is to list specific action items, report on the status of each item, record any major accomplishments of the week, report any new issues that have come up, and report what was learned during the week.

Every month, we have a state-of-the-business meeting. Here we hold all the teams accountable for the goals set down in writing. Progress towards reaching each of the goals is evaluated. The goal of the monthly state-of-the-business meeting is to keep each team member maximized, improving his or her own judgment, and therefore carrying out responsibilities more effectively.

Every six months, all conduct a self-evaluation plus an evaluation of their peers' strengths and weaknesses. We've found this to be initially disconcerting to the participants, but ultimately of great benefit. Rather than focusing on weaknesses, which everyone has, we focus on the strengths of each person and capitalize on those. We've found that's the key to building a strong and effective team. Not only can you use these methods inside the organization, you can apply them to outside relationships with public relations firms, marketing consultants, computer firms, etc.

What information is important, however, is often open to question. The goal is to move from the noise of the everyday to information that is really important. Numbers are essential in evaluation and the numbers must be reliable. Every process needs to be benchmarked. Each team member must become an entrepreneur in his or her own right. Every member must walk the talk. Operations must become transparent, with each key person understanding the finance, operations and marketing strategies. Each person on the team must be held responsible for his or her decisions, and make the right decisions. The numbers must be there.

We've created a semi-annual full-day retreat to conduct a business plan review. We do this prior to the 15th of December and the 15th of June. It's also an opportunity to think about the future, to dream a little. During each of these full-day planning meetings, there's an opportunity for everyone to have input. We hire an outside facilitator or a professional human relationship coach—facilitators are readily available through local universities. The cost for hiring an outside facilitator is somewhere between $1,500 and $3,500 per day. They're relatively expensive for most small businesses, but well worth it if you find the right one. In most cases, you will want to contract with the same facilitator for all meetings so there is continuity. A good facilitator will make these meetings as productive as possible. It is advisable to meet with the facilitator before and to introduce him or her to core issues.

Each team member comes prepared with his or her goal sheets. In the planning session, we look at the company as a whole.

What are our goals?

What is the vision of the company?

Has the mission changed?

Should we be in this business?

Where does our future lie?

After the meeting, each team member prepares an individual goal sheet consistent with the plan and submits it by the 15th of January and July each year. Collectively, those goals are integrated into the business plan. It's both a top-down and bottom-up approach. In the monthly team meetings, there is a review to determine if each person is on track. Every six months, each employee's performance is evaluated.

How Do You Find Qualified People To Work For You?

This process identifies individuals suitable for participation on a team to ensure the workability of the group. It is preferable not to run an ad. That's the least effective filter available. Instead:

- Write a description of the job and the type of person you would prefer in the position.
- Identify the most likely places such a person would be working in a similar job.

176

- Consider hiring an identification firm (not a headhunting firm).
- That firm makes the call and identifies the people at the targeted companies who hold such a position.
- Once you've identified the individuals, describe the job and ask them to send in résumés. With this approach, typically, the response has been between 10 to 100 résumés, depending on the position.

Candidates need to have something at risk and something to gain. We like to see how they work under pressure. Hire a candidate as a consultant to draw up a proposal of how he is going to add the most value to your organization over the next 12 months. Give him two weeks to interview the team members that they are going to be working with and a few of your clients. Then he should prepare a presentation for the group. This helps you not only evaluate their presentation skills but their ability to hit the ground running successfully. The team evaluates the candidate. This creates a sense that everyone is involved in the hiring. If each team member feels personally responsible for bringing that person in, everyone is more likely to do everything possible to help the new person succeed. You want to create the reality that your company is one of the most difficult firms in which to get a job, but once on board, everyone will work together to help each other succeed.

To come up with the right compensation package, we first identify what the market is paying. Our policy is to pay market wages. Shame on us if we ever lose an employee to a competitor over compensation. That wastes a lot of time and money. Create a learning organization to keep employees up-to-date and growing. Invest time, talent and money in your employees, with the goal of having as close to zero turnover as possible.

Recognize that you're going to have some turnover, but you don't want it to be because employees are dissatisfied and prefer to work for a competitor. Provide opportunity for growth. Many of our internal people want to become advisors. As they mature in the process and become more knowledgeable, we give them the opportunity to do so within the organization.

KEEPING MOTIVATION HIGH

Profit sharing is tied directly to goal sheets and performance. Ultimate responsibility for keeping the key people who are vital to your organization lies with the team leaders. Team leaders are responsible for informing and motivating members. Team leaders keep team members informed by meeting with them weekly, giving them status reports, and sharing what the score is. Above all, the team should have fun. Every day unexpected obstacles and opportunities appear. Every day each person is faced with the enlivening challenge of doing something a little better, a little smarter than before. The team should feel excited about matching wits with the marketplace. Every month, team leaders should tally up the score and communicate to team members what happens if they win. (They get food on the table, money in the bank, a more secure future, and an opportunity to play again.)

When you follow this type of system, everyone shares in the excitement of working together and making a difference. And it keeps you on track towards building a multi-million-dollar business.

CHAPTER THIRTEEN

THE FINANCIAL PLAN

L et's take a look at three different financial professionals. We start with an advisor who is primarily commission-based, another that is fee-based, working on
his own, and the last, working with a turnkey asset management program (TAMP).

THE OLD COMMISSION MODEL

Let us paint a picture of the first fellow, Bob. He's got an "Old
Co." He's stuck in the old paradigm of delivering business on a
transactional basis. He doesn't consider himself an exclusively
commissioned player as he also does some fee income, but it's primarily 12(b)1 fees, a little bit of income tax return preparation,
financial planning fees, and pretty much everything that you could
ask him to do that involves personal financial planning.

He's quite successful—a combination of the high payout from
his independent broker-dealer paying him about 90% of the commission and the fee revenue he realizes through his own RIA, totals
$900,000. Other miscellaneous income is about $10,000, a little

consulting revenue from workshops that he's done for corporate executives. So, his total gross revenue is about $910,000. Bob would be an individual who is often recognized at his broker-dealer meetings as one of the top financial planners.

Statement of Operations

Bob's "Old Co."
Commission-Based
Money Management Business

Revenue

Commission fee revenue	$900,000
Other income	10,000
Gross revenue	910,000

Operating expenses

Salaries, wages & benefits (7 employees)	420,000
Marketing	50,000
Rent (400 sq. ft. per employee)	67,000
Equipment and furniture	42,000
Professional services	40,000
Licensing, education and insurance	28,000
Travel and entertainment	40,000
Other operating expenses	24,000
Total operating expenses	711,000
NET INCOME (owner profit)	**$199,000**

Figure 13-1: Statement of Operations

Now, to do all the work, because he doesn't have systems, it takes a lot of employees. He has seven employees, not counting himself. He has someone helping him in marketing and client service. Because he's sold so many different investments, he needs a whole bunch of administrative assistants that can make this all work. Worse yet, he has to have people watching the people that he's hired. So, he's got an office manager.

We know this person real well—we were Bob. It's a painful cycle because you're generating a lot of revenue, but you're spending it. Almost half your revenue is just going out for wages and benefits. In addition, to generate this business, because most of it's first-year business, you've got to spend a lot of money on marketing. $50,000 is a pretty low estimate because you're doing some major workshops, running ads in the local paper, going ahead and buying radio spots and so forth. You've got to house the people. You need a larger office because now you have seven people.

You've got 2,800 square feet—we're assuming 400 square feet per person and rent of about $67,000.

Outside professional services? Bob needs accountants to get the records all straight and file the tax returns. He is also going to need attorneys, unfortunately, for the litigation that Bob is involved in because with so many clients—so many products—there's the likelihood of an error. Also, Bob needs a consultant to keep his system going and help get organized because Bob doesn't have any system.

Further major expenses are licensing, education, and insurance; errors and omission insurance; going to the conferences; trying to find the "hot" new product—all these things add up. Then, there is travel and entertainment. Unfortunately, when Bob's taking a client out, the entertainment doesn't count for quality of life. Bob travels more to go to conferences to really understand all the different products and markets. Other miscellaneous operating expenses include depreciation, utilities, supplies, postage and phones. Also, equipment and furniture, buying new PCs for the people, and trying to keep them happy.

The bottom line—Bob is making $199,000 a year. This would make many a parent proud. It makes the broker-dealer very happy. It makes the product vendors very happy. However, Bob doesn't always make the clients happy. As a matter of fact, there is a large turnover of clients and even though he's attained a high degree of success, he feels that he's on a treadmill that he can't get off. At the beginning of the year, everything starts all over again. It's a terrible job and who would want to buy it?

CONVERSION TO FEE-BASED ON YOUR OWN

Let's contrast Bob's success with Gene who's made the conversion to a fee-based business, working on his own. This is a forward-thinking individual who reinvented himself into "New Co," converted many of his assets and followed the steps on our business plan, including marketing and sales. A few years later, after he's implemented the marketing and sales process, he has a $100 million under management, averaging 90 basis points or $900,000.

Statement of Operations

Gene's "New Co."
Fee-Based
Money Management Business

Revenue

Fee-based management revenue	$900,000
Other income	10,000
Gross revenue	910,000

Operating expenses

Salaries, wages & benefits (5 employees)	300,000
Marketing	30,000
Rent (400 sq. ft. per employee)	48,000
Equipment and furniture	30,000
Professional services	40,000
Licensing, education and insurance	22,000
Travel and entertainment	20,000
Other operating expenses	20,000
Total operating expenses	510,000
NET INCOME (owner profit)	**$400,000**

Figure 13-2: Statement of Operations

Gene also has an additional consulting income of $10,000, doing workshops for the executives. Gene's total gross revenue averages $910,000, but Gene doesn't need as many people with their different functions. Gene doesn't do aggressive marketing anymore. He has a client base. His job is managing and administrating his business. He has one staff member who's really good with computers. His staff is down to five employees. Gene has expenses of about $300,000. It's cheaper for Gene to get the insurance he needs, which brings down his insurance costs to $22,000. His travel and entertainment are cut in half. Gene's clients take him out to dinner. Other expenses are lower because of his smaller office space. Total operating expenses for Gene's operation are about $510,000 and the net income is $400,000. All of a sudden Gene has created equity and his business is probably worth approximately $1.5 million.

Think about the transition this commission-based financial planner has made to be a financial advisor of a $100 million asset management business. Gene's making double the amount of money as Bob, plus Gene's creating a business worth substantially more. He has fewer employees, less stress, and more time with his family.

THE NEW TURNKEY ASSET MANAGEMENT PROGRAM MODEL

In the past, these have been the only two options. Most financial advisors have stayed with the commission, just putting their feet in a tiny bit, to move to the fee-based. What we have found is that you have to have a deliberate plan to move to "New Co." as soon as possible. Many advisors felt uncomfortable in trying to do it all on their own, with all the risk associated. Now advisors can work with a turnkey asset management program to make this transition a reality or, if already fee-based, to improve their business model. We have provided a list in chapter two.

Let's look at an advisor who has formed a strategic alliance with a turnkey asset management program. This advisor's name is Larry. If we examine his profit and loss statement in the next few years, he has $100 million under management. A typical TAMP is going to have a higher fee of approximately 150 basis points, with a 50% payout to the financial advisor. This higher fee would be justified to the advisor by the increased services provided by the TAMP, which in the case of RWB, is very high level investment management consulting combined with several value adds such as the Personal CFO^{TM} program for their clients. This will result in the $750,000 of net income to Larry (50% of the gross fees) plus $10,000 of other income for continuing consulting. Even though Larry's gross revenue has gone down to $760,000, his net income has increased significantly.

What about Larry's expenses? Larry needs three employees. Most of the advisors working with us, who have approximately $100 million, have one to two employees; but in Larry's case, we're going to assume more. Marketing is much less because the TAMP program provides that support. Larry's rent is around $29,000 (it's less because of the fewer number of people). Equipment and furniture again is less, being a function of the number of employees Larry has. Professional services are much less since Larry no longer has to buy the software from the database providers. High-quality consulting is included in a true turnkey asset management provider. Education, licenses, and insurance should also be a lower number. Travel and entertainment are about the same. Other expenses are again lower because of the number of employees. This would result in revenue income for Larry of about $451,000. This is a pretty dramatic increase revenue over the commission-based advisor, plus if Larry wants to sell his business, he has built a business worth over $2 million of equity.

Statement of Operations

Larry's "New Co."
Fee Based
Money Management Business
Using Turnkey Asset Management Program

Revenue

Fee-based management revenue	$750,000
Other income	10,000
Gross revenue	760,000

Operating expenses

Salaries, wages & benefits (3 employees)	180,000
Marketing	10,000
Rent (400 sq. ft. per employee)	29,000
Equipment and furniture	18,000
Professional services	20,000
Licensing, education and insurance	16,000
Travel and entertainment	20,000
Other	16,000
Total operating expenses	309,000
NET INCOME (owner profit)	**$451,000**

Figure 13-3: Statement of Operations

One other advantage is that Larry has an additional strategic buyer of his business, the TAMP, the turnkey asset management program he has been working with. Everything the TAMP has done has systematized Larry's business, to create a huge amount of equity with less effort.

CREATING YOUR FINANCIAL PLAN

One of the big mistakes that financial advisors make in the attempt to build a successful financial asset management business is focusing on the top line, which consists of either the number of assets under management or gross revenue, or both.

But the only thing that really counts in the short term, and which also turns out to be the most significant in the long term, is free cash flow. Free cash flow is simply the profitability of the business adjusted for non-cash items and the owner's compensation.

The key: Whether or not you are ever going to sell your business, you want to build your business as if you are going to sell it. That's the avenue to getting maximum value out of the business you are building. Focus on creating as much free cash flow as possible to maximize the value of your company. To accomplish this, set up the appropriate financial systems. Fortunately, today there's great software available: Intuit's Quicken; Quickbook's program, MYOB (Managing Your Own Business); and others which will allow you to run your business very efficiently, even if you're a one-man show. Stop by your local computer software store to purchase.

It's critical that you have an 18-month budget. This means that you need to look at every major line item of your business and what you expect to spend on each monthly. Every month you should prepare—or better yet, have someone else prepare—a financial statement showing exactly what happened regarding revenue items, expense items, and free cash flow. Then look at the variance and see if you're above or below—and determine what you can do to maximize the situation.

Every six months, you should update your budget going forward 18 months. You don't want to go beyond 18 months because this business is so fast-changing that changes can't be anticipated too far into the future. Most of us won't be able to recognize our businesses five years from today. Just look back five years and realize the huge differences.

In creating an exit strategy, you have to look at the variance, carefully considering your profit and loss statement. It's critical to have your financial statements prepared by a high-quality CPA firm. We use one of the Big Six. In some areas of your business, it's wise to over-hire, and this is definitely one of them. The firm you choose to work with needs to understand the financial market and financial services business so you'll get expert advice and a sounding board on how to improve your business, including the reporting end of it.

Free cash is a business term that better defines profitability. It adjusts income before tax for non-cash items such as depreciation and amortization of good will. Small businesses, typically subchapter C corporations, are, on the other hand, tax motivated and therefore likely to strip out all the profits at the end of the year. Paying the owner a salary and bonusing everything that's left over leaves very little, if any, corporate tax to pay. This, however, makes it very difficult to determine the profitability of the business. For instance, if a business pays the owner a $50,000 salary and then the owner pulls out a $250,000 bonus at the end of the year, was that $250,000 free cash flow? Not necessarily. We'd have to compare what the owner paid himself with the market rate for an employee in that position. If that were determined to be, say, $150,000 annually, adjusting for the $50,000 in salary, $100,000 would be applied to fair salary compensation. That leaves $150,000 to be considered as free cash flow. To complicate the situation further, many business owners run their car purchases, vacations, meals, etc., through their businesses. Although adjustments can be made for these factors, an advisor building value in the business should consider these factors and plan ahead. A buyer would naturally be hesitant to make too many adjustments.

Another use for having detailed financials is that your employees can have a clear picture of the business too. By using the strategies of an open-book management style and sharing big picture information with employees, they can more readily be empowered to become "intrapreneurers." They will be able to make informed business decisions. Owners often expect employees to take tremendous responsibility and make difficult decisions but don't provide them with enough detailed information. By providing employees with complete financials, your employees are going to have the same level of information and knowledge that you do. They'll become infinitely more valuable to you in building your business.

This open-book management does not include sharing salaries. One of the challenges in any organization is having effective differentials on compensation. We all take our pay very personally. In the detailed financials shared with employees, it's wise to group all the salaries together as one number. As an example, in our organization, every six months we walk our employees through the financials of where we are now and where we're going, and review if we've hit our goals. The most powerful aspect is that we assign every single line item to a specific employee. That employee is responsible for that budget item and for any variance.

In our company, open-book management provides employees with all the information and tools we have at our disposal. As a result, we've been able to hit our budget time and time again. An example: We hired a young lady to work in our mail room and gave her responsibility for the budget in that department. We explained how our open-book policy worked. Then, on her own initiative, she negotiated with Airborne over Fed Ex and saved our company $3,000 a month as a direct result. Cutting costs affects the bottom line more directly than increasing revenue.

Another of our employees had worked previously for a paper company. When he noticed how large a line item paper was in the company's budget, he took it upon himself to make a few phone calls. Subsequently, he and the head of his department were able to save the firm over $10,000 a year. It can definitely be worth the effort to list major line items on a report distributed to all employees with a request for ideas on how to cut costs. People need to know what they should be on the lookout for.

It is definitely positive motivation to start off with a projection of a goal to reach for and an analysis of what it's going to take to get to that point. Then it's crucial to do comparisons all along the way of actual results, then match them to budget projections. You need to know where you should be at each interval to get to the end point, yet to be prepared to make adjustments in response to actual events. The budget versus actual, that's an important measurement. The first requirement is actually knowing where you want to be at an established end point in time. Then it's a matter of building consistently towards that point.

In your case, the goal may be to build a million-dollar business. Towards that end, certain monthly checkpoints have to be established. There are certain indicators that we look at regularly, such as bottom line net income and cash flow. We prepare a cash flow statement monthly and hand it out quarterly. In our view, that's even more important than an income statement because without a healthy cash flow, a company is doomed. On a cash flow statement, it's easy to see cash coming in and where it's actually being spent. You can see just what's being spent on operations and capital purchases, plus the in-flows and out-flows from investing and loans.

The next measurement device that we consider imperative is the balance sheet or statement of financial position, because that reveals just how strong a company is. A statement of financial position is a balance sheet which shows how much cash is on hand at any one particular point in time, how much liability has accrued, and the current ratio. It's a checking device to see if there are sufficient assets to cover current liabilities.

Financials

A balance sheet, however, is not going to have much value for a company with, say, $5,000 in cash and perhaps $50,000 in equipment. Such a company is very low capital intensive, probably a service business. Our company is in the service industry, yet we have $1.5 million invested in the company in internal systems. In fact, we have spent close to $1 million on developing our portfolio management system. As the company grows, we must buy more furniture and computers and software. But for a small service-oriented business which operates on a cash basis, keeping track of liabilities can be the most important aspect of the balance sheet.

It's crucial to find out if important liabilities are not showing up on the balance sheet. When we are performing an evaluation for a company, we ask a lot of questions. We talk to a company's attorneys and CPAs, plus the vendors they regularly use. We need to delve into the possibilities of lawsuits arising from past programs and relationships, for instance.

188

One question we routinely ask: Has your company ever guaranteed an employee either a salary or employment? Written guarantees have the most potential for liabilities arising in the future. When a company is being sold, the new owner must pick up the promises; that's a lot of baggage to carry in some cases and can jeopardize a sale. Another potential liability is a long-term lease hard to get out of or, on the other side of the coin, does the company have a good lease on the premises it occupies if the desire is for the company to stay at the present location? Are there hidden conflicts that do not show up on the financial statement, such as a claim of sexual harassment? Due diligence requires uncovering the potential for liability in all areas possible.

In the effort to create equity in a business, it's important to act judiciously and wisely in all aspects relating to that business. One aim is to not get locked into anything that you're not really sure about, such as signing a lease without knowing a lot about the future of the business. On the other hand, if your business is solid and growing, it may be important to secure a long-term lease that ensures stability.

One of the key tools for determining and confirming liability and risk comes from developing professional relationships outside the firm with CPAs and lawyers. Such relationships can provide a valuable sounding board for clarifying gray areas.

What do most advisors look for in a CPA firm? Low cost. Wrong! Again, this is an area where it's worth "over-hiring." In most situations, the up-front cost is justified in the long run many times over.

Most people want to pay the lowest cost for the minimum services required from their relationships with CPAs and law firms. A better approach is to get the maximum value from these interactions by getting expert feedback. Our firm wants big value added from our attorneys, for instance, and there is cost attached to that, but the tradeoff is well worth it. Instead of simply focusing on the compliance issue and getting the minimum statement out, we give the professionals we work with a lot of information about our business so they can give us the full value of their expertise in many areas.

Another way to add some protection and value is to segregate duties within the company, even a small company with few employees. For example, make sure that the person opening the mail and receiving checks for payment is not the same person who makes the deposits. That's really tough within a small shop, but it's worth thinking out the separation of duties. Establishing an internal control structure will impress a person looking into buying your company, and it looks good if you get audited.

It's also more impressive to hand someone reviewing your company information well organized in a three-ring binder versus a few papers held together by a paper clip. The immediate reaction is, "This looks great. Everything ties together. There are internal controls." The box is checked in your favor. The SEC or IRS comes in. "Looks like they've really got their act together." And they're out the door. A potential buyer thinks, the records are really thorough. This business is being run well.

In valuing a company, the key factors are assets under management, gross revenue, and bottom line free cash flow or net income. Number one: How much gross revenue is coming in? Secondly, look at the expenses. By examining costs, it's possible to see where expenditures can be reduced. There are studies that indicate it's more difficult to raise the revenue side than it is to reduce the expenses. For most financial firms, compensation is the largest component of their cost structure. Do you have any idea what your return on investment is for your compensation program?

To create value in your company you must deliver more value and consistent experiences to your investors. You need all your employees' help in achieving your vision. Your most valuable assets, after all, are your employees. But have you really given them a stake in the business to maximize their performance and abilities? One of the biggest internal structural challenges is how to motivate your employees to help your businesses be hugely successful.

Your Compensation Program

By its very nature, compensation is the reward for a job well done. To continue to work as an incentive, compensation must keep up with what is offered in the marketplace. Compensation and status within the company increase as a person brings more value to the business. Ideally, it's a win-win situation for both the company and the employees.

Your goal should be to effectively redesign your employee contract to read: "If we're successful, you're successful." If your employees get to share in the rewards of the company, they'll be more interested in their work. Unfortunately, most of us reward our employees with increased pay for increased tenure; rewards need to be tied to results.

You want your employees to be more self-directed and motivated to move from considering themselves simply employees to being entrepreneurs within the company structure.

Most of us place a high value on teamwork, but our compensation plans don't reward teamwork. If anything, individual performance is rewarded. We talk about wanting to deliver a "quality experience" for our investors, but there is no incentive pay for employees to ensure this happens.

We believe a better way to design compensation is around what's important to those being compensated. For everyone, the motivating factor will be a little different. If we're smart about it, we will design compensation around what will help our employees address their needs by accomplishing our goals and values. Include your employees in any compensation planning; they know what will motivate.

A major component of any new compensation program is an assessment program, which results in pay for the desired performance. Too often what happens is that a good employee ends up with one big reward—more work. There is usually very little difference in pay for a great employee over a mediocre employee. Look at your own employees—often only a few dollars a week take home pay difference exists between your best and worse employee.

Your new compensation structure needs to be horizontal rather than vertical, focusing on team functions. It should be flexible, variable, and reward the team for being focused on the customer. Employees need to be concerned with the firm's success and productivity; management also needs to keep an eye on cost control and align pay with performance. Unfortunately, most employees believe that they have little or no impact on overall productivity. If they are able to save the firm a little money, they don't personally share in the gain. They also have little sense that their pay is tied to performance or affected by it.

In a study by Meek and Associates, 73% of employees felt quality and effort have little or no impact on their pay. Only 9% believed they would personally benefit from productivity gain.

Our company's experience: Our firm is state-of-the-art, not only in the investment field but also in management strategy. Realizing the importance of compensation strategies, the company has hired consultants to help with the design and implementation of a new performance program. However, we made the goals too difficult to obtain in the first year. The employees collectively were not able to reach their goals in the first year of the program. It didn't work as we had hoped.

Our company struggled with whether employees should be paid their bonuses anyway since it had been such a great year in other respects. What good was a pay-for- performance program, if you paid whether the goals were obtained or not? Would employees look at this as another entitlement program? It was decided only a partial bonus would be paid since the incentive program had been based on hitting a mark within a specified time frame. Employees were disappointed. They didn't want any more to do with variable pay. Many didn't really understand the risk-reward of pay for performance.

As a company, we had to take a step back and reassess; we had learned that compensation is not a quick fix. It was decided that a four-year program would be installed to replace the former one-year program, which was too short a time period to make significant changes.

We hired another consultant to survey our employees and compare their salaries to the market. We made a commitment to pay market wages and subsequently adjusted our pay scale to reflect the market. If wages were above market, however, we didn't adjust down. We also eliminated cost of living pay—the 4% employees automatically received, just for living another year. We recognized that our failed incentive program had created some mistrust and decided to hold off on the program until we got all our employees up to market wages.

Today we structure increasing pay for performance each year. The first year would consist of 90% base pay, 10% incentive; the next year would be 85-15; then 80-20; and finally 70-30. The idea was to reach an average rate of 30% incentive pay so that wages would become more aligned to corporate goals, the company's success, team success, and individual success within the next five years.

The result: We're no longer giving merit raises, or cost-of-living increases. We may never be able to lower anybody's salary, but we're not going to increase salary arbitrarily either. Incentives are now going to come from the bonus program and be tied to company success and achieving goals. Employees are beginning to become entrepreneurial.

The Meek study revealed that approximately only 1% of compensation for employees in the United States is on an incentive program of variable pay. We all talk about pay for performance but we're not successfully implementing the concept.

It's even tempting to give up on the concept. It does require a major paradigm shift. But if we're really going to meet the challenge of being the best that we can be, we need to design our businesses around what we value. We owe it to ourselves, our employees, and—most importantly—our investors to design our firms for maximum success.

Such a major shift first takes a commitment from the top to make a change, and then there needs to be open and frequent communication. As with most any change, there's going to be uncertainty, fear, and resistance. If there isn't clear communication, the results can too easily be confusion and a lack of trust. The goal is to take compensation from the traditional design where focus is on base pay to the focus being on variable pay based on performance.

Individual and team performances both need to be rewarded and recognized. In the past, compensation was based on tenure and status; we need to shift to pay for performance and results. The intended result of a new compensation structure is for employees to commit to continuous improvement in their knowledge and skills, and to focus on teamwork and results. There needs to be improved flexibility in a rapidly changing environment; compensation based on meeting customer needs assures a response that better matches demand.

Your compensation programs need to reinforce teamwork and create more open channels of communication. Variable pay will be based on the success of the company, partly due to teamwork and partly, individual performance. There are three equal parts to the equation: First, the company. Second, the team. Third, the individual.

Not only should variable pay be introduced, a recognition program should also be established. Such a program can be extremely low cost, involving a simple presentation of an award or gift for a job well done. We all enjoy getting recognized.

To make your new compensation program work, you need your employees to assist you in determining the company goals, team goals, individual goals, and the resulting compensation. We've all been taught that if we just do our job and stay with the company, we can automatically expect to get an increase in pay as time goes on. Approximately 90% of pay programs are based on this assumption. If you want your employees to become entrepreneurial, you must let your employees share in the risk-rewards of creating a hugely successful asset management business. Together you will make it happen.

IV

CREATING AN EFFECTIVE MARKETING AND SALES PLAN

You have a unique opportunity to create a hugely successful asset management business, if you take advantage of today's window of opportunity. However, your competitors—the big brokerage firms, banks, insurance companies and many others—are rushing to capture these assets. To compete effectively, you must develop marketing strategies and sales systems that will provide you an endless stream of pre-qualified and pre-endorsed people. This will allow you to reach the next level of success.

In the next three chapters, Strategic Marketing, Public Relations, and Relationship Selling, we will share with you what has helped our advisors and us to grow dramatically. Each of these strategies and systems has already been field tested by many other advisors. They've been refined, perfected, and simplified into a step-by-step process that works. These step-by-step systems are the quickest and easiest path to success in the asset management business.

CHAPTER FOURTEEN

STRATEGIC MARKETING

M arketing can best be defined as creating an environment conducive to sales. Our goal is to develop a
steady stream of pre-qualified, pre-endorsed
prospects. The way to meet this goal is to create an ongoing
process that provides a continuous stream of prospects that
come to you systematically on purpose. Creating this process
will be one of the key ingredients to creating equity.

There are five key strategies in building a hugely successful marketing action plan.

CREATE A COMPELLING VISION OF SUCCESS

The first step to your marketing plan is to create a compelling
vision of success. You need to know where you want to go so that
you can begin with the end in mind. In chapter 10 we discussed
how to use visual planning to see what your business will look
like in five years. You should have painted in your mind a very
accurate picture of what your business will look like five years
down the road. It has become clearer as you have begun to reduce

these thoughts into writing your business plan. You've begun to create the plan for your team and a financial model of success for your business. Now you need to begin laying out the marketing component in order to reach your vision.

DEVELOP A TARGET MARKET

We discussed previously one of the main challenges in developing a marketing plan—learning to say "no." There are so many opportunities out there that most financial advisors jump from opportunity to opportunity and never establish a long-term business strategy. They never get firmly established in one marketing sphere or become known to one community of prospects. They're island hopping instead of making the most of where they are.

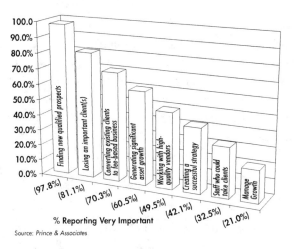

Source: Prince & Associates

Figure 14-1: Growing Assets Under Management Concerns Independent RIAs Most

The marketing challenge for the nineties is narrowing your focus, specializing in your target market. The benefits of targeting are several. First, targeting allows you to focus your resources on only high payoff activities. Once you've identified a market that you can service extremely profitably, you can

198

focus in on it and, more importantly, leverage your time. It will be easy to get referrals because you understand the deep and narrow issues that affect this target group. You will become known inside this community as the expert that really understands their issues because you do. Working with only one target market will allow you to become extremely proficient in assisting that market in addressing their financial challenges.

Suppose you decide to become the number one financial advisor in your major metropolitan area of a million people. How long would it take to accomplish that? And at what expense? Five years? A million dollars? More likely, 20 years and many millions of dollars. You would need to effectively mass market. That requires a huge amount of capital and is not very effective. However, if you decide to become number one in a niche market of perhaps only a thousand people, you will quickly own that market. With very little effort you can learn their unique needs and then help them solve these, effectively positioning yourself as their expert.

In Tom Stanley's book, *Marketing to the Affluent*, he tells readers to find money in transition, money that's in motion, and pool capital from small, targeted groups. Then you will be hugely successful. Many successful advisors do focus on money in motion, whether from the rollover market, divorces, executives who receive large bonuses, inheritances, settlements, salable assets such as businesses, pools of capital in retirement funds, qualified plans, endowments, and foundations. Most advisors do not have any plan. They worry that if they every turn away business from a market they are not currently working with, it will be a missed opportunity. They do not realize that the penalty of working with everyone is not only a dysfunctional marketing plan, but the whole business becomes dysfunctional. You end up trying to be all things to every type of clientele with very little leveragability of knowledge and experiences through systems in your market.

You want to penetrate your market accurately and quickly. If someone is selling a business, there's going to be capital generated. These are major events, oftentimes once-in-a-lifetime events. By getting systematically deep into your target market, you can identify important events that will occur and that are unique to this market. Developing a marketing plan that addresses these needs will cause you to be perceived as the expert in that area. While people in a group have similar needs, there will be slight differences; you need to position yourself as the expert who can handle the details.

Unlike the tax shelter days when many advisors focused on affluent investors with high income, you should focus on wealthy investors with large pools of capital. In most cases, your minimum will be $100,000. These individuals are typically business owners and retirees.

You want to contact business owners before they sell and as close to the impending sale as possible. You want to reach soon-to-be-retirees. You're trying to identify areas where money is in motion—industries, for example, that have gone through a consolidation or which are downsizing.

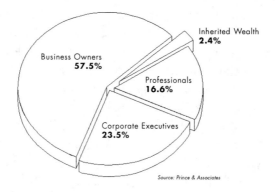

Source: Prince & Associates

Figure 14-2: Business Owners Are the Primary Market for Independent RIAs

Another market that several advisors working with us have focused on are individuals going through divorces. Unfortunately, most people in these circumstances, whether male or female, have serious erosion of capital and retain only one-third of their net worth. One-third generally goes to each spouse and the other third to the attorney, but it's still new money in motion. In most divorces, there is little capital to invest unless there has been a family business. Typically, in a divorce where there's a business involved, the husband keeps the business. The wife gets everything else, and she usually doesn't have an advisor. She's the "out" spouse that you want to focus on. You can provide great assistance and be very well rewarded if you work in the affluent marketplace. Many divorcées have support groups that will allow your delighted clients to refer you to other affluent divorcées if you establish trust and really impress them.

Another focus is wealthy widows or widowers; in death, of course, significant assets are often freed up. This market can be effectively targeted through other professional advisors such as attorneys, CPAs, and life insurance agents who serve this market. Jointly working through strategic alliances with other professionals should be considered for any target market that there is a mutual interest in.

There's a lot of discussion now about the $10 trillion that will soon be moving from one generation to the next. In reality, though, the wealthy are just giving it to their already wealthy kids. Wealth is extremely concentrated and most people with large amounts of money over $5 million investable are already working with advisors, so it's unlikely that this will be a great new target market.

Some advisors will want to work in the institutional market. Although this market represents over $5 trillion, it's so competitive and there are such huge opportunities elsewhere, that we recommend you avoid the institutional market unless you already have existing relationships. It's hard to have a competitive advantage against the firms that are already entrenched. While, on occasion, you will pick up an institutional account due to a pre-existing relationship that you have with a private client, don't be fooled into focusing on that market unless you have a long time horizon and a competitive advantage.

DISCOVERING NICHE OPPORTUNITIES

A niche opportunity is simply a market that's particularly suited to your talents, skills, and interests. All of us have unique talents. We all have comparative advantages and skills, and interests in different areas. You want a high quality of life and that comes from working with a group of people you have an affinity with. The choice could even hinge on an interest as specific as sailing, marinas, and large boats. But whatever it is, look at the market that you would enjoy being in. Make sure, though, that this market has a high concentration of qualified prospects that have money in motion or pooled capital available. In identifying a niche, you want to make sure prospects have a shared perception and similar problems, values, and desires for solutions.

Niche opportunities exist everywhere, but you have to do some research. There are two types of research: one, internal, where you query your existing client base; and two, external, where you go outside your existing client base to gather information. We have found it extremely effective to interview key clients, centers of influence, local experts, and industry leaders to identify new niches. The interview process allows you to discover specific opportunities that are available that you're not aware of.

As you drive around your community, you'll see a myriad of opportunities. But by doing research and asking key people, the search becomes very focused and targeted. It's okay to initially jump around and look at all the opportunities, but then you want to focus in on no more than three niches that you might fully develop. There is a likelihood that the most successful niche of these three will end up, long-term, as your only niche. You need to gain specialized knowledge to work effectively in that niche.

What are the inhabitants of your targeted niche looking for? By interviewing people who aren't your existing clients and finding out what they're looking for in a financial advisor—without trying to sell yourself, just gathering information—people will be open because they won't feel you are trying to sell them anything. You are not. You simply want to better understand the financial challenges that they face so that you can better serve their market. More often than not, you'll end up with a client or at least a referral. People want to help you. The four most powerful words in the English language are, "I need your help."

When you ask someone properly who's had success in life to help you, he or she will most likely want to help you. This applies to many areas of life, including uncovering new markets and converting prospects to clients.

How do you get started in doing interviews? First, you want to identify your favorite clients. Develop questions that will both reveal opportunities and lead to referrals. Some of the things you want to find out are: What are your clients' motivators? What do they like about working with you? Are there any problems that they have that you're currently not solving? How is your communications process? How did they learn of you? Are they happy with the job you're doing? Do they have any marketing ideas?

Other people you should consider interviewing are centers of influence in the niche you want to work with, such as CPAs, attorneys, and other professionals that share the same target market. It's easy to get together with anyone in the world; you're simply two phone calls apart. One, a call to set the stage, such as a request for an introduction by someone you both know; and the second, a call to the person directly. When you make those calls, you need to have a deliverable win-win attitude about how you're going to help that person achieve a higher level of success.

In doing research, you want to identify people who need your services. Uncover their values, problems, challenges, and opportunities. Identify individual prospects and centers of influence. Begin building strategic alliances. Commit these steps to writing in your marketing plan.

POSITION YOURSELF AS AN EXPERT TO ATTRACT QUALIFIED PROSPECTS

Communication is something that we all want to do immediately. The key to communicating, however, is properly positioning youself first. Positioning is the art of controlling your clients' and prospects' perceptions.

How many brands of soap can you name? Or toothpaste? Most of us can name three to five brands in each area. Some of us struggle to name even that many. As a financial advisor, you have to stand out in a very crowded marketplace. Think of the number of competitors in the financial marketplace. You have to design your position so that you're first in mind when it comes to the asset management business. The goal is to be perceived as different and better than your competition. Your main challenge is beating your number one competition—the brokerage industry. However, 53% of affluent investors don't trust brokers. The means of meeting this challenge is to develop a process through marketing and sales that instills a high level of initial trust that differentiates you from the brokerage industry. Then deliver such high level experiences that your clients are dramatically impressed.

If you are perceived as a specialist to a particular niche community, you've got a huge advantage. For example, a divorcée going through perhaps the most traumatic experience of her life has major financial decisions to make. She can work with a general practitioner or she can work with you, a known specialist in the community in working with divorcées. You've got it beat, hands down if you are that expert.

Many affluent people view financial specialists as merely product pushers. You want to be perceived by the affluent, in contrast, not as a "problem solver" but as a person who meets challenges. A person with $5 million in net worth does not have "financial problems;" he or she has "challenges." You want to be known as a person with expertise in meeting those financial challenges. That's your ideal position and it's a powerful one.

In *Cultivating the Affluent* by Russ Alan Prince and Karen Maru File, affluent investors were surveyed to find what they considered as the most important services provided by a discretional money manager. Number one, by far at 56.7%, was asset allocation; they expect good investment advice. Second was financial and estate planning. And next was tax planning. After that, nothing was over 2%. You want to design your business so that you offer these services with the competitive advantage of understanding your targeted market's specific needs. Position yourself as someone who is uniquely qualified to address his or her concerns.

Affluent investors want trustworthy advisors. You have to earn that trust every step of the way, and be impressive in doing so. Empathize with their problems, understand their values and their goals, and help them get what they want. One of the keys to positioning yourself is to capitalize on trends, and the asset management business is a trend that is growing dramatically.

You want to develop a "unique selling proposition." A unique selling proposition consists of benefits that you uniquely offer to prospects. You also want a strong "positioning theme." A positioning theme is a perception you create that will turn on qualified prospects but turn off people who don't qualify.

Verbal benefit statement: State a strong promise of benefit. This statement can become the subtitle of your business. For example, if you specialize in working with executives, you might state, "I help executives make work optional."

You also need to make your collateral material consistent with your positioning. The first thing most financial advisors want to do is print up a glossy corporate brochure with matching everything. Our firm has well in excess of $1 billion under management and we don't have a formal corporate brochure. In fact, we try to never mail out any marketing or sales material. We want to meet face-to-face so that we can better understand the prospect's issues. Then, we can decide whether the prospect is a candidate for our services and how best to present our services. There are a million different ways to present your services to an individual prospect. There are usually only one or two effective ways. Many advisors go out and spend $10,000 on a great-looking corporate brochure as if it is the silver bullet. If the paper is glossy, it's perceived as mass marketing and more likely to turn off your affluent prospect. You want everything to be customized to the individual client.

COMMUNICATE YOUR BENEFITS COST-EFFECTIVELY

You need to deliver the right message to the right prospect at the right time. The right message should touch upon a prospect's emotional as well as financial needs.

Select the right channel for communicating with prospects: There are three main channels, the relationship channel, credibility channel, and number channel.

Relationship is one-on-one, usually through referral or a strategic alliance.

Credibility is established through public relations.

Numbers are achieved through direct response.

Most financial advisors recognize that if they could be constantly contacting qualified prospects, they'd be hugely successful, so they try to do this through mass marketing techniques. That's not effective.

In a survey of independent RIAs completed by Prince and Associates, financial advisors recognized the need for marketing support in their communications efforts.

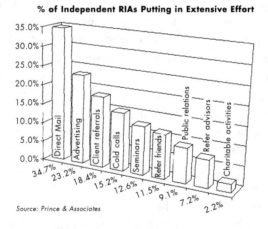

% of Independent RIAs Putting in Extensive Effort

Source: Prince & Associates

Figure 14-3: Independent RIAs Need Marketing Support

Well over half of those surveyed wanted help in direct mail and advertising. Stop and think about this for a second.

Wouldn't it be nice to have a direct mail piece that would bring in multi-million dollar clients on a systematic basis? On the other hand, if you were a multi-million dollar prospect, how would you find your financial advisor? Would it be through a direct mail piece? A flyer that somebody stuck in your mailbox? No. What about through an ad in the local newspaper? No, that's not how you'd go about finding a financial advisor. You'd go to a trusted friend or business associate and ask whom they'd recommend. Only if that friend or business associate truly trusts and is impressed by his or her financial advisor, would a referral be forthcoming. So why do we try to contact our prospects the way we would never want to be contacted? You shouldn't. Relationship marketing is developing a systematic way of building relationships with your future clients. It's the only way that makes sense.

But you have to fight your instincts. Everyone wants to do direct marketing. It seems easy. Our firm, in its early stages, did a tremendous amount of direct response, advertising, mailings, etc. Today, however, we do no advertising. If you have a brand name already established and you're a major player, direct mail and advertising can be effective, but it's not a good avenue for most individual financial advisors. Instead, concentrate on doing a good job at relationship-based marketing by generating personal referrals through client recommendations. You'll be much more effective.

Credibility-based marketing, however, does work. It complements relationship-based marketing because being published gives you instant credibility with prospects. Media interviews, public speaking, and publishing a newsletter can be so valuable that the next chapter will focus only on these.

Number based channels: Advertising, special events, cold calling, and mass mailings don't work with affluent investors. On the contrary, these are effective ways to make sure you won't work with the affluent. When working with the mass market, these avenues can be very effective. Don't forget what market you're aiming at.

By following these four steps, you will create tremendous success:

Find out who the profitable prospects you want to work with are and target them.

Identify no more than three niche opportunities. Work down to one that you can stay focused on.

Position yourself to attract qualified prospects. Differentiate yourself from your competitors.

Communicate cost effectively on a relationship basis and establish a high degree of credibility.

Steve Moeller, with American Business Vision, has been a key contributor over the last five years in the development of our very successful marketing plan. He helped us move from tactics to strategy. This was one of the major reasons for our growth. If you would like to learn more about Moeller's marketing services, call (703) 716-7280. We were glad we did.

Now let's learn how you can build your credibility effectively into your business plan for almost no cost.

CHAPTER FIFTEEN

PUBLIC RELATIONS, THE "WRITE" WAY

W hy settle for being quoted in someone else's story? Here's how to publish your own articles and position yourself as an industry expert. Over the years, we've experienced both success and failure with our public relations programs. Our biggest challenge was duplicating our successes and establishing consistency. That was because we were treating PR as a part-time job. Once we started giving it full-time effort, our success increased overnight and the benefits surpassed the costs tenfold.

When it comes to the media, many financial advisors do not discern the difference between public relations and publicity. Some are under the misconception that if they get their name in the press or if they are quoted in an article or two, that is enough to double their business instantly. This just isn't the case. In fact, that form of publicity has very little value unless it is part of a well-conceived and consistent marketing effort.

Getting your name published is publicity; getting your byline published is public relations. Understanding the difference is essential to successful marketing.

UNDERSTANDING PUBLIC RELATIONS

The first step in improving your PR results is to consider what public relations really is and how it can be implemented effectively in your marketing plan. Public relations is the method and activity employed to promote a favorable image and relationship with the public. Publicity, on the other hand, is the act or process of disseminating information to gain public attention; it's just one facet of PR.

In order to work with journalists, it's important to understand how they think. Most reporters have no particular interest in quoting or promoting one adviser over another. They are interested in writing newsworthy stories that will capture the attention of their readers.

The best way to win favorable press is to provide reporters with ideas for great stories. If you make yourself valuable to reporters, they are likely to repay the favor. Once established, you can enhance the relationship by offering disinterested advice. Sometimes this means referring a reporter to another adviser or source with expertise in an area where your knowledge is limited. The more journalists learn to trust you, the more likely they will call you and quote you.

After we gained a clearer understanding of the relationship between publicity and public relations, we started to design an overall PR program. We visualized what we wanted to happen to our business as a result of our efforts. One of our goals was to shorten the sales process. To do that; we would have to be perceived as experts in the field. That became our primary goal, which we accomplished by publishing articles in industry and trade association journals.

We began to write magazine articles explaining how asset-class investing, our primary business activity, works. This enhanced our visibility not only in our local community, but also in the financial services industry. Our professional status grew. We weren't afraid of giving away our marketing and investment secrets—in fact, by sharing them we established trust with the public and with other professional advisers.

Perhaps you want to double your business, gain more credibility in your community and be able to distribute reprints from a professional article as a promotional piece. Factor these goals into your marketing plan. Your public relations program should be designed to enhance and complement an already existing marketing plan. As with other aspects of your business, you need to think strategically and make a long-term commitment to building your financial business.

GETTING PUBLISHED

Write articles and get them published. Local press is great for providing immediate recognition and feedback, and articles that appear in national publications and trade journals add even more value.

While getting into the press is effective, it can be time-consuming. You can either do it yourself by writing articles (try to do a minimum of two per year) or by hiring a public relations firm to do it for you. Check your firm's policy toward a financial advisor hiring his or her own public relations or advertising firm. Many national firms have strict guidelines that must be followed and require all information released to be approved by the corporate office. Take this into account, because the approval process may cause delays.

Understand what your PR fees will buy; there's a wide range of prices within the industry. The fees that are charged by a typical PR firm might shock you. You may also find that most firms have very little background in writing financial articles. Make sure the firm you hire understands what your business is about.

If you do it yourself, write about what you know. Pick some aspect of investment management you enjoy, or explain how to solve a problem. Use an experience you've had personally to show how by implementing a certain process, you overcame a particular obstacle. Some broker-dealers or turnkey asset management programs will provide you with a finished article you can use as a boilerplate; copy the format and add your own words. We maintain a database of articles on our Intranet for advisors working with us.

GETTING PUBLISHED, STEP BY STEP

The following are five steps that will help you get in print, even if you are inexperienced in public relations.

Step 1: Identify your target market.

Your strategy should revolve around how to deliver your message to your target audience. Write down PR objectives, market segments, and how you intend to reach them. Your written PR plan can be as detailed as the statement of investment objectives you write for a client.

Start by examining your existing client base. Most investment professionals have a large number of clients in a relatively small number of industries. Surprisingly, most ignore their own inherent knowledge of existing clients' industries. Instead, put this information to use. Trade journals and newsletters have credibility and prestige among influential members of various industries.

If you are a financial adviser writing for a trade magazine targeting your own industry, you have missed your market (unless your market is other financial planners). More than likely, your clients and prospects will never see it. You should be writing for your local newspaper, regional business magazine, or better yet, the trade association magazine for your target market.

Step 2: Identify what publications your target market reads.

Determine who your publishing prospects are by asking your top clients what they read. They may be devotees of obscure trade journals such as *Associations Management, American Fire Journal, Public Accountant* or *Cemetery Management.* In addition, most trade associations have their own publications and these are relatively easy to break into.

The Writer's Market (Writer's Digest, 1995), a compendium of periodicals with information useful to the freelance writer, gives editors' names, addresses, and brief editorial guidelines for trade and business magazines. The library will have the Encyclopedia of Associations—a guide to more than 30,000 national and international organizations, including trade, business, commercial, legal and government organizations—as well as the *Gale Directory of Publications and Broadcast Media.*

Step 3: Pitch your article.

You can either take your chances and write a story, send it to a magazine with a cover letter explaining what your article is about, or do what most professional writers do: Write a query letter to the editor first or pitch him or her over the phone.

Bear in mind that editors are interested in providing informative, entertaining articles to their readers—not improving your business. No editor is going to simply hand over editorial space so you can promote your company.

Before attempting to contact an editor, make sure you read several recent issues of the publication. Study the subjects, style, and tone of the articles to see if you can write in a similar fashion. When you write your query or make your pitch, tell the editor why you think your article is appropriate for his or her publication, why you think the magazine's readers would find your article interesting and why you are qualified to write it.

Step 4: Write the article.

If you're lucky, an editor will agree to consider your article (it's highly unlikely he or she will accept it solely on the basis of a query). At this point, you've sold the idea—but you still have to sell the story. Keep that in mind when you are writing. If your tone is too promotional or self-congratulatory, expect to have the article returned with a brief note: Thanks, but no thanks.

Write to inform the magazine's readers about a particular product or trend, or offer a solution to a common problem. Don't simply describe yourself or your services (any magazine that would publish such an article will probably publish a similar article from your competitor next month, and then where will you be?).

When submitting the article for consideration, offer to provide additional information if needed, as well as references and data to back up your claims. Most publications will insist on independently verifying information furnished by free-lancers, regardless of how established they may be in their respective careers. Magazines do this to protect themselves (their credibility is at stake, too), and writers who are reluctant to cooperate are all but admitting that they've played fast and loose with the facts.

Step 5: Send out reprints.

Once your article has been published, leverage it. Call the magazine and ask for reprints, then distribute them heavily. You have much more credibility if you are in a position to show a prospect or client some of your ideas that were published in his or her own trade journal or local business magazine.

After a presentation, leave behind copies of your reprint-ed articles. This gives the prospect additional evidence and a visual to refer to long after the marketing presentation has been made.

Beyond reprints, the real benefit of a published article is that it can communicate your message to a greater number of people than you could reach by yourself. The communication process becomes geometric if the articles are published in media vehicles that influence high concentrations of specific readers, such as doctors, attorneys, CPAs, and business executives.

If you take these steps to make publishing an important part of your public relations plan, you will see your business take on a life of its own.

CHAPTER SIXTEEN

RELATIONSHIP SELLING

There are four steps to achieving a successful relationship selling strategy. Most financial advisors are tempted to jump straight into creating strategic alliances. It's great to be action-oriented, but first the groundwork must be established. We have to be able to tell our story about the investment management consulting process, step-by-step. The way to accomplish this is to practice until perfect. The best way to get started is with yourself. Convert your own investments to your new asset management program. If you do not believe there is enough value to change, none of your clients will. Then, you are ready to get started. Your existing client base will give you many opportunities for practicing and refining your story, so that you can then work with new prospects or strategic alliances.

CONVERTING YOUR CLIENTS

First, identify existing clients who could benefit from your new asset management services. Sort your clients into three groups. The first group includes those with a minimum of $100,000 in liquid assets, such as individual stocks, bonds, mutual funds, and money market funds. The second group is made up of clients with assets in semi-liquid form, such as annuities, CDs, or mutual funds with large redemption fees. The third group includes clients with illiquid investments, such as limited partnerships and real estate. Know when these various illiquid investments might be sold or otherwise liquidated.

Set up one-on-one presentations and fact-finding meetings with your clients. These are the first two steps of the investment management consulting process we discussed in chapter eight. Typically you will want to combine these meetings for existing clients. You have already established a relationship and they will be more open to discuss your new business.

You may be uncomfortable telling clients that you're now doing things differently and you will be inclined instead to test it out with new prospects—but that's a big mistake on two fronts. First, you really don't know the story well enough to tell it to new prospects. The second reason is more important as it focuses on the benefit to the client. You have chosen to build this asset management business because of huge potential benefits to your clients. You should not penalize them for being an existing client.

Call your clients and tell them that you are changing the way you are doing business in order to give them the highest level of value-added service and that you now have the ability to offer institutional asset management to individuals. Tell them this is an opportunity usually only available to billion-dollar pension plans. Explain that you'd like to update your clients' investment plans to see if they would personally benefit from this new approach.

Tell each client that you plan to review his or her values, goals, and current financial picture, in order to prepare an updated Investment Policy Statement. You will find out exactly where your client is now and where he or she wants to go, and how—if you were in those shoes—you would optimally modify the existing investment program, if needed.

216

Do not make it too hard on yourself. It's really not that complicated. You first need to update where your clients are. You should be doing that anyway and they expect it. Then you need to find out where they want to go. Since you now have access to institutional asset class investing, they will want to hear about it. By telling them that you're changing the way that you're doing business in order to give them the most value and that you would really appreciate their input, they'll be even more excited to meet with you.

Advisors who are good public speakers can leverage their time very effectively in the conversion process. Instead of time-consuming individual meetings, public speakers can meet with many clients at the same time through workshops. Invite clients who have already converted to the meetings. Often, they will share their perspective unsolicited and will be outspoken, pre-sold advocates who can increase your success dramatically.

Some clients feel less pressured in a group seminar than at a one-on-one meeting. Many feel they get more out of a seminar because they hear answers to questions asked by other people that they might not think to ask. Close the seminar by offering to do individual Investment Policy Statements for participants. Schedule individual meetings at the end of the workshop, or call attendees the next day to do so. Most advisors would agree that if they could readily present their services to pre-qualified, pre-endorsed individuals, they would be able to more than double their business each year. Since your client base is qualified, you have the framework to make this happen.

As you progress through the Investment Policy Statement to the 45 day meeting, ask your clients for referrals. Many advisors are not comfortable directly asking for referrals and feel they should come unsolicited. When you have earned them, they will come. Nothing could be further from the truth. You owe it to your clients to allow them to help you with your marketing and prospecting.

Your clients want you to be focused on solving their financial challenges, not spending that time on marketing and prospecting. The best way to have clients refer pre-qualified and pre-endorsed prospects is to tell them the truth. The truth is that if clients realized how much of the average advisor's time is spent on marketing and prospecting, they'd be shocked. It is estimated that most financial advisors spend well over a quarter of their time marketing and prospecting. For some financial service salespeople, it can be more like 90% of their time. Their clients would certainly be distressed if they knew that.

Position yourself effectively. You've gone through the investment management consulting process, established trust, and truly impressed your clients. Now, allow them the opportunity to help you help them. Our sales consultant Bill Bachrach tells our advisors to tell their clients, "Many people don't realize that the most expensive and time consuming aspect of being a financial professional is finding new clients. We often spend a substantial part of our time and efforts prospecting and marketing. This takes away from the time we can devote to the activities that make us better resources for our clients. As one of my best (favorite or newest, for your new clients) clients, how would you rather I spend my time—looking for new clients or thinking about your money and keeping an eye on issues that could affect your personal financial health?"

Without exception, clients answer correctly; they want you focused on solving their financial issues. You respond, "Of course, and you're not alone. All my clients feel that way. For me to spend the time you want me to spend on looking after your financial best interests, I need your help. It is important for you, and all my clients, to help me keep my appointment calendar full by introducing me to people who meet my guidelines." Then, show them a profile of your target market's ideal prospect that you've developed and ask them for names and phone numbers. Our experience is that we get, on average, two to three new prospects at each quarterly meeting held with a client.

CLONING YOUR TOP CLIENTS

Once you've converted appropriate existing clients to your new asset management business, you want to expand your business not only through the referral process, but through a cloning process as well. This is a simple system that will allow you to stay focused and expand vertically within your favorite clients' markets.

Identify your top 10 clients. These are not necessarily the top 10 by revenue alone, but also the ones you most enjoy working with. Quality of life is critical, and you need to enjoy the people you work with. By cloning your favorite clients, you have more favorite clients, and you can build the ideal business. The quickest way to burn out is to work with people you don't enjoy working with. Life is just too short.

Often, these 10 people are the ones who have made the biggest financial impact on your business and whom you most appreciate. They are likely to already be giving you unsolicited referrals. Gaining an understanding of why these clients choose to work with you will help you understand what future clients will be looking for. If you can uncover your unique abilities through these relationships, you are on your way to developing a profitable and enjoyable business.

Let's say you are working well with a few key physicians and have an understanding of their unique needs. When one of their financial parameters change, it is easy for you to emerge at the right place at the right time with the right solution. You are uniquely positioned to solve a particular market need or problem. These physicians will be pleased to refer you to other physicians like themselves.

Marketing research shows that, in most cases, 80% of an advisor's revenue is generated from the top 20% of his or her clients. Find out everything you can about the top 20% who generate this revenue for you. These top clients will each provide you with two or three qualified referrals each quarter, if you make it easy for them to do so. The top 20% of your clients will be replicated, and you will be working with high-quality people with whom you most enjoy working. Not bad.

The most efficient way to upgrade your business is to become an industry expert. Go to your top clients' trade shows and meetings, and become familiar with their professional fields. Build a name as a financial advisor for their market. Each new market contains a whole supply of new qualified prospects. You've got to take the time to learn how to solve their financial problems and their challenges, not just sell them products. If you specialize in providing investment advice to a narrowly focused target group, you will understand that market and will be well on your way to having a multi-million dollar asset management business. Position yourself as a trusted ally of this market niche, not as someone on the outside. Your job is to gain a reputation as an industry insider, not a salesman. It is best to position yourself early in the game. Your clients can also help you uncover a delivery system into their marketing niche.

Clients are familiar with or are often members of trade associations or organizations that represent their market. All you need is one contact. This could be your client or someone your client knows. Ask your client to be an advisor to you. Ask him or her to be on your marketing team and get that person started working on your behalf. It often only takes one call for a meeting to get this going.

We personally get calls on a regular basis from individuals wanting assistance in our profession's area. We almost always meet with people who are referred to us by someone we know. This type of alliance and networking is a powerful technique.

Colleagues and associates will invariably be willing to help you out, give you names, and offer suggestions on how to build your own strategic network. Call your favorite clients and tell them, "I need your help. I am developing a more focused approach to my marketing. I have created a profile of my favorite clients and you are one of them. I really respect your opinion. Would you let me take you out to lunch? I would like to get your ideas and opinions about marketing to people like you in your field."

This works. We have never had a client say no to this. When you tell somebody he or she is one of your favorite and respected clients, and that person has already entrusted you with his own life savings, you're going to get a positive response. At the luncheon meeting, we take out a worksheet that's made up of 22 questions and we walk the client through it, question by question, taking notes. You'll be surprised by the answers you get.

One of our advisors felt that this really wasn't a valuable exercise when she first undertook it. On her first client interview, however, she found out she was not assured of getting the million-dollar rollover that her airline pilot client was going to soon be receiving. Even though she had been his financial advisor and tax preparer for many years, he didn't see her as an asset manager. Questions 11, 12 and 13 bring up competitors. In this client interview, the advisor found out that the client's co-pilot friend was a financial advisor as well, and this was the person the client was considering to manage his assets. Had she not conducted the interview, she would have surely lost this million-dollar sale. Instead, she found out whom she was up against, she presented her story, and made the sale. She's now convinced.

QUESTIONS TO ASK:

- What are your lifetime financial goals?
- What have been your greatest personal financial frustrations?
- What are the major financial challenges that people in your situation (industry, etc.) face today?
- What else could I do to help you solve your problems or achieve your goals?
- To what business organizations do you belong?
- To what social organizations do you belong?
- What sports or other activities do you enjoy?

- What publications do you like to read?
- How did you first hear about me?
- What originally prompted you to do business with me?
- With whom else did you consider working?
- Who do you feel are my competitors?
- How do I compare with my competitors?
- What is important to you in your relationship with a financial advisor?
- What are the major benefits you have enjoyed by working with me?
- If they asked, what would you tell your friends about me?
- The most compelling thing I could say to someone in your situation that would interest him or her in doing business with me?
- Knowing what you know, if you were me, how would you market to people like you?
- Do you have any friends or associates whom you think might benefit from meeting me or attending one of our workshops?
- Do you know of anyone who works for a company that is about to downsize their work force?
- Do any of your friends own their own businesses?
- Do you know of anyone who would like to sell his or her highly appreciated house or business?

Once you've gone through the questions, thank your clients for their help. If they've done a good job and you'd like to continue the conversation over the years, tell them that you're creating an informal board of advisors for your business, and ask them if you can call them occasionally to get their opinion and ideas on your marketing plan. Almost always, they will say "yes."

Some of the situations uncovered by advisors working with us during their client interviews are:

A good friend of a client has just inherited a large amount of money and needs the help of a financial professional to preserve it.

A friend of a client is just about to retire and will receive a $500,000 lump sum distribution from his retirement plan. He needs a money manager for the first time in his life.

A local corporation, where a client was previously the CEO, is downsizing. He identifies 1,200 people who will soon receive over $200,000 each in lump sum distributions.

A friend of a client has just taken his company public, thereby increasing his net worth. This friend wants to prudently diversify his wealth and needs a fee-only advisor to help him do it.

A client's colleague is selling his $2 million house and wants to be shown how to avoid capital gains tax by using a charitable remainder trust.

A client's relative is a wealthy small business owner who wants to transfer his business to other family members, without the government taking a huge chunk out for taxes. He wants to find out how family partnerships might solve this problem and how to get the rest of his financial house in order.

This simple system of cloning your best clients will allow you to easily double the total number of clients in your business, thereby doubling your income. And you can continue this process as long as you'd like. If you don't have existing clients or your favorite clients are not in the marketing niche that you want, then call on CPAs or other centers of influence who are in that target market and do the same exercise.

CONDUCT GROUP PRESENTATIONS

Most financial advisors have experienced the phenomenon we referred to as "post seminar letdown." You probably know the feeling. You've just conducted what you consider a wildly successful seminar, but after the warm glow of the high fives, back slapping, and congratulations fades, you realize you didn't really do any significant business. Something went wrong, but you're not sure what. All you know is that you failed to turn qualified prospects into clients. Why? Because most advisors have a vague idea that they want more clients, but they get so caught up in the event that they forget why they're there.

By beginning with the end in mind, we never lose sight of the purpose of our workshops, which is to provide an endless stream of pre-qualified, pre-endorsed prospects for entry into the sales process. You should plan your workshops backwards, starting with the follow-up, then the workshop, and last, getting attendance. Here is a typical example of beginning with the end in mind planning.

You should chart out a time plan for follow-up meetings. Decide on the number of workshops you will be doing and an approximate number of prospects that will be attending. This will give you an idea of the amount of follow-up you will need to do. If you do not have a client base which you can clone in your desired target market, or if you are new to the business, we recommend that you hold small workshops on a monthly basis. This should be the same basic workshop each month, allowing for constant improvement as you move ahead.

PHONE CALL FOLLOW-UP STAGE

If your workshop is on a Thursday, don't wait until Monday to begin making your follow-up calls. Start the day after or, better yet, the day of the event. Make contact with everyone within three days. Before calling a prospect, be sure to go over his or her response sheet so that you have a good idea of the type of person you are talking with. When you make your first follow-up call, make it clear that the meeting you hope to set up is part of the investment consulting process—and, as you promised in the workshop, you are willing to put together an Investment Policy Statement especially for this person's situation.

THE WORKSHOP

Built into each workshop is a call to action that creates excitement and motivates participants to want to personally meet with you after the workshop. We offer participants something that usually only the largest pension plans provide—an Investment Policy Statement that addresses each person's own unique objectives and spells out exactly what we would do if we were in his or her shoes. Our strategy is to create a win-win situation. We do this by teaming up with a good speaker who has the same target market and who will share expenses as well as help promote the workshop.

Depending on your targeted market, the ideal time for workshops will differ. For retired individuals, days are best; for executives, evenings or Saturdays work better. We have been very successful with Saturday morning workshops that run from 9:00 to noon. We have greeters hand out name tags and address cards for each attendee. We have the attendees check the registration material for accuracy. Having the wrong address for a prospect at this stage is not a major disaster, because he or she will correct the mistake, but letting the wrong address go uncorrected can be as bad as having no address at all. The registration personnel also hand out seminar workbooks.

It is a good idea to have at least two people speaking and to schedule a refreshment break between speakers. The break gives people a chance to approach and talk with the presenters. In fact, presenters often find themselves surrounded by people with questions. It is a golden opportunity to make personal contact with those attending the seminar. Obviously, it is important for the presenters to be relaxed, friendly, and sincere.

EXPLAIN THE INVESTMENT MANAGEMENT CONSULTING PROCESS

The last part of the seminar process involves getting those in attendance to want to have an Investment Policy Statement done. We always have participants complete a response sheet. The aim of the response sheet is not to grade how well you did, but to determine what participants liked, what they didn't like and, most importantly, to find those who desire a complimentary follow-up meeting that will result in an Investment Policy

Statement. Prioritize the follow-up request forms. We give the participants the opportunity to mark "yes," then "maybe," and then "no." If they mark "no," we don't call them.

THE PRESENTATION

In the workshop, your presentation should start with addressing the audience's values. Use the value-based selling techniques discussed in chapter eight. Start by telling participants that the four most powerful words in the English language are, "I need your help." Then ask, "How many of you are confused about investing?" (Show of hands.) Pause and tell everyone to look around; almost everyone in the audience should have raised a hand. Make sure you give them time to respond and then acknowledge them. Then say, "If you're not confused about investing, you're not paying attention." That should get a chuckle and helps them begin to see what is in it for them; you are going to help them through all the confusion in the investment arena.

Next, try to determine the level of sophistication in the audience. Ask how many in the audience consider themselves to be sophisticated investors. (Show of hands.) Typically in groups of thirty, we have one fellow in the back of the room raising his hand defiantly. That person is likely to be your biggest challenge. Then say, "Let me share with you our definition of a sophisticated investor: someone who has lost money at least once and did not enjoy the experience. Now, how many of you are sophisticated investors?" (Everyone raises a hand.) It's a very powerful method to get people involved in the process.

We then enter the noise versus information discussion using a flip chart and walking the audience through each of the four quadrants as we did in chapter three. Point out it is your job to help them move from being noise investors to being information investors who understand how markets work. Then outline the five key concepts from chapter five and illustrate the building block approach we discussed in chapter six. This is a very powerful way of introducing institutional asset class investing.

Throughout the presentation, we mention the various steps of the investment management consulting process, and reiterate the importance of the Investment Policy Statement. By the time we're ready to close the workshop, attendees are extremely comfortable with the thoughtful discipline of not only our investment approach, but also the process whereby we work with new clients. We then ask the audience to check off on a response sheet whether they would like a complimentary personal Investment Policy Statement prepared individually for them.

Don't judge success by the number of people in the workshop. Don't judge success by the number of people who check off that they want to meet with you. Judge success by the real results you achieve—new assets under management. We've done workshops for as many as 400 and as few as 10. In most cases, groups numbering 10 to 30 have been the most successful.

PROMOTION

Promotion basically consists of both relationship marketing and direct marketing. Let your clients know that you are holding monthly workshops and that their colleagues and friends are invited to attend. If your clients perceive that the process you use to work with new investors is consistent and high in quality, they'll be comfortable giving you the referrals you ask for at each quarterly meeting.

In addition, when you are getting started, it can be advantageous to conduct a very targeted direct mail campaign. You might be tempted to simply run a newspaper ad, but you may find that does a better job of having competitors attend your workshops than qualified prospects. Teaming up with a radio personality who runs the top local financial show can be successful. If you are just getting started and don't have existing relationships, this might be something to consider. Think about how you prefer to be contacted and you will begin to understand why teaming up with a CPA or other financial professional can greatly enhance your success.

The most successful workshops we've done were sponsored workshops, rather than public workshops. We enlist another organization to co-sponsor the workshop, such as a charitable organization or professional association. This not only reduces costs dramatically, it gives a foot in the door to their specialized donor or client lists. Choose the association or professional organization wisely, however, to make sure it is consistent with your ideal client profile.

CREATING STRATEGIC ALLIANCES

In almost all surveys of wealthy investors, CPAs rank the highest when it comes to whom investors trust for financial advice. Attorneys usually rank second and financial advisors third. No surprise. So what can you do as a financial advisor to meet CPAs who are centers of influence?

What if we could show you a way not only to meet with the senior partners of the CPA firms in your community, but also engage them to be your strategic marketing partners? Would that be of value? Of course it would. Strategic alliances work not only with CPA firms, but also with other professionals such as attorneys, life insurance agents, and property casualty specialists—in fact, with anyone who shares a target market with you.

By creating a strategic alliance, you can open doors, build trust, and create new business opportunities for both organizations. A strategic alliance is a synergistic and mutually beneficial partnership that results in a win-win arrangement. In the past, financial advisors would call other professionals and invite them to lunch with the misplaced hope of getting referrals.

We'd spend most of the lunch meeting attempting to differentiate ourselves from other financial advisors so that the accountant would be comfortable sending their clients to us.

The fact is, however, that financial advisors look pretty much the same to CPAs, much as all CPAs look pretty much the same to financial advisors. To build a strategic alliance, you need to focus on being perceived as an ally, helping the CPA firm to be hugely successful. By focusing on this, not on how you differ in investment approach, you will become successful at partnering with CPAs.

WE HAVE FOUND THAT THERE ARE FIVE STEPS TO DEVELOPING A SUCCESSFUL STRATEGIC ALLIANCE:

Step 1 – Formulation and Preparation

Prepare a list of the local and regional CPA firms in your area. Identify the senior partners. For most financial advisors, it doesn't make sense to go after the Big Six firms. You'll end up frustrated at their inability to move quickly due to large bureaucracies. Local and regional firms, on the other hand, are under tremendous pressure to develop marketing strategies. They need your help. Identify firms that are in your existing target market. You're likely to have access to a local business journal which publishes a list of the top firms. Use this as a resource and aim high. Look for top firms that share your targeted market and are regional or local.

Step 2 – Make the Call

Call the targeted CPA partners and set up an appointment to discuss joint marketing opportunities. Be bold. The purpose is to explore ideas of how strategic alliances might be mutually beneficial. Our experience has been that every time we've called a targeted CPA firm, they've wanted to get together. Why? They need help with business development. When they hear you are in the process of exploring strategic alliances with CPA firms and you're interviewing three or four to identify which would be the best partner, they are going to want to meet with you. On the first call, explain you're not looking for referrals, but a true strategic alliance-marketing partner. That will differentiate you from almost all the competition.

Step 3 – The First Meeting

Take a few moments to introduce yourself – but no more than three minutes.

Remember, CPAs can't tell the difference between investment advisors. Immediately shift the conversation to their concerns and how an alliance might address those concerns. Even if you see opportunities, don't move on them immediately. Go slow and create a larger opportunity. Take notes. Share with them what marketing research suggests are their challenges. Ask how the firm is currently addressing each of the challenges that CPAs face:

The liability of working with any marketing partner. CPAs are concerned with liability. Most CPA firms have been sued and certainly the Big Six have had high profile lawsuits. Share with them up front that you are also concerned with liability, and would like to discuss this issue with them in more detail. Also mention that you are convinced that because you use an asset class investing approach (since reading this book), they will have no liability exposure in working with you.

Developing new business clients. Ask them what they're doing currently to develop new business. Have they worked in the past with a financial advisor? Has it been successful? What are some of the most successful marketing projects that they've undertaken in the past? Don't be surprised if they haven't done anything. Most firms are just beginning to be proactive in marketing.

New revenue from existing clients. Explain that you understand many CPAs are losing revenue from existing clients because of other readily available tax services, such as the computerized software programs. What are they currently doing to generate new revenue? Would they be interested in exploring other avenues with you?

Retaining existing clients. CPAs are under a lot of pressure from the increased competitiveness and the availability of software programs. Ask what they're doing to retain their

230

existing client base and tell them you have some ideas.

Maximizing client benefits. Tell them about the benefit of working with you. Ask if they have ever thought about increasing the benefits that they offer clients by developing a strategic alliance with a high-quality investment advisor.

Tell them that you want to share any information they've given you with your marketing people. Hopefully, you have some marketing people, or at least an informal marketing advisory board you can bounce things off. (If you have followed the steps properly, you do have an informal marketing advisory board.) Tell the CPA partner that you'd like to set up a second meeting for brainstorming and kicking around possibilities of how you might work together. If working with this CPA firm looks like an exciting opportunity, discuss looking at the next two years. If it doesn't, thank them for their time, ask for some of their business cards, and move on.

Step 4 – The Second Meeting/Market Exploration

The purpose of the second meeting is to discover shared opportunities, goals, and expectations for the future. This should not be done over a meal. You should allocate at least an hour to explore shared expectations from having a strategic alliance over an initial time period of 12 months. Compare their vision and yours of how you might jointly accomplish your mutual expectations. You want to have a series of questions prepared that will be stimulating and open-ended—and listen. Take detailed notes of the points discussed. If the meeting is successful and you want to work with this person further, set up a third meeting where you will present a draft of a plan to maximize the opportunity to work together.

Step 5 – The Third Meeting/Planning

Prior to this third meeting, you've reviewed all the notes from the previous meetings and have written up a marketing action plan, which delineates ideal goals and minimum goals of this strategic alliance. Typically, goals are expressed for the CPA firm in revenue and for your asset management business by the amount of assets you acquire under management. The ideal goal is what it takes to make a very successful program over the next 12 months. The minimum goal is what is necessary to achieve in order to continue. By having goals, you will get much more focused on working together. Then write up the strategy.

We have found that setting up systematic workshops together serves a number of purposes. One, by having workshops, not only do you get exposure to the other firm's client base, but you also develop consistent markets together. Most importantly, your strategic alliance partners finally get to hear your story in a very professional manner when they sit in on the meeting. That alone is worth conducting the workshop.

Write out specific tactics and for what each of you will be responsible in developing workshops or other events and strategies together. Once you have this strategic plan in writing, you are ready for the third meeting. This meeting is simply about getting agreement on the structure of fulfilling your initial project together. Review the overall plan, the strategy, the goals, and the targeted action steps to reach your mutually agreed upon market. Discuss both short-term and long-term expectations. Review the budget of expenses and how they will be shared. Typically, expenses are shared 50/50. Look for points of leverage and opportunities that weren't explored in the initial written plan. For each step, reach an agreement as to whom, what, when, and how each step will be accomplished.

Developing an ongoing series of workshops for your mutual clients and prospects is a great starting point and very powerful. It will consistently reinforce the relationship and allow you to learn more.

Utilizing the relationship-selling strategies that we have discussed will all but ensure the success of your asset management business. You must stay focused and go through each of the four steps in order to achieve the highest level of success you are capable of. If you work the plan, you will realize your goals.

PART

V

LEVERAGING YOUR SUCESS THROUGH OPERATIONS

N othing can kill a good firm quicker than failing to build the infrastructure to handle growth. In the next three chapters, we look at the infrastructure that will support your success. You will learn how to develop the systems that will reinforce the trust that you've established with your clients through the marketing and sales process and continue to impress them at every stage.

CHAPTER SEVENTEEN

THE BACK OFFICE AS A PROFIT CENTER

The key to a hugely successful asset management business is having clients who trust you and are impressed with what you do. Most financial advisors focus on marketing and sales to accomplish this. Unfortunately, it is difficult to measure how effective you are beyond the number of new accounts you obtain. Most prospects who decide not to work with you, tend not to provide you with any quality information regarding why they did not choose you as their advisor. If you are reasonably successful in marketing, you may fool yourself into believing you are doing well even if you are making many mistakes. With operations, your clients will not let you fool yourself.

Now is your opportunity to really impress your client by focusing on the details. Unfortunately, most firms fail because enormous growth strained operations and they lost the confidence of their clients to manage the day-to-day details. To manage the day-to- day details, you need to look at operations proactively and as a true profit center.

The first step in building great operations is to focus on results that you want—no errors. Starting with the new account process and continuing through every time you touch your client, you have an opportunity to impress your client and continue to earn the confidence with which they entrusted you.

Clients trust you with their life savings. If you can't even provide an acceptable statement, it raises serious questions about your competency in their minds. As well it should. Your clients are constantly making judgments about you. They compare you subconsciously with your competitors and with their friends' financial advisors constantly, no matter how "good" your relationship. They may forgive an error the first time but it puts them on guard. The second time, they're not as forgiving. And the third time, they're probably gone. It's the three-strike rule! Self-checking mechanisms save you from the embarrassment of showing a client a report that's wrong. Great systems insure the success of your back office.

In designing your system, you must address each of these processes and make them appear effortless to your clients. The best analogy that I have heard is that your operational systems should appear to your clients as a swan on a beautifully sunny day effortlessly gliding across a tranquil lake. A very peaceful picture painted for our clients' minds. That is what your clients should see even if the true picture is the view of the webbed feet scrambling madly underneath the surface of the water.

CHOOSING YOUR CUSTODIAN PARTNER

To make this a reality, you must choose your custodian partner well. This is an extremely competitive market with each custodian provider attempting to differentiate their offering. Currently, Charles Schwab has a significant lead not only in technology, but also in their overall package. They command almost 80% of the market place. With over $70 billion in assets, Schwab currently has more than two times the assets of their next five competitors combined in this marketplace. These assets represent one-third of Schwab's total asset base.

The other custodians are all playing catch-up, but Schwab can hear their footsteps and has been able to effectively meet this competition head-on.

The four main competitors in providing custodian services for independent financial advisors are as follows:

Datalynx	(800) 525-2124
Charles Schwab & Co.	(800) 648-6021
Fidelity	(800) 771-1332
Jack White	(619) 678-5110

In our firm, we have five main operational processes for all accounts. You need to ensure that each of these processes is error free. The most humbling experience for an advisor comes at that moment of truth when you're with a client who has placed all of his or her faith in you, you present the paperwork at the meeting—and it's wrong. Develop the systems so that this will not happen.

OPENING NEW ACCOUNTS

Common embarrassing mistakes are signatures that are missing, and blanks that aren't filled in. Much of whether the paperwork goes smoothly, or not, depends on the custodian, but it also depends on your thorough understanding of the paperwork requirements. Always take the time to adequately prepare for meeting with a client. Use a highlighter to mark all the areas you need to fill in with information so you don't pass something by. Don't go into the meeting, full steam ahead, everything's on, and then later bother the client with some detail you should have taken care of up front. It's better to be prepared than to be embarrassed later.

We encourage every advisor to open his own account and to go through the steps of opening an account with each new custodian he or she begins working with. Practice:

Step 1: Walk through the process from A-Z.

Step 2: Money doesn't have to be deposited; just open the account.

Step 3: Fill out all the paperwork; make all the mistakes.

MANAGING DISTRIBUTIONS

One area which we have seen custodians make mistakes is distributions. A client may require monthly income to be paid out of her account on a certain day. When we first got started with our custodians, there often was a disconnect surrounding who was responsible for the distribution and it was not consistently executed. Of course we thought it was the custodian's fault. They thought it was our fault. The client did not care; they wanted their check. In your clients' minds you are responsible for any mistakes the custodian makes; you selected the custodian.

To correct any chance of error, we have a process that records when a custodian should pay a distribution. Our office compares what we expected to be distributed with what actually was withdrawn from the account using the download we receive the business day following the expected distribution date. We then track if the correct amount went out from the proper account at the right point in time. We want to know right away if the custodian has executed all instructions properly. More importantly, we want to solve the problem before it can be effected or noticed by the client.

We also have a computerized system for tracking every distribution, including a list of incidents that have happened and the details surrounding them. If a distribution is not received by the client, we can readily create a running chronology. We alert the custodian to the specifics of the incident and get an explanation back. We're immediately on top of it. As a business grows, the tracking of all transactions becomes increasingly important. We make a complete record of each error, noting all the details and the contact person's name at the custodian's office who dealt with the matter. We analyze how we could have improved results and note that on the record. We can pull these records up from our database at any time.

INSURING DATA INTEGRITY

Another concern is data integrity. With massive data coming in, we have to ensure that all that information is streaming

238

correctly. Every time a transaction goes up, the computer must record and reconcile it—whether it's a deposit, a distribution, a trade, a name change, an address change, whatever the details—no matter how large or how small.

Data integrity helps in figuring out what to do in specific situations that arise and in establishing procedures. For example: What if a transaction hits an account and you don't recognize it? What if there is a split on a stock? What if there is a merger? What if a stock is coming in at a zero basis? How do you report this to your client? More importantly, how does your portfolio accounting software track these anomalies? How does your portfolio accounting system handle these and other types of transactions?

How do you ensure that the stock doesn't drop into your system at a zero basis, which generates an incorrect tax report?

We've developed a data integrity system in which people are in charge of looking at all the information on a specific transaction and coming up with an analysis and solution. A person isolates the situation, learns and understands it thoroughly, and determines how it should be handled by the firm's portfolio management accounting system and ultimately it is reported correctly to the client.

Your goal is to work with the custodian to ensure that a particular transaction is not going to "contaminate" your database, but rather will ultimately improve the database by being handled well. Repeatable procedures can develop out of individualized solutions that work.

We have clients with multiple accounts making up one larger portfolio. In calculating internal rates of return within that portfolio, it is important to determine a starting date of management. Rather than using the date money is received, we use the date that trading and billing actually began. We set it up so that we can easily look at each individual account, or at the portfolio as a whole. It's important to be consistent in the way an internal rate of return is calculated. Always keep the same pattern, never deviating, and you'll avoid one way of getting into trouble in an audit.

If your custodian makes a mistake or takes forever to get money into an account, the advisor is blamed. Advisors are thought of in the same light as the custodians they use. The company you keep, good or bad, is often how your clients judge you. Only work with the best. It is too costly not to.

As an advisor, cross-checking on your client's behalf is a large part of compliance and fiduciary responsibility. As the quantity of clients and the dollar magnitude of your business grows, your systems become even more crucial to the protection of not only your clients but also your professional standing. You need to build in systems that will ensure you won't get blind-sided by a bad trade that the custodian puts through or incorrect commission charged.

FACILITATING TRANSFERS

We also do the same thing with transfers of money from one financial institution to another (contra broker) say from Franklin/Templeton Funds to Charles Schwab. Clients are rightfully concerned when their money is in transition for any period of time. Transfers are notoriously slow since most financial institutions are very reluctant to relinquish dollars. At our firm, we've created a transfer process, which ensures double-checks of every transfer, and watches all transactions to make sure they happen correctly. We establish a close relationship with the custodian's transfer specialist and develop a tag—team spirit with the custodian to ensure expediency and to "trap" any errors or blow-ups that may have occurred.

There is an established system for assisting you in properly executing a transfer efficiently. One is the ACAT (Automated Customer Account Transfer) system that allows three to five days for execution of a transfer—or at the very least, to have it on line.

Our firm handles transfers carefully, tracking every step of the way. We know when each transfer was initiated, exactly what point in the process it's in, and when the last follow-up occurred with the broker-dealer or contra firm. If something blows up, we know within the week. If the money is to go straight to the custodian, an advisor may not find out about a problem for two or three weeks. We also enable advisors working with us to use our Intranet to track the status of all accounts, which can create huge value. They have the ability to see everything we do. It's important to have state-of-the-art systems in place so that anyone looking at your firm perceives quality, even if you're a very small firm.

There are many nuances and details with respect to transfers. For instance, if the transfer involves a partial account transfer or a proprietary fund, the ACAT system cannot be utilized. If there's a limited partnership or an asset that the custodian can't handle, the ACAT will reject the transfer. Then you've got to go back to your client with your tail between your legs. You need to let your client know up front what can and what cannot be transferred on a timely basis. Remember to manage their expectations before you manage their money. Transfer blowups typically happen within seven to 10 days of their initiation with the custodian, so a week has been lost in the process. The client is not going to be happy and you're back at square one.

You need to work with a custodian closely to make sure your transfers are "clean" and that all the dollars you're asking for can come over within your custodian's parameters. Can the custodian handle X-Y-Z mutual fund? Can the custodian handle X-Y-Z limited partnership? Or does the client need to sell those holdings at the broker where his funds are currently residing? On an ACAT transfer, if everything is clean, you're done within seven business days, whereas in a non-ACAT transfer, the process normally takes 20-30 business days. If you must step out of the automated transfer process, make sure your client understands how long the transaction might take. With a normal brokerage account transfer, the process normally takes 20-30 days.

Transfers—Key Points:

• Make sure the client's assets are where you think they are and in a form that can be transferred from the existing financial institution to the target one.

• Send the transfer by certified mail, if it's going direct.

• Make sure your custodian sends the assets to the proper person at the contra broker.

• For direct rollovers from a client's 401(k) into an IRA account, make sure the client received and completed all forms received by his employer to transfer his 401(k).

• Explain the process in its entirety to the client.

• Manage expectations.

Often the quickest way to transfer your client's total position at the brokerage house is to liquidate it. The transaction cost will most likely be higher than it would be if the new custodian handled it—but your client has saved 20 days. Another big advantage with liquidating at the original brokerage house is that if the market runs up or runs down, you have access to the client's funds immediately. With an ACAT transfer, the funds are frozen until the process is complete. You can't start entering orders within that account and the broker's liability is potentially open. The client may be stuck in the middle, watching the market sink as their funds are in transition.

After tracking any problem, we close the loop by sharing the records with the financial advisor whom can then give feedback to the client on the solution arrived at.

EXECUTING TRADES

Trading can be complicated and expensive to your business if not properly handled. Building a close alliance with your custodian can help smooth out the process. Remember, your role as a fiduciary to the client is to get the best execution possible and to manage their emotions. You do not want to violate that role or lose the trust of the client. You also don't want to blow it for yourself and run up costs due to trade errors. A common mistake made by new advisors is impatience.

Be patient in selling for your client. A panic sale or emotional sale can be not only detrimental to your proceeds, but to the overall price of the stock or bond in trading. When doing

242

a block trade (over 10,000 shares), you definitely should use your custodian's institutional brokers. Their job is to isolate what the market is, who's buying, who's selling, and generally help you work the order in the best way. They can help you set limits. For orders, make sure you or the client doesn't rush in and "blow out" a position without knowing the consequences, and ensure that the transaction costs of the trade are beneficial to your client. When selling greater than 5,000 shares, don't be afraid to negotiate with your custodian or institutional broker. They love this type of business and it's easy for them. If you're not an expert, find one.

Unfortunately, trade errors will happen. Create a separate database to record these trade errors. This will not only help you in audits from the SEC and NASD, but it will allow you to track and ultimately eliminate recurring errors. The SEC and NASD will want to know what kinds of trade errors have arisen and what was done about them. Keeping your records clean is compulsory from a compliance standpoint, but it's also a good management tool. You can see what went wrong and a better approach to use for the next time. You also have a better chance at getting an improved result from the custodian if you've got specifics about what went wrong where.

DATABASE PORTFOLIO MANAGEMENT SOFTWARE

If we were to start up a new asset management business today, the first thing we would do is get a state-of-the-art computer system, a Pentium 200 with Microsoft Office 97. We would explore the best asset management software, with a preference toward a relational database that would be compatible with Microsoft Windows. This would become the central hub of our business. Today the players in the asset management software business are Advent, Centerpiece, and dbCAMS. However for most advisors, Advent or Centerpiece would be a better choice even with the flat-file technology. dbCAMS tries to do too much, serving all the financial planning issues. The other two software programs are much more focused. We started with Advent and had very good success until our growth required us to build our own propriety system using a Microsoft SQL database running on a Window NT platform.

Database Portfolio Management Software Providers

Advent	(800) 523-4708
Centerpiece	(800) 528-9595
dbCAMS+	(301) 341-8000

Once your computer system is set up, you should select a custodian to house your clients' assets in mutual funds, stocks, or bonds within their brokerage services. We would pick one custodian to focus on and stay with that one, if at all possible, for all clients. By focusing on one custodian, you will understand their subtle nuances and build relationships that you can leverage to continuously improve your business.

Once you have set up your computer system, purchased asset management software, and picked the custodian you are going to work with, you need to learn how best to work with the custodian. Visit in person with your custodian firm's regional representatives, talk to the servicing team you are going to be working directly with, and begin building a working relationship. This custodian relationship is going to be most helpful delivering quality service.

CHAPTER EIGHTEEN
_____

USING COMPLIANCE TO YOUR ADVANTAGE

Most successful brokers and financial planners think of regulatory agencies as an anti-sales group that sets up road blocks without understanding the business, certainly not with an interest towards helping sales. The reality however, is that the compliance department of your organization can be a competitive advantage, especially when the time comes to sell your practice. By doing business by the book, and incorporating the key addresses and disclosures necessary to appease the regulatory groups, you are creating a very powerful presentation.

Any otherwise strong exit strategy can get derailed by a compliance problem. Seaboard Investment Advisers, Inc. learned this the hard way. A company with over $1 billion under management, they appeared to have great performance and well-satisfied investors. But in 1994, the SEC launched a compliance investigation. Unfortunately, the key officers didn't immediately react; instead they buried their heads in the sand by not taking the SEC seriously. Because of not following proper compliance, millions of dollars of equity and years of work were wiped out in a relatively short period of time.

For most advisors, it makes sense to utilize their broker-dealer's compliance department. Make sure you get everything approved; don't try to sneak anything by. Be aware, however, that the rules governing registered representatives and registered investment advisors are not the same. The NASD, for instance, considers communication to 10 or more persons to be advertising. On the other hand, registered investment advisers advertising is communication to more than one person. You and/or your compliance officer need to understand many sets of rules.

Compliance procedures should include monitoring incoming and outgoing correspondence, but when Internet e-mail is used, that's difficult to do. Most companies now are putting in spot-check mechanisms, as opposed to checking every piece of correspondence. The NASD and the SEC have new directives and have funded monitoring of the Internet. They now search the Internet to find potential violations. The biggest risk, however, comes from your competitors not approving of what you're doing, because they're likely to report any unusual or suspect activities.

When our asset management business was in its early stage of development, we had an unexpected visit from the California Department of Corporations. The visiting official said the Department had a whole file full of complaints received about our firm. We were shocked. We'd had no complaints from any investor or client on file. We asked why an unsatisfied customer would send a complaint directly to his department. He said, "Well, the complaints are not from your customers." We then asked if the complaints had arisen from our public workshops, but we couldn't imagine why the public wouldn't write us first. He replied, "No, the complaints aren't from the public." We asked, "Well then, just who are these complaints from?" He said, "Your competitors."

When the State of California conducts a review, they bill the company being reviewed. So if a competitor turns you in, and that's who is most likely to turn you in, the result can be real costs to you, even if you have done everything right.

246

Financial services professionals must register with the SEC as well as state regulators and it's natural to feel a sense of victory when the regulatory authorities approve your registration. In reality, however, your regulatory obligations as a Registered Investment Advisor (RIA) have just begun.

YOUR RECORD-KEEPING RESPONSIBILITIES

The SEC lists 16 record-keeping points that advisors should have in order to survive an SEC audit, and sooner or later the SEC will audit the operations of your advisory firm. One of the easiest ways to successfully survive your SEC examination is to set up 16 separate files corresponding to each of the 16 major record-keeping responsibilities imposed by the Investment Advisors Act of 1940 (the "Advisors Act"). Set up all 16 files, even if a few of the 16 files are empty or merely contain a single sheet of paper indicating the rule is "not applicable." This approach will show the SEC examiner that (a) you are familiar with all of your record-keeping responsibilities; and (b) even though a specific rule may not apply to your particular operation, you are cognizant of the rule.

Fifteen of the 16 record-keeping rules come directly from Section 275.204-2(a)(1) through 9(a)(15) of the Advisors Act. The 16th rule comes from the Insider Trading and Securities Fraud Enforcement Act of 1988.

You should keep the following 16 files:

Journal: Keep a journal in accordance with generally-accepted accounting principles.

Ledger: Maintain a ledger in accordance with generally-accepted accounting principles.

Securities Purchases: Keep a complete record of all securities you have purchased or recommended.

Canceled Checks: Save all of your canceled checks and bank statements for a five-year period. (Caution: The five-year period is a federal standard but some states such as Pennsylvania and Wisconsin, require retention for a six-year period.)

Paid and Unpaid Bills: Assemble and save all documentation of paid and unpaid bills.

Trial Balances and Financial Statements: Retain all trial balances and financial statements of the firm for a five-year period (or longer depending on state requirements). The trial balances MUST be run on a quarterly basis. The SEC will not be pleased if you are unable to provide these trial balances on a quarterly basis for the last five years.

Written Communications: Keep records of all written communication between you and your advisory clients.

Discretionary Accounts: Maintain a list of all accounts in which you have been granted discretionary authority.

Evidence of Discretionary Authority: Retain all documents that grant you discretionary authority.

Written Agreements: Save all written agreements executed between you and the advisory client.

Communications Recommending Specific Securities: Keep a copy of all advertisements, notices, or circulars which recommend specific securities to clients.

Securities Transactions Where the RIA has Direct or Indirect Ownership: Maintain a separate record of all your recommendations of a specific security in which you or your principals have direct or indirect ownership. This is the most difficult step to follow. It means that you must maintain this independent log documenting when you or any associated person of your RIA entity recommend to a client a specific security in which you, your spouse, your children, or any other entity which you control also has a position.

Securities Transactions Where RIA has Direct or Indirect Ownership, but is Primarily Engaged in Business Other than Advisory Activities: Comply with the requirements of the previous item even if you are not primarily involved in the investment advisory activities.

Brochure Retention: Keep copies of brochures (copies of your Form ADV-Part II or substitute disclosure brochure) given to clients. Keep a signed receipt from all advisory clients. Also, don't forget that at the end of each year, in accordance with the "Brochure Rule," you must offer to deliver an updated version of ADV-Part II or your substitute brochure—even if it has not changed—to all advisory clients of the prior year.

Solicitors' Documents: Retain copies of all disclosures signed by paid solicitors who refer advisory business to you and with whom you share advisory fees.

Insider Trading Compliance: The Insider Trading and Securities Fraud Enforcement Act of 1988 amended Sections 204A and 214A of the Advisors Act to require all RIAs to adopt a written Firm-Wide Policy Statement and a Written Procedures to Implement statement. The Firm-Wide Policy Statement sets forth what specific steps the RIA is taking to police the dissemination of material, non-public information. The Written Procedures to Implement statement sets forth how the principals of the advisory firm are making sure that the firm-wide policy is observed. Federal securities laws require even small shops to adopt these two written statements. All officers, shareholders, directors, associated persons, and clerical personnel must receive each of these two statements. They should sign them as well.

What You Do When the SEC Visits

Some people don't call before they visit. Among them are industry examiners. Knowing that, it behooves each of us to be ready to welcome examiners at any time. Being prepared implies agreeing who has responsibility for representing the firm during the audit process, having our systems in order, and knowing the kinds of documentation that are likely to be requested.

When auditors first show up they will want to speak with the company's control people, generally the officers of the firm. Usually they'll tell you the audit is "for cause" or is a routine audit. This meeting sets the tone of the audit. Essentially, it's the place for setting the ground rules. You'll designate a point person (generally the compliance officer) to handle requests from the auditors and to answer questions. In our firm, employees are instructed not to talk with auditors unless the point person is present, and we ask the auditors to respect that request. (Even a casual conversation in the hallway could lead to unwanted inquiries.) We want to ensure that one person hears all that is said and to clarify any misunderstandings

We also want to make auditors comfortable, and we want the visit to provide as little disruption to our normal business activities as possible. To that end, we provide them with workspace including tables/desks, phone, and access to a copy machine.

It's important that we know what's been provided to the auditors in case of any necessary follow-up. We also have a strong sense of confidentiality and do not provide any more than is asked for. Therefore, we ask for all requests in writing. If the auditors want to see a specific file, we'll get that file for them.

Auditors can ask for any of your records. Generally, they start with accounting and then review client files. They are looking for evidence of the firm's attention to details—to receipts matching bills, to Focus Reports matching internal reports, to signed account agreements in every investor file, to the documentation of proper licensing of representatives. They will ask for a compliance manual and compare the firm's written procedures with actual procedures. They'll ask to see the correspondence files and look for the appropriate sign-offs. There is a good chance that, if you've done some advertising, the auditors have seen it and will be looking for a copy in the advertising files. If you've provided performance numbers, they'll want to check the calculations, so back-up information is crucial.

We always request an exit interview. If there are any problem areas, we can discuss them and clarify any misunderstandings. When all is said and done, an audit is an educational experience. Viewed positively, it forces us to review our business practices periodically, and it points us to those areas that need improvement.

250

EFFECTIVE MARKETING MATERIALS

In public relations, you're building the firm and your name is attached to all marketing materials by definition. Everything you say via advertising must be carefully considered and balanced. If you're telling the advantages of something, you must also tell the disadvantages. You're required by law to give balanced presentations.

One of the requirements of the regulatory agencies is that registered representatives with outside business activities inform their compliance departments, in writing, of those outside activities. The compliance department must be aware, for instance, if you are selling real estate. In addition to the notification requirements of the representative, there is a requirement for the written acknowledgement by the supervising firm.

Reprints are not pre-approved advertising material. If you plan to send reprints out to investors or potential investors, you must first receive reprint permission. Then you are required to file the material with the NASD (if you're in an NASD firm) and receive approval for use as marketing material.

In 1994, the NASD came out with a ruling that broker-dealers must oversee the activities of investment advisors. Broker-dealers are still adjusting to this ruling because many had an attitude of, "I don't want to know about or participate in any advisory activity." Now there is a responsibility to know and to oversee which, if you are a registered representative, you must honor.

The SEC doesn't like the use of hypothetical performance numbers, but they're allowed when actual numbers aren't available. When actual numbers are available, the SEC requires the presentation of those numbers. In Clover Capital, several guidelines were issued. An advisor must disclose, if applicable, that the advisor's clients had investment materially different from the model. He must disclose prominently that the results do not represent actual trading, and he must describe the effect of material market or economic conditions on the results.

The rule in compliance is not to take anything for granted. You can't stick your head in the sand in this area. Set up your 16 files as suggested. Keep accurate records; it will pay off. When a buyer is interested in your firm, one of the first things he or she will ask for is to see your compliance files. The best way to prevent any roadblocks is to stay ahead of any compliance issues. Have a system in place, follow the system, and document in writing your process. It will pay huge dividends when and if you decide to sell your business.

CHAPTER NINETEEN

COMPUTER SYSTEM

Technology provides an opportunity to leapfrog over your competition. Why not use it? Many of your competitors are still stuck in old legacy systems, unable to take full advantage of today's technology. This gives you an enormous competitive advantage.

When traveling around the country, visiting with some of the large brokerage firms, we were surprised to see many still using mainframe and mini-computer technology. The time delays and costs of implementing new technology for this group are painful.

Our firm has the good fortune of being located in the heart of Silicon Valley, where technology is a major part of life. Every day, there seems to be a new announcement of a breakthrough that our industry can harness to take us to the next level of success. It's important to utilize changes in technology, as they become available. You want to be on the leading edge, but not the "bleeding edge." So often, program announcements are merely of "vaporware" that have great promise, but the software doesn't quite yet exist. Don't be fooled by all the noise in the computer marketplace and make considered choices.

253

When updating your computer system, you want access to the best tools available. To your advantage, the cost of having the best tools has gone down dramatically. Technology that costs $5,000 today, was hundreds of thousands of dollars only 10 years ago.

Rule of thumb: Over-buy your needs because software requirements are growing as quickly as hardware technology. Currently, we recommend that you buy computers with Intel's highest platform only. At the time of publication of this book, that's the Pentium MMX, either 166 Pro or 200 Pro, with at least 32 megabytes of random access memory (RAM). In our office, we run desktop applications using Windows 95 as our primary desktop platform and Windows NT for the network environment. Each of our desktop computers typically has a 2-gigabyte drive or higher. The reason for such large drives on the local desktop is that we utilize Microsoft's Office 97 suite of products that includes Excel, Microsoft Word, PowerPoint, and Outlook.

We have standardized our office around Microsoft. At this point in time, Microsoft has such a commanding lead that it makes sense for financial advisors to standardize around Microsoft products. Because of Microsoft's lead, any new technology will be introduced as an upgrade, not startup, making it much easier to learn and implement.

THE MICROSOFT SOFTWARE PACKAGE (OFFICE 97)

While many new software programs sound overwhelming, they aren't. No matter what your previous computer background may be, Microsoft has designed this office suite of software packages for you. They are designed to work extremely well with beginners as well as the most advanced users. The overall Microsoft package is broken down into a number of key components, as follows:

MICROSOFT WORD 97

This is the most popular word-processing program in the world. You can use Word 97 to write letters; create proposals, dramatic reports, brochures and newsletters; and even design web pages for your new Internet site.

We particularly like the spell-check and the grammar check, which was used throughout this book. We used a lesser-known piece of software within this package, Microsoft Binder, to bind all the chapters together and otherwise manage this very large document. Word 97 provides you with an array of tools to write and present anything you want to, very effectively.

POWERPOINT 97

If you've witnessed our firm making a presentation; there's a 99% chance that presentation was made in PowerPoint. Many of the tables and graphs that we've used in the book were created in PowerPoint. It's an extremely powerful tool for creating slide shows, overhead transparencies, and on-screen computer presentations.

EXCEL 97

I can remember back to the days of VisiCalc, the first spreadsheet program developed just over 10 years ago. Some of you who have been in the financial planning profession for some time can remember how excited we all were to have this simplistic spreadsheet available on our personal computers. The progress that has been made by Microsoft in those 10 years is unbelievable. Almost anything with numbers can be done in Microsoft Excel. The evolution from VisiCalc to Lotus 1-2-3 to the now leading product, Microsoft Excel, has been built on an expanding platform of tools built into the spreadsheet. The nice thing is, you don't have to be concerned with these tools unless you need them. Most importantly, all integrate within the Office 97 products. Every chart with numbers in this book was calculated in Excel 97. It's a very powerful program for converting raw data into graphs, charts, and tables that will truly impress your clients.

OUTLOOK

Microsoft Outlook is a desktop information management program that helps you organize and share information on your desktop and communicate with others. It can effectively manage your messages, appointments, contacts, and tasks. It can track all your activities, view open files, and share information with others inside or outside your office. Outlook is organized into folders that are very intuitive.

When you first start-up Outlook, the e-mail in-box folder opens. Use the in-box not only to read or send mail messages, both internally and externally through your Internet provider, but also for the organization of tasks. Outlook can be used as a substitute for Microsoft's Internet browser—the Internet Explorer. The strength of Outlook is that it allows you to integrate all your tasks and organizational tools within one place. Each employee can open up Outlook and access his or her mail, both internally and externally.

We are tied to the external world in each of the desktop applications through a T-1 high-speed data phone line. For our employees who work at home or who have additional computer systems at home, we make an ISDN line available. For our laptops, we currently use at least a 28.8 modem. The speed of connection is critical in the ability to work with and move information between programs.

In today's world, everyone needs to be connected by e-mail. This will allow you to communicate with clients, peers, strategic alliances, custodians, turnkey asset management programs, and anyone else who is technology-proficient. Outlook allows you to coordinate your e-mail system with your calendar, notes, tasks, contacts, and journal entries—all in one program.

Let's say that you receive an e-mail which requires action. You first drag it to the task icon. The program instantaneously establishes the task as one to be undertaken and asks what time frame is required, the task's level of importance, and who should do it. Are you going to undertake the task or will it be

256

delegated? To whom? Also, the program sets up an automatic follow-through. For many of us who aren't good typists or well-organized, this is a fantastic tool.

An e-mail task may lead to a calendar event or you can deliberately move the item to your calendar and establish the appointment. The whole program is very object-oriented, whereas in the past, computers were extremely text-oriented; Microsoft has been moving progressively towards object-orientation, where the user simply clicks on an icon and moves it to another item. You're grabbing objects of information rather than text, and once you're comfortable with this process, it's very intuitive. The look and feel of each Microsoft product is the same; so comfort of use and familiarity are inborn. The calendar program is a very sophisticated program that will allow you to share your calendar with everyone else in the office or in any remote office.

"Notes" allow you to clean up all those little yellow Post-It notes from your office. Instead of leaving them all over your desk, wall, etc., you can now just stick them on your computer pages electronically. Let's say an e-mail comes in that you'd ordinarily write down on a note. Now, you just drag it over to the "yellow stick-um" icon and the e-mail becomes a note that you can save on your desktop. If it's a task that you need to follow up on, drag it over to the "task" bar. The computer will make a copy and file it under the subject of the e-mail, then ask you if there's a due date and when you're going to get started, whether the task has priority status, and what percentage of the project is completed. The task can be assigned to someone else. You can send out status reports on the task, mark the project as completed, and file the project. If you ever need to review the information, there's a search engine that will very quickly pull the information back up.

THE PAPERLESS OFFICE

Unfortunately, not all information is going to come to you electronically. By adding just a simple $300 scanner with a software program made by Visioneer, called PaperPort, you can have a paperless office. Every piece of paper should be handled only once. In our office, paperwork that should be saved or shared is scanned at the desktop and saved. This can then be distributed through e-mail, internally or externally, or saved as a task. If it's information that should be saved for the company, we e-mail the information to our Webmaster, who adds it to our Intranet site.

Think of all the opportunities missed because you've misplaced something or didn't act on it in a timely manner. Now, every piece of information is at your fingertips. Also, from a compliance standpoint, at the push of a button, a paper trail is there for the SEC or your broker-dealer to review.

From a marketing standpoint, information can be readily accessed and e-mailed to a client. If the client doesn't have e-mail, you can simply drag the information to the fax icon on your computer and it will be sent through WinFax, Faxworks, or another fax program on your system.

Very powerful tools are now available to small businesses. Now, it's up to us to use them. The amount of contact you have with clients will increase dramatically when these tools are in place. Remember, clients want this. Affluent investors demand a tremendous amount of service and contact from their asset manager. Automated processes can enable you to make frequent contact, which will truly delight and impress your most demanding clients.

To make this happen, however, you have to stop using the "Old Co." computers. Many advisors have old 386s, and installing Windows 95 on these simply won't work. The whole suite of products in Office 97 takes up almost 200 megabytes of disk drive space and that's before any information is entered. It's critical to use the new technology or you'll be frustrated by the slower speed and inaccessibility of tools. Outlook also has a low-level contact management system that's suitable for some small financial advisory offices of five or less people.

SALES FORCE AUTOMATION

It's likely that you'll need a sales force automation tool that can be be integrated into your business process. Few software programs have produced the tremendous rewards that sales force automation can accomplish. When properly designed and implemented, sales force automation can dramatically increase your business productivity, your profit margin, and, ultimately, the bottom line. However, most people misuse sales force automation or contact management systems and the expertise ends up frustrating everyone in the office. Sales force automation improves your sales process, enables you to serve your clients much more effectively, and creates powerful competitive advantages. This software, however, requires a major cultural shift in your office that will not only affect those people who work directly with clients, but the team that supports them.

The first step is to understand what sales force automation software is. Structurally, it's simply software with a database and text notes attached. It allows you to store, retrieve, and process customer information and notes about your relationships with clients. Unlike accounting and portfolio management software that really only tracks quantifiable numbers, both quantitative and qualitative information can be tracked with effective sales force automation. This will allow you to build a huge database of information about your clients and their interactions with you or anyone else in your firm. You can easily convey all the information to anyone who needs to know it. You can create a priceless information base that will enable everyone in your organization to build strong client relationships and provide outstanding customer service. This personal service creates equity by building customer loyalty.

A good decision to initiate the creation of sales force automation for a business has little to do, however, with software or hardware. First, you need to have a clearly defined sales process thought out and how you are going to service customers, as we discussed in Chapter 8. The questions you need to ask are: What is my sales process now? What would I like it to be? How can I design a system to support the desired sales process and the outcomes I am trying to achieve? Once you understand the sales process you want to have in place, you need to define the information needed at each point in the process. What information do I need to collect in the fact-finding meeting? What information do I need to gather for sales support? How can I effectively manage the relationship with an established client?

Today, there are two tiers of programs available in sales force automation. The first, ranging in price from $50 to $500, is designed primarily for individual financial advisors, not sharing information with other employees, except to a very limited extent. The number one seller in this marketplace is ACT. It is available at all computer software stores.

While we have utilized ACT in the past, we've found it extremely difficult to work with as an enterprise system. We are just completing a joint development project with Resource/Phoenix in Mill Valley, California, to build state-of-the-art sales force automation for the financial services industry for larger organizations such as broker dealers, mutual funds, and large RIA's. We believe it will redefine the sales force automation marketplace. For more information, you can call Resource/Phoenix (800) 266-2344.

PORTFOLIO MANAGEMENT DATABASES

One of the key databases you will need is a portfolio management system. We initially started with Advent, by far the leader in the industry. We always believe in working with the best and the brightest. For most advisors who go it alone, Advent should be the tool of choice.

We found however, that Advent, while good at performance management for a relatively small number of accounts, did not incorporate the business process systems needed for our firm. For that, we developed proprietary software to handle our portfolio management system. We used a platform of Microsoft SQL, which is Microsoft's state-of-the-art database program, with Microsoft's visual basic front end for a clean, crisp appearance. We then released this package in an Internet application that any advisor working with us can pull up at our website (*www.rwb.com*). Any information about the advisors' client can be quickly accessed. The status of transfers, distributions, and demographic information on any of their clients is only a double-click away. This has allowed us tremendous flexibility in managing the business. Representatives from Microsoft, after hearing how we applied their technology, spent eight hours videotaping our operations. They then created a 3-minute videotape that highlights us as one of the best examples of client/server technology utilization. You can view this clip on our website.

It is important to surround yourself with the best and brightest in every field, and technology is no exception. No one person can be all things to everyone, as we've stated many times. Do not try to be the technology expert. Align yourself, either through an employee or a service provider, with someone who has the expertise necessary to make great technology applications happen in your firm.

Be very thoughtful about whom you choose because this person will become the backbone of your organization. Many people sound good at first, but have real problems actually applying the knowledge and making it work for you. Before hiring anyone, make sure that you reference their established accounts and determine their ability. Then start the chosen person as a consultant, with one fixed project. Make sure you see the end results that you expected on a timely basis before going any further. We've had a number of our advisors hire consultants to help them out in their own offices, only to later receive their computers here in our office via FedEx, preceded by a phone call begging our tech people to clean it up. Don't make that mistake. And even more importantly back up your systems religiously.

USING THE INTERNET

Most financial advisors view the explosive growth of the Internet as cause for alarm. Many are concerned that investors will no longer turn to them, but rather to Internet direct marketers, such as Intuit, Microsoft, Vanguard, and Fidelity for solutions to their financial problems. To remain competitive, our challenge is to find ways to keep pricing relatively low, provide substantial value that is perceived by the client, and become more accessible.

To accomplish this, we must first understand what investors want; then we must embrace technology to assist us in providing effective solutions. Those financial advisors who readily accept this new force and use it to their advantage will position themselves as leaders in investors' minds, and attain the advantageous distinction of offering a high-tech, high-touch solution that on-line competitors cannot offer.

Investors place high value on asset allocation, followed closely by financial and estate planning, then tax planning. They perceive little value in advisors managing managers, or in asset protection. Why are these findings important? If you are aiming to position yourself high on the value matrix, you must know what investors perceive as valuable. The next challenge is to deliver it. Most financial planners have discontinued the creation of comprehensive financial plans because the activity isn't very profitable. Should you restart? No. Instead, use the Internet to deliver information online directly to clients and/or in your quarterly meetings.

As we previously discussed, our firm has engaged Coopers & Lybrand to establish a site to support the Personal CFO™ project. A corporate CFO helps the CEO maintain and improve the financial health of the company; this application is the computer equivalent for advisors. A good CFO does not know everything there is to know but can readily find the resources when needed, plus the CFO coaches the CEO by holding him accountable. In this Intranet site, advisors will have access to financial planning modules they can use in coaching clients. Coopers & Lybrand's Personal Financial Planning Group updates this online site often so that it's always current. This is a very low cost way to share information effectively and to add value without a large investment of time. (Unlike the Internet, which is an open forum, the Intranet is a private community. Typically a company will use an Intranet site to communicate with its employees, staff, vendors, and so on.)

Advisors interested in greater client contact can achieve this without ever leaving the office. The rising cost of office space and the need for greater productivity are driving the trend towards telecommuting. By the year 2000, 30 million people will be telecommuting, according to Gartner Group, Inc., an information technology advisory firm in Stamford, Connecticut. The number of Internet users available for you to access will increase dramatically in the near future.

Vital information and key customers become easily accessible with the low cost installation of an Internet connection. Remote users can access their home or office PCs from afar to look up a phone number, scan their e-mail, update a file, or access network resources and shared databases.

To facilitate this access, we will be making our clients' performance reports available to them on our Intranet site after the first of the year. Making your reports available to your clients will draw them into your site on a regular basis for updates, and you can then provide them with additional information.

Financial advisors are relatively conservative as a rule and aren't usually comfortable working at the cutting edge of technology. Most planners, therefore, will wait until the Internet becomes an established norm. In the book, *Crossing the Chasm*, by Geoffrey A. Moore, the author describes two marketplaces for emerging technology. There are the innovators and early adapters who are willing to deal with the frustrations of new technology not working perfectly because they're excited by being the first ones out there, and they're able to be part of the creative force. Then there are those who simply want an effective tool they can step up to and use for communication and the dissemination of information to clients. That second marketplace is opening up in our industry now, and you want to be part of it.

Applications	Today		In 5 Years
Communication	59.9%		79.6%
Research	12.8%	➡	28.0%
Prospecting	0.7%		19.3%

Source: Prince & Associates

Figure 19-1: Independent RIAs Use and in the Future Will Predominately Use the Internet as a Communication Tool

Amicus Networks, an Internet consultant specializing in the financial services industry, found that investors rank interactive communication the number one criterion for an online system. This would include news reports, chat rooms, e-mail, plus audio and video broadcasts. When you surf the web, if you like what you see, you look a little further; if you don't, you hop to another place. Interactive communication alters that by allowing a two-way communication flow where people can get questions answered and real needs addressed. That's what survey respondents reported they're primarily looking for.

Independent financial advisors are in the business of developing relationships. After all, there's no business without a relationship to a client, and technology can enhance communication in a relationship or establish a new one. Do not design a site without facilitating some form of interactive communication.

A few advisors are already having some early successes and there's infinite potential. As a hobby, one of our advisors participated in the Prodigy Bulletin Board—which led to a prospect flying out to meet with him and ultimately investing $600,000.

So, how can you best present yourself on the Internet? There was a time when simply converting a company brochure to a web page was enough to get you noticed—but in this day and age, that doesn't cut it. Each day, 17,000 domain names are registered. The key is to differentiate yourself from the 200,000 new pages that appear on the World Wide Web each day. When we used the Alta Vista search engine to identify websites which contained the words "mutual funds," over 200,000 matches were identified. For the words "Financial Planning," 800,000 matches came up. The noise on the Internet is increasing all the time.

One important way to differentiate yourself is to focus on developing a sense of community. That means answering people's questions, interacting with them, and providing needed services.

Chances are users aren't merely going to surf your Web site, then call you up and hire you as an advisor. If you're simply displaying a web page and users happen to come across it, the chances are they won't be ready at that moment to make an investment and you won't have made enough of an impression to motivate them to come back to you when they are.

Our firm is experimenting with using technology to hold live broadcasts; advisors address members of the community who want to gain information relevant to their concerns. An advisor can easily broadcast into a chat-room and initiate a Q & A session.

Going back to origins, commerce has always occurred within a community. In the heyday of the gold rush, for instance, commerce was born when enough miners were in one place to support a tavern. A post office would be established when there was a critical mass to support that, and so on. If you interact with and bond with a community on the Internet, when users are concerned with an investment problem, they are going to come to you for assistance.

Positioning yourself as an expert requires a consistent business and marketing plan. You can create high visibility on the Internet, but you must deliver a message that's relevant and consistent. We established a bulletin board on Prodigy, but that shotgun approach did not produce profitability for the firm; results simply did not justify the work entailed. On the other hand, the forums we hold on CompuServe have been productive for two reasons: First, we are able to communicate directly with a vast number of people. Secondly, the media got wind of it and we got coverage there as well. We're definitely continuing with conferences, and we would suggest this as an effective medium for advisors to direct prospects to a Web site.

You want to develop an online community that includes both your clients and prospects, and which is in alignment with your marketing plan and goals. You then need to figure out how you can provide useful information to that community on a systematic basis for low cost, but with high-perceived value.

THE INTERNET DEMOGRAPHICS

Five percent of the American population is now on the Internet. Users are typically male with a reasonable income. Most people currently online are good potential prospects for financial planners. Blue-collar workers are not yet participating in large numbers, so you're likely to be in touch with the more educated and affluent.

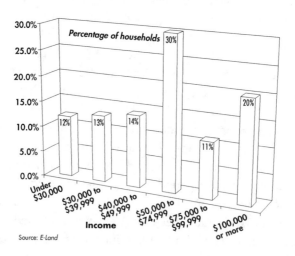

Figure 19-2: Internet Users by Income

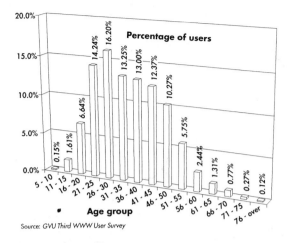

Source: GVU Third WWW User Survey

Figure 19-3: Internet Users by Age

The Internet can be very impersonal, however. The challenge is to create relationships within an online community. This does not replace the need for one-on-one contact; most advisors still need to get together with each client a minimum of once a quarter.

You want to know exactly who is looking at what pages on your site. If you know that a certain user is accessing a topic, say "Children's Education: Saving For College," you already know a lot about the needs of that prospect. That's extremely valuable.

Amicus Networks (512-418-8828) has a product called "Community Builders," which reveals the user's name and e-mail address, so making contact becomes easy. Anonymous users are not part of the network; qualified users are. That's a great head start.

The number one item that investment business professionals want from technology is interactive communication; number two is security. The emergence of improved security and transaction support will make electronic commerce even more pervasive. It's not an issue of whether this is commonplace; it's a matter of when. At this time, 87% of business professionals who do not have a Web site are interested in developing one; 82% want to develop a Web site for customers; 50% are planning on implementing a Web site over the next nine months.

When we first looked at the Internet, we thought it wasn't very practical. Now the Internet is not only turned on in our office every day, it's turned on all day!

HOW TO GET STARTED:

Step One. To get started on the Internet, first choose an Internet provider. The provider will supply you with the browser software. Use either Microsoft's Internet Explorer or Netscape's Navigator. Don't even bother with America Online, CompuServe, or Prodigy for your Internet access; they are not effective solutions at this time. Three Internet service providers you might try are: Netcom (800-NET-COM1), PSI (800-827-7482), and AT&T (800-831-5259). If you get stuck at this point, hire a teenager to get you started; they can be remarkably proficient and inexpensive. You may even have a teenager in your family who would love to get you started.

Step Two. Have fun and surf the net. Allocate several hours over the next couple of months to just browse. Spend time exploring various financial and non-financial sites. Look for what you would like to display on your own site. Three of my favorite financial sites to search through are *The Wall Street Journal*, Financial Planning Online, and Advisor-Works.

The Wall Street Journal on-line (www.wsj.com) is available for a small charge. *The Wall Street Journal* site not only provides each day's stories from the paper version, but also includes many of the Dow Jones wire services. Many stories are also updated regularly throughout the day. They provide a search engine which allows you to search all their stories easily since the beginning of this year. The Wall Street Journal also provides useful special sections, including company-briefing books on individual securities.

The *Financial Planning* online (www.fponline.com) is another valuable resource to investigate. It updates the hot news from the industry daily, provides a discussion forum for planners, and much more. This site will give you a good idea of how a community can be supported through an Internet site.

Advisor-Works (www2.advisorworks.com/aw/) provides one of the most complete listings of resource sites that financial advisors should try. Look for the Bookmark File in its preview section. Check out their hot links to these valuable sites.

Step Three. Review your marketing plan. Understand just who your target market is. What is the "unique selling proposition" that will not only differentiate you from your competitors, but also position you as the market leader in that niche? Discuss with an Internet consultant how you can utilize the Internet most effectively to maximize your own World Wide Web site. Show the consultant Web sites that are similar to what you want.

Step Four. Build your Web site. You will not get it right the first time. The Internet is constantly changing, and your site should be as well. Plan a systematic review every few months to see how effective it has been and what you can do to improve it. The Internet must become an integral part of your overall marketing structure.

You need to develop a site for your established investors and possible prospects. The net is a delivery vehicle where you can create high-perceived value for low cost. For the effort to be effective, however, it must be consistent, well-planned, and support your firm's comprehensive marketing strategy. The tools are now available for financial planners to reposition themselves as truly high-tech and high-touch, just what investors value.

VI

CONCLUSION

You now know what it takes to build a hugely success-ful asset management business. In the last two chap-ters, we will focus on realizing your equity creation goals. In Chapter 20, "How To Sell Your Business," you will learn how to maximize the equity realization in the sale of your business. For many advisors, this will be the single most important personal transaction that they ever complete. You don't want to make any costly mistakes.

Chapter 21, "Pulling It All Together," will review the building blocks of your hugely successful asset management business. We believe by following each of these steps, you can create the systems that will ensure your clients' success and thereby, your own. In this chapter we show you how to get started with bite-size pieces of your business plan.

CHAPTER TWENTY

HOW TO SELL YOUR BUSINESS

The most difficult challenge you will ever face is preparing for the sale of your company. There are a number of issues that need to be addressed:

What is your business worth?

In Chapter two, the valuation of firms was discussed historically. Valuation of your business is more an art than a science. There is a wide range of methods to arriving at a valuation that is acceptable for both the buyer and you.

When is the right time to sell?

The right time is when you're hitting the steepest part of the upward slope and growing dramatically, but before business reaches a plateau. Most of us want to get to the uppermost peak and then sell, but you actually want to sell prior to reaching that point.

When do I begin the sales process?

At the beginning of the company, begin building up to a healthy valuation. It's never too early to begin preparations.

Who should I sell to?

There are a lot of potential buyers. The key is to identify someone who you fit in with strategically.

What kind of help do I need?

A lot. For most financial aadvisors, this is the first time they will ever be personally involved in a sale of a business. When you combine the emotions in selling your baby after all the hard work you have put in and the lack of "deal" experience, it is hard to complete a transaction without at least a sounding board such as your CPA or attorney. Some advisors may choose to be represented by someone who is in the merger and acquisition ("M&A") business.

Let's look at the common mistakes that financial advisors make when attempting to sell their businesses.

Most financial advisors don't have any idea of what their businesses are worth. They start sharing with everyone that their business is for sale. They talk to all comers with the hope, "this is the one." They focus first on key employees, then on competitors, then on suppliers, then on key customers. All of these potential markets present inherent problems.

For relatively low cost, key employees can "move across the street" and take your clients with them. Employees, therefore, are going to be the least willing to pay much for your company. They can effectively buy your business for book value. Simply replacing your tangible assets would allow them to get started. That certainly is a much lower price than any knowledgeable financial advisor is going to sell for.

Competitors are high risk because they can use the situation to their advantage. First, they can get information that's proprietary to you, such as your client list or processes you have in place. This can be obtained during the due diligence phase before any dollars have changed hands. Second, there is a negative connotation to selling, particularly if you've been on the market for a long time. They will use this to their advantage. Third, even though you might ask potential buyers to sign a confidentiality agreement, people talk. It might not be the principals involved in the negotiation but someone else at their office who learns about you selling your firm. The temptation to share a secret almost assures that word will get out.

Given the above, you don't want to go to your employees or competitors. What about approaching your clients to buy your firm? You would have to tread carefully here. If the deal doesn't go through you will likely lose the client. The approach may cause some loss of your credibility as their financial advisor even if you can figure out a way to approach them, given the regulatory environment.

Let's say someone approaches you out of the blue. You are flattered. We all like to feel that we have value. It is even better to be offered a lot of money to enhance that feeling. It's easy to get seduced by the offer into trying to close the first deal and negotiating it on your own. It is a common mistake to negotiate with only one buyer from our employees, competition, or clients. Maybe you would be much better off focusing on strategic buyers and having an expert handle the negotiations. It's difficult to run a business and consummate a transaction at the same time. A buyer, interested in acquiring your firm may take nine months to decide on the terms. The business, if it's ignored for the duration, will no longer be as attractive to the buyer.

WHEN IS THE RIGHT TIME TO SELL?

When asked how he got so rich, J. Paul Getty answered it was by selling too soon. Everyone is waiting for the peak time to get the maximum value. When things look good and you don't want to sell, that is probably the best time to sell. The temptation is to wait until midnight. When "things" start falling apart it is to late.

In preparation for selling your business, you should set a goal with a time frame of when you would ideally sell. Remember to begin with the end in mind. Most buyers will require you to stay for a minimum of two years and more often, four years. With the average time from initial contact taking almost nine months, you need to begin shopping your firm to sell almost five years before you are fully out of the business.

274

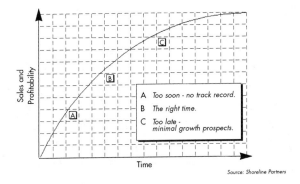

Source: Shoreline Partners

Figure 20-1: The Right Time to Sell

How Do You Maximize the Value of Your Business?

You need to study your financial statements and clean up your act by getting rid of aspects of your business that are a drain. Sort through the junkyard of assets that you have. Clean up your books and business operations. The most important determinant in the value of your business is free cash flow. Design your business to maximize this prior to sale. Then consider recasting your prior financial statement so that it reflects your true earning power. You can show the buyer a financial statement that's different from your tax forms. Most financial advisors like all small businesses attempt to minimize taxation while maximizing personal benefit from the company. For example, it might be that you're receiving $600,000 in salary, but the cost to replace you might be only $200,000.

In recasting, you could show more realistic numbers, and thereby demonstrate higher earnings. In most cases, a buyer will be interested in your earnings before income tax, but will also request to see your IRS forms. It's easy to substantiate business expenses that have a personal nature. You should also trim down your company as much as possible in preparation for selling it, getting rid of any excess expenses and non-operating activities.

In recasting your financials, you want to examine your own compensation and other key principles. Examine your retirement contributions; ownership through the business of cars, boats, or airplanes; any low interest loans; miscellaneous perks; other companies you own where there are transfers between businesses; or company owned real estate. You can also make some adjustments for capitalization policies, debt services, discontinued product lines, or defunct aspects of the business. If you've made the conversion from commission to fee, this involved a number of expenses. In recasting, you'll be able to adjust for these.

However, you will not be able to tell the buyer that you took $100,000 in cash that you did not report out of the business. Fraud is another story. Your credibility would be eliminated and your ability to do a clean transaction negated if fraud is apparent. The potential buyer might even be tempted to turn you in to the IRS for the 10% finder's fee. They should. Keep the deal clean and above board.

Another technique to increase value is to share your business plan, particularly the vision plan. Most of us have ideas and strategies for taking the company to the next level. You want to document in writing all the opportunities you perceive. A file that records every potential opportunity that you're either exploring currently or considering for the future is of enormous value to a buyer. Include reasons why you've chosen to do something, or not do it. Do research on all potential opportunities and record your findings.

The key is managing your exit strategy. Get prepared from day one. Establish repeatable systems. Most financial advisors, if they do have systems, carry them in their heads. To the extent that you have documented procedures, your business will be much more valuable. The buyer is going to get a great deal of confidence out of seeing operations and marketing plans.

The backgrounds of key personnel should also be in writing. Tell what they do for the firm. Share your team-building approaches. Make sure your compensation plans are in writing and that there are no promised compensation benefits that are not disclosed.

Any lawsuits where you're the defendant should be settled, if possible. The buyer does not want to be exposed to any additional risk beyond the normal course of business. Contingent liabilities will substantively reduce the purchase price. Worse yet, it may kill the deal. If you're a plaintiff, it's not as much of an issue, though you must disclose this too.

Image is critical. When a buyer walks into your office, how does the place feel? Is it a showplace? Think of selling a home. Most people fix their houses up, making all the improvements their spouses always wanted them to do just prior to sale. Why? It increases value dramatically by showing a sense of pride. You need to do that same dressing up of your business environment.

There's a managed series of events involved in the process of selling your business. The first is the valuation of the firm, then identification of strategic buyers, then marketing, then negotiations, then closing. It starts out as a clearly defined process, but as you get closer and closer to the closing, it becomes much more anxiety prone. You need to be prepared for this.

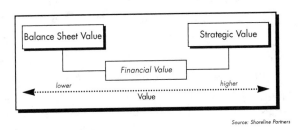

Source: Shoreline Partners

Figure 20-1A: Continuum of Value

THREE TYPES OF BUYERS – WHICH ONE IS RIGHT FOR YOU?

The first, and worst, is balance sheet valuation. This is what someone would pay for business based on your balance sheet alone. A financial advisory firm with $100 million in assets might only have $100,000 of book value or tangible assets. This is what your key employees could set up the firm next door for. The only time you'd ever consider a balance sheet sale is if you're in dire distress.

The next is financial value. This is attractive to someone buying the business for the income stream it can provide. Typically, such a buyer is interested in income immediately. The valuation is simple a present value calculation of the future income stream discounted for the business risk inherent with a small business. Many of your local competitors will make an offer based on this valuation.

The last is strategic value. In this case, the buyer is interested in dramatically leveraging their profitability with the inclusion of your business. Such a buyer needs you and is willing to pay for it.

To understand how a strategic and financial valuation differs, consider the following story. About 15 years ago, the owner of Duraflame, the manufacturer of fireplace logs, was interested in selling the firm. He contacted 20 of the most obvious candidates, including Clorox. Since he was asking $3 million for a firm grossing $17 million, Clorox was not interested. Only one of his 20 prospects got as far as the due diligence.

He was frustrated and decided to take a step back. What he needed was a strategic buyer. What would this buyer look like? It would be someone that could accomplish more with his company then he could currently. A strategic buyer would be one that could address his major challenges and leverage his advantages successfully. The number one challenge his company was up against was distribution. He had a regional company doing $17 million. If he could hook up with a company with national distribution, he could do ten times the business, pushing sales to $170 million. Another challenge was that stores only stocked his products, fireplace logs, during the winter. If he could find a company with sales primarily in the summer, his company would be the perfect complement.

He decided on charcoal products. They were distributed nationally and only during the summer. The number one player in charcoal was Kingsford, which was owned by Clorox. In effect, the owner of Duraflame sold to the same company he had originally propositioned, and not for $3 million, but for $15 million. The difference was in the strategy.

To the extent that you can find a buyer who can use your company to reach the next level of success, you're going to get the best value both on purchase price and long-term compensation.

How do you identify strategic buyers? The strategy begins with scheduling time for preparation. You also need the means for doing effective research. The Internet provides opportunities for searching out potential strategic buyers. You want to identify major players in your potential market who would consider acquiring your type of business. There are databases that list the different players, as do trade publications. In preparation for this book we tried to identify firms that are currently buying asset management firms with assets below $500 million. Many are beginning to talk about it. Our firm has just received approval of the board to begin acquiring firms between $100-$500 million in assets under management that are consistent with our belief system. We expect that there will be several other firms entering this market soon.

You want to identify a minimum of 10 potential buyers. Create a four-page executive summary, which describes your business and the opportunities. In addition, create an offering memorandum that has all the information necessary for creation of an effective letter of intent. Both of these documents should be focused on what the buyer is interested in. The buyer's interest will be largely based on expectations for the future. In studies, 65% of valuation is based on the future, 25% on the present, and 10% on the past. You should design your document with those same percentages. Historical content should be 36 months, the current 12-month period, and the future 60 months. Market the future, show the present, document the past.

Be realistic about the future, because in most cases you will be signing an employment contract. You'll be responsible for meeting those numbers. In marketing your business, make sure that you have the processes in place.

Before distributing the memorandum agreement, ask potential buyers to sign a confidentiality agreement to protect the information and your processes from being exploited. Not all will be willing to do this, however, because of potential liability.

Qualify the buyer to make sure entering into negotiations makes sense. Review financial statements. Make sure the buyer has the ability to actually make things happen. The buyer should have access to capital—or better yet, have it in place. Review the buyer's corporate strategies and culture to make sure all are consistent with yours. Especially if you're staying, review the buyer's management practices and the personalities of top management people. Also, location is very important. How often are you going to be required to make trips to the home office? What are the strengths and weaknesses of the buyer's existing products and marketing systems? Are those going to help your company reach the next level of success?

Conduct initial off-site meetings. Don't meet in the office. First find out if your business cultures match and then schedule further contact meetings. Secure a letter of intent from the buyer. It's advantageous to have at least two letters of intent so there's some competition. Only after you have the letter of intent in your hands should you allow the due diligence process to begin. Many letters of intent will require you to stop negotiations with other buyers. You can ask for this qualification to be removed, but not all firms will drop that clause.

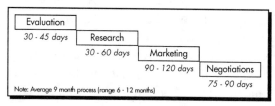

Source: Shoreline Partners

Figure 20-2: Sales/Acquisition Process

Initially, the selling process is a routine science. Then a problem invariably hits near the end. Then the skill of negotiating really comes into play. Here's where it's very worthwhile to have a seasoned facilitator. Facilitators come in many forms: business brokers, management consultants, lawyers and attorneys, intermediaries, and investment bankers. You should consider engaging one of these specialists, for the sake of both the deal and your confidentiality. One business intermediary we have worked with successfully is Phil Currie at Shoreline Partners in San Diego at 619-546-4822.

It's extremely difficult to carry through all negotiations yourself. You should consider employing a facilitator who has a good handle on the whole sales process, including valuation, research, and marketing, thereby lightening your emotional load. A good facilitator is familiar with deal structuring and restructuring and can help you keep several offers in place. In selecting such a consultant, you want to make sure he or she does indeed have expertise in negotiation.

Typically the sales acquisition process takes 30-45 days for valuation, 30-60 days for research, 90-120 days for marketing, and 75-90 days for negotiation. The average acquisition takes nine months. The range will be between six and 12 months.

Payment can be in the form of cash or a note. The final deal will most likely include a non-competition agreement, a consulting agreement, and/or an employment agreement—plus some earn-out. Make sure you have good tax advice. These deals can become quite complex.

By following this process, you can maximize the value of your business and more importantly realize it. You earned it.

CHAPTER TWENTY-ONE

PUTTING IT ALL TOGETHER

In assembling this book, we've presented the building blocks for creating a hugely successful asset management business. Starting with no existing clients, we believe many financial advisors will be able to create a business with equity in excess of $1 million in five years or less. There are times when this journey of building a multi-million dollar business will seem overwhelming for both new and old financial advisors. We need to take a step back and break the process down into bite-size pieces. We feel that, by focusing on 90-day increments, the task becomes very manageable. Let's review the key elements of each of the chapters you will need to implement if you are going to achieve the success that your clients and you so richly deserve.

THE OPPORTUNITY OF THE INVESTMENT MANAGEMENT BUSINESS

Reading Chapter 2, it's difficult to comprehend that there is over $13.3 trillion in investment management today; and that number looks like it's going to become much larger very quickly. This isn't new information for everyone. This amount of capital hasn't gone unnoticed by your competitors.

The good competitors, the full service commissioned brokers who control 38% of the marketplace, are getting ready for a frontal attack on this business. You have to be aware of what your competitors are doing, particularly in your local market, if you are going to be able to develop an effective marketing plan. Timing is everything, and the window of opportunity is closing.

THE AFFLUENT INVESTOR

Today's affluent investor has between $500,000 and $5 million available to invest. The fastest-growing segment of the affluent market is projected to increase at a rate of 19% over the next five years. The good news is, that's your market.

The great news is that these individuals have not been properly served in the past. You will gather assets very quickly by focusing on this group. It's important to spend time understanding what they want, what they value, and what they need. Then help them achieve their needs, reach their objectives and address their concerns.

CREATING A HUGELY SUCCESSFUL ASSET MANAGEMENT BUSINESS

Many of us got into this industry to capture the American dream, but we only captured part of it. We got the opportunity to work in a job, not a business and we did not create the equity from our livelihood that we expected. More importantly for many of us, our quality of life suffered. We have no balance between work and family and many of our outside interests.

We need to recognize and understand that if we continue in the same pattern, we're not even going to have the same results as we had in the past. Today, as never before, there's an opportunity for small businesses to create tremendous equity—on purpose—by implementing the systems and serving your investors' needs. Becoming more systematized will allow you to build in the quality of life that's important to you and your family.

The business is going to be valued based on the assets, gross revenue and most importantly, the free cash flow that it generates. By building your business for the long- term return, you can better serve your clients. You will be successful to the extent that you help your investors move from being noise investors, caught up in the day-to-day media activity, confused and making costly mistakes, to systematically becoming information investors who understand how markets work. This client focus will differentiate you from the vast majority of your competitors who are market-driven to make profits, rather than to serve their investors' needs.

THE FIVE KEY CONCEPTS TO INVESTMENT SUCCESS

Some of the simplest concepts we've learned have been the most important. We've narrowed successful informational investment strategy to five key concepts. You will need to be able to communicate these concepts effectively to your investors. If you are new in the industry, you might still have that hope that maybe you're the next guru. Well, maybe you are; but the only way you can be sure of building your business and delivering consistent value to your investors, is to promise only to deliver market returns through asset class investing.

1. Utilizing Diversification Effectively to Reduce Risk.

Investors don't understand risk, but they do understand volatility. To the extent that you can mitigate losses and reduce the violent ups and downs of individual markets, you will have a client who is much more comfortable. Simply including assets that don't tend to move together will help manage their expectations and dampen the volatility of the portfolio.

2. Dissimilar Price Movement Diversification Enhances Return.

The most effective way to accomplish diversification is through investments that have low correlation to each other;

284

thus, increasing returns by lowering risk. It is a simple mathematical fact that if we have two portfolios with the same rate of return, the one with the lower volatility will have a higher terminal wealth resulting in a higher compounded rate of return.

3. Institutional Asset Class Mutual Funds.

The only way we can be sure that we can increase clients' returns is to lower cost. Your clients will enjoy buying wholesale over retail. It will differentiate you effectively. Institutional asset class mutual funds not only lower costs and reduce taxes but, most importantly, maintain that market segment so that you can have that consistent asset allocation.

4. Global Diversification.

Our industry environment is a global village. We currently invest in 25 different countries. That allows us even more effective dissimilar price movement than we could ever accomplish in the U.S. alone. It's not that we expect higher rates of return overseas. On the contrary; it's simply that we expect that stocks of similar risk are going to have the same expected rates of return, no matter where they are in the world. However, we don't believe they're going to get there at the same time in the same magnitude. By including global securities, you will increase the probability of your client's success.

5. Designing Portfolios That Are Efficient

Markowitz taught us that we should no longer look at investments individually. It's only when we combine the investments and understand the characteristics in the portfolio, that we can build the optimum portfolio. In this book, we introduce five model portfolios that are good starting points for your clients.

BUILDING YOUR MODEL INVESTMENT PORTFOLIO

Three risks make up the equity market: market risk, size risk, and the book-to-market risk. We need to understand the relationship between risk and reward, since our job is to capture those risks effectively for our investors. Most investors should mitigate the risk of equity exposure by including a short-term fixed investment portion.

Don't be tempted by active management. The temptation of beating the market and adding just a little bit more value will be overwhelming. Remember there's no empirical evidence or academic basis for believing that you'll be successful. Instead, it's one of the easiest ways to cause your investors to make costly mistakes and the quickest way to reduce the equity value of your business. Your job is to prevent them from making costly mistakes and provide them with peace of mind.

TAX-EFFICIENT INVESTING

We believe you should focus on private clients in the affluent marketplace. Almost every single investor in this category feels that they are paying more than their fair share in taxes. We need to address their tax sensitivity. Utilizing institutional asset class funds will inherently reduce their tax liability over actively managed mutual funds. In addition, some new products, particularly the no-load variable annuities with fees well below half the cost of the typical broker-marketed product, will enhance their after-tax rate of return dramatically.

THE INVESTMENT MANAGEMENT CONSULTING PROCESS

Systems are the solution. It's crucial that every one of your clients has the same experience with you. The only way for that to happen is if everyone in your firm understands the process you follow. The investment management consulting process will position you effectively above most of your competition, particularly if you employ the concept of becoming your clients' Personal CFO^{TM}.

Almost every commission-based financial planner who made the transition to fee-base initially fought this process. It is time consuming; however, it's an extremely effective use of your time. Don't be tempted to shortcut what will ensure that the most valuable asset in your business, your relationship with your client, endures a lifetime. The bottom line is that, without systematically reinforcing your relationships with your clients on purpose, you don't have any equity.

BUILDING YOUR BUSINESS PLAN

Once you understand the opportunities, you're ready to create a business plan. Your mission statement is to be focused on creating a better life by building equity for your clients and for yourself. You now have an investment philosophy that you should put in writing, which will differentiate you from your competitors and more importantly, will work successfully for your investors.

Each of the business planning sections will prompt you on how to actually implement your new asset management business. Most advisors should plan on spending one month per section to really work with your employees and your key relationships to develop and write a clear plan for each area.

Nothing is more important than being able to visualize what you are trying to create. Remember, everything is created at least twice: first in the mind; then in reality. We'd like you to create it one more time in between, in writing. It will make the processes much more real to you. Even if it doesn't work out exactly as you envision, you will have much more clarity of purpose and dramatically increase your likelihood for success.

Take the exercise in the vision planning chapter and sit down with a trusted friend or advisor. Have them ask you the questions, tape your responses, have it transcribed and then from that, create a written summary that you can share with every one of your employees. This becomes your vision plan for your business.

WHERE ARE YOU IN THE BUSINESS CYCLE?
A REALITY CHECK

Each of us is starting from a different beginning point. It would be very easy to get off track, since we don't know what normal challenges we should face at this point in our business.

Abnormal challenges may derail our business success. Normal challenges are simply those issues at any given point in the growth cycle that every business has to deal with. If you understand where you are in the business growth cycle, then you will recognize the issues that are going to be natural to encounter. These are just part of the growth process. You will be able to plan how you are going to deal with those issues before they become roadblocks.

Creating Your Business Team

Your most valuable assets are your employees. You need to build a team that understands where you are now and where you want to go. They have to share your vision, have an understanding of what challenges and problems are normal at this stage in business, and know how to address them.

Have realistic expectations about what you can accomplish together and most importantly, make accommodations for them to share in that success. It's not only compensation, but the ability to participate in creating an intrapreneurship. They should be fully empowered with the information and understanding of how the business works, so that they can help you in making quality decisions to achieve that hugely successful asset management business.

The Financial Plan; Putting the Numbers in Writing

It's never been easier, with the Microsoft Excel spreadsheets, to put numbers together extremely quickly and extrapolate the results out a million years. Although it's going to take some time to build the business model, they look great. We've provided some model one-year illustrations in the financial plan chapter, which you can use.

Remember, you're developing your new company: the ideal company. Lay out what you would like it to look like from a financial standpoint as it relates to your vision. Share this with the employees. If they don't understand the financial issues, they won't be able to make informed decisions. If you are willing to empower them and to share some of the responsibilities, as well as the rewards for success, you will have extremely loyal and productive teammates.

STRATEGIC MARKETING

Marketing is the creation of an environment conducive to sales. It's the strategic plan. Strategic comes from the Greek word meaning general, long term, big picture plans and activities designed to enable you and your organization to achieve your business goals. Marketing strategies focus on targeting, positioning, allocating resources, and developing specific industry approaches and alliances.

Most of us don't spend time on marketing; we move immediately to sales. Allow yourself the time to think about and develop a written marketing plan. We don't usually think strategically; we think tactically. Sales is a tactic under the umbrella of strategy.

Once we've developed a compelling vision plan, we can then target the market we choose to work with, uncover niches to research, and position ourselves so that the affluent individuals in these niches will want to work with us and seek out our services. Then, and only then, should we begin to communicate our benefits.

PUBLIC RELATIONS

The most effective way to build your communication plan within your marketing plan and to establish immediate credibility is to have a very high visible presence by utilizing public relations. Unfortunately, many people get confused with the difference between publicity and public relations. Publicity, in the traditional sense, is to create many millions of impressions. While this is great for the ego, it's costly and not very effective.

To develop into a recognized star, the quickest road to success is through getting your advice published. A book is a great project, but it's not without great effort. Writing a regular series of articles, preferably monthly, to your targeted market audience will give you immediate recognition and credibility.

TACTICAL SALES PLAN

Tactical is from the Greek word meaning to arrange. Your tactical plan is comprised of those short-term focused activities which accomplish specific steps in your strategic plan. Tactics are prospecting, advertising, direct mail, public speaking, and selling.

The first step of a tactical plan which will immediately start building your asset management business is to convert your existing clients. You owe it to your clients, if suitable, to share with them the knowledge you gained in this book and to help them achieve financial success. In so doing, they'll help you learn better how to communicate your benefits.

Second, clone your top clients. Create an endless stream of pre-qualified, pre-endorsed referrals. If you enjoy public speaking, develop a presentation that's powerful and concise, with a message that separates you from your competitors. The most powerful message we've heard is simply letting the prospects know the difference between noise investors and information investors, and how you can help them become information investors and achieve success.

Lastly, once you know your story well, you're ready to team up with the top professionals in your community who have the same target market. Strategic alliances are powerful, but time consuming. Allocate no more than a day a week to your strategic alliances, and only after you have fully completed each of the other tactical steps in your selling plan. Long-term strategic alliances will be one of your most successful strategies.

CHAPTER TWENTY-ONE

THE BACK OFFICE AS A PROFIT CENTER

Advisors are usually either very technical in nature, resulting in analysis paralysis, or are great salesmen who do not pay attention to the details. Very seldom are they both. In either event, they don't spend the time necessary to solidify their business by having their operations and customer service fully in play. With the growth that you'll experience through implementing the strategy in the book, you will face operational growing pains. Recognize that typically it will last from six to nine months and be prepared that anything emotional that lasts from six to nine months can be painful. Consider working with an advisor who can help guide you through the process. You must have the systems firmly in place to address this growth.

COMPUTER SYSTEMS

Small businesses have a competitive advantage. Since most financial advisors have no legacy systems in computers, they can make huge changes and utilize the latest technology more easily than their larger, encumbered competitors. Only after you've designed your systems so they work manually, should you build them into the computer. Think of it like building a house. It's much easier to change the house while it's still being designed versus being built. You must use technology to your competitive advantage.

THE INTERNET

Don't ignore the Internet; it's going to change your business, and possibly, your life. Get familiar with it and utilize it effectively. There will be many opportunities that no one has even thought of yet. If you become familiar and comfortable with it now, you'll be positioned to recognize those opportunities as they develop and seize them.

GETTING STARTED

To accomplish all this—developing a plan to build the asset management business over the next five years that you visualize and cutting that into 90-day incremental goals—you have to make a fundamental decision: do it on your own or do it with a turnkey asset management program. If you work with a turnkey asset management program, the provider will coach you through building your business plan, as well as provide you with many of the back office, marketing support, and sales support tools that you'll need to build your business. If you choose to do it on your own, you need to find someone who can act as your coach. Most importantly, you need to get started on your journey. Your clients are counting on you.

Appendix A: Asset Classes

Date	Annual CPI	Annual TBill	Annual 20yrTBnd	Annual S&P500	Annual USHBiM	Annual Rus2000	Annual EAFE	Annual IIntSm	Global Defensive	Global Conservative	Global Moderate	Global Aggressive	Global Equity
12/31/72	3.41%	3.82%	5.68%	18.97%	15.98%	-0.27%	37.65%	64.87%	9.95%	15.91%	20.79%	24.51%	27.80%
12/31/73	8.77%	6.93%	-1.10%	-14.67%	-2.76%	-38.96%	-14.17%	-12.81%	1.30%	-3.72%	-7.69%	-10.62%	-13.15%
12/31/74	12.20%	8.00%	4.34%	-26.46%	-22.40%	-28.64%	-22.13%	-28.23%	0.34%	-8.20%	-14.79%	-19.58%	-23.59%
12/31/75	7.02%	5.81%	9.18%	37.23%	51.92%	65.71%	37.04%	50.55%	19.31%	30.72%	39.95%	46.92%	53.07%
12/31/76	4.82%	5.07%	16.77%	23.85%	44.98%	51.06%	3.79%	11.55%	13.44%	17.83%	21.32%	23.92%	26.31%
12/31/77	6.76%	5.13%	-0.65%	-7.18%	0.76%	26.81%	19.37%	74.58%	9.30%	14.77%	19.29%	22.77%	25.80%
12/31/78	9.03%	7.21%	-1.19%	6.58%	6.63%	25.80%	34.33%	66.06%	11.66%	17.67%	22.56%	26.28%	29.49%
12/31/79	13.33%	10.39%	-1.21%	18.42%	23.80%	41.96%	6.16%	-0.54%	11.98%	13.23%	14.17%	14.85%	15.42%
12/31/80	12.40%	11.25%	-3.96%	32.40%	16.53%	38.58%	24.45%	34.76%	16.83%	19.36%	21.30%	22.70%	23.97%
12/31/81	8.94%	14.72%	1.86%	-4.91%	11.23%	2.00%	-1.04%	-4.83%	16.04%	13.10%	10.68%	8.82%	7.30%
12/31/82	3.86%	10.53%	40.37%	21.40%	27.36%	24.88%	-0.83%	0.99%	18.21%	16.98%	15.90%	15.04%	14.51%
12/31/83	3.80%	8.80%	0.69%	22.52%	26.78%	29.09%	24.55%	32.51%	14.21%	19.74%	24.28%	27.75%	30.81%
12/31/84	4.01%	9.79%	15.54%	6.26%	14.07%	-7.27%	7.88%	9.97%	11.89%	10.79%	9.88%	9.17%	8.64%
12/31/85	3.76%	7.72%	30.94%	32.17%	29.46%	31.06%	56.73%	59.59%	20.76%	28.61%	35.13%	40.16%	44.84%
12/31/86	1.14%	6.16%	24.45%	18.46%	20.38%	5.69%	69.98%	50.13%	18.24%	24.80%	30.16%	34.24%	38.04%
12/31/87	4.43%	5.48%	-2.71%	5.23%	2.32%	-8.78%	24.93%	71.34%	10.30%	14.00%	16.63%	18.38%	19.78%
12/31/88	4.42%	6.35%	9.67%	16.81%	24.66%	24.90%	28.60%	26.91%	11.54%	17.07%	21.61%	25.09%	28.13%
12/31/89	4.65%	8.37%	18.11%	31.49%	28.36%	16.24%	10.78%	28.49%	13.64%	18.52%	22.51%	25.56%	28.25%
12/31/90	6.09%	7.81%	6.19%	-3.17%	-13.94%	-19.51%	-23.20%	-16.97%	2.97%	-3.13%	-8.00%	-11.65%	-14.77%
12/31/91	3.06%	5.60%	19.26%	30.54%	29.84%	46.05%	12.47%	5.24%	14.17%	17.58%	20.29%	22.31%	24.23%
12/31/92	3.02%	3.49%	9.41%	7.68%	21.15%	18.43%	-11.81%	-20.05%	6.15%	6.43%	6.64%	6.79%	6.99%
12/31/93	2.75%	2.89%	18.24%	9.98%	20.21%	18.89%	32.87%	24.34%	11.54%	18.07%	23.47%	27.63%	31.40%
12/31/94	2.66%	3.90%	-7.77%	1.31%	-4.55%	-1.71%	8.03%	17.16%	1.59%	2.38%	3.00%	3.47%	3.82%
12/31/95	2.66%	5.61%	31.66%	37.59%	38.37%	28.44%	11.55%	1.47%	11.35%	14.74%	17.50%	19.59%	21.62%
12/31/96	3.33%	5.12%	-0.93%	22.92%	20.22%	16.48%	6.35%	2.57%	7.22%	9.15%	10.69%	11.85%	12.93%
Average	5.61%	7.04%	9.71%	13.82%	17.25%	16.28%	15.37%	21.99%	11.36%	13.86%	15.89%	17.44%	18.86%
Maximum	13.33%	14.72%	40.37%	37.59%	51.92%	65.71%	69.98%	74.58%	20.76%	30.72%	39.95%	46.92%	53.07%
Minimum	1.14%	2.89%	-7.77%	-26.46%	-22.40%	-38.96%	-23.20%	-28.23%	0.34%	-8.20%	-14.79%	-19.58%	-23.59%
Median	4.42%	6.35%	6.19%	18.42%	20.22%	18.89%	11.55%	17.16%	11.66%	15.91%	19.29%	22.31%	23.97%
Std Dev.	3.36%	2.78%	12.64%	16.69%	17.39%	25.03%	22.61%	30.54%	5.64%	9.35%	12.80%	15.49%	17.88%

297

Appendix B: Internet Portfolio Modeling (Screen shot)

Reinhardt Werba Bowen Advisory Services - Microsoft Internet Explorer

File Edit View Go Favorites Help

Back Forward Stop Refresh Home Search Favorites Print Font Mail Edit

Links

Address http://www.rwb.com

RWB Model Selection Program

Instructions for Advisor: John J. Bowen, Jr.

Please complete the following questions regarding your custom portfolio model. Upon completion, please sign and date a printed copy and forward to RWB.

Is this an existing portfolio?

◯ Yes   What is the title of portfolio? [Sample Portfolio]
◉ No

Reason for creating a non-standard model [Client has stock portfolio with low cost basis]

Value of Portfolio: [$500,000.00]   Is this a company retirement portfolio **with employees?** ◯ Yes ◉ No

Define Custom Model

1) What percentage of Equity do you recommend in this model? -------------------------------- 025% [025] % 099%

2) What percentage of Fixed Income do you recommend in this model? -------------------- 001% [075] % 075%

3) What percentage of Money Market do you recommend in this model? ------------------ 001% [001] % 008%

298

4). What percentage of Domestic Funds do you recommend in this model? ------------> 040% [070] % 070%

5). What percentage of International Funds do you recommend in this model? ------------> 030% [030] % 060%

6). What percentage of US Large Cap stocks do you recommend in the Domestic portion of this model? -----> 050% [050] % 080%

What percent of Market Neutral--------> 000% [050] % 100%   v.s. Value -------> 020% [050] % 050%

Note: The large Market Neutral v.s. Value position must be the same for US and International allocations

7). What percentage of US Small Company stocks do you recommend in the Domestic portion of this model? 050% [050] % 080%

What percent of Market Neutral--------> 000% [050] % 100%   v.s. Value -------> 000% [000] % 006%

Note: The Small Market Neutral v.s. Value position must be the same for US and International allocations

8). What percentage of Int'l Large Cap stocks do you recommend in the Int'l portion of this model? -------> 020% [050] % 050%

What percent of Market Neutral--------> 000% [050] % 100%   v.s. Value ------->

9). What percentage, if any, of Emerging Markets do you recommend in this model? ------->

Note: The maximum percentage of International exposure is reduced by the amount of Emerging Markets you select.

10). What percentage of Int'l Small Company stocks do you recommend in the Int'l portion of this model? ----->

What percent of Market Neutral--------> 000% [050] % 100%   v.s. Value ------->

Are there any comments you wish to record?   ◉ No ○ Yes

299

Appendix C: Materials Sources

Inflation: CPI
Source: SBBI (see below)

T-Bills: Thirty-Day Treasury Bills
Source: SBBI (see below)

T-Bonds: 20-Year Government Bonds
Source: SBBI (see below)

Large Company Stocks: S&P 500 Index
Source: SBBI (see below)

EAFE Index: Courtesy of Morgan Stanley & Company. Europe, Australia,
and Far East Index.
  Jan 1972 - present: EAFE Index including gross dividends ($)

Small Co. Stocks: U.S. Small Company Stocks (Deciles 9&10)
Source: DFA Small Company Universe Returns (Deciles 9&10) - ALL
Exchanges
  Jan 1926 - June 1962: NYSE, Rebalanced Semi-Annually
  July 1962 - Dec 1972: CRSP Database, NYSE & AMEX, Rebalanced Quarterly
  Jan 1973 - Dec 1981: CRSP Database, NYSE & AMEX, OTC,
    Rebalanced Quarterly
  Jan 1982 - Present: DFA Small Company Fund (9-10)

CPI stands for Consumer Price Index, a measure of change in consumer prices,
as determined by a monthly survey performed by the U.S. Bureau of
Labor Statistics.
SBBI stands for Stocks, Bonds, Bills, and Inflation. Data Courtesy of Roger G.
Ibbotson and Rex A. Sinquefield, Stocks, Bonds, Bills, and Inflation: The Past
and The Future, Dow Jones, 1997. Updated annually.
S&P stands for Standard and Poor's. The S&P 500 Index is generally considered
representative of the U.S. large capitalization stock market.
EAFE stands for Europe, Australia and Far East
CRSP stands for Center for Research in Security Prices, University of Chicago

THE FOLLOWING ASSET CLASSES WERE USED TO CONSTRUCT THE
HYPOTHETICAL PORTFOLIOS:

Thirty-Day Treasury Bills Source: SBBI

DFA Two-Year Fixed Income Portfolio: Data courtesy CRSP.
  January 1972 - June 1996: Simulation using 2-yr maximum maturity
    U.S. Treasuries.
  July 1996 - Present: RWB/DFA Two-Year Corp. Fixed Income Portfolio net
    of all fees.

300

U.S. Large Stock: Data courtesy Fama and French; CRSP
January 1972 - March 1993: Fama-French Large Cap Value Strategy.
April 1993 - Present: Dimensional's Large Cap Value Portfolio net of all fees.

Small Co. Stks: January 1972 - December 1972: CRSP Database, NYSE &
AMEX, rebalanced quarterly
January 1973 - December 1981: CRSP Database, NYSE & AMEX & OTC,
rebalanced quarterly
January 1982 - Present: U.S. 9-10 Small Company Portfolio net of all fees/Small
Company Subtrust net of administrative fees only.

DFA International High Book to Market Portfolio:
January 1972 - December 1974: EAFE Index including gross dividends ($).
January 1975 - March 1993: International High BTM (Value) Value-weighted
Unhedged $ (Top 30% BTM). Simulated DFA Strategy (Maximum Japan 38%),
Courtesy of Fama-French & MSCI. Includes Japan, U.K., France, Germany,
Switzerland, Netherlands, Hong Kong, Australia, Italy, Belgium, Spain
(rebalanced quarterly).
April 1993 - June 1993:EAFE Index (MSCI) substituted temporarily.
July 1993 - Present: DFA International High Book to Market Portfolio net
of all fees.
Countries include all of the above and Sweden as of October 1994.

The International Small Company Strategy:
January 1970 - June 1988: 50% DFA Japanese Portfolio, 50% DFA U.K.
Portfolio net of all fees.
July 1988 - Sept. 1989: 50% DFA Japanese Portfolio, 20% DFA U.K. Portfolio,
30% DFA Continental Portfolio net of all fees.
Oct. 1989 - March 1990: 40% DFA Japanese Portfolio, 30% DFA U.K.
Portfolio, 20% DFA Continental Portfolio, 10% DFA Asia/Australia Portfolio
net of all fees.
April 1990 - Dec. 1992: 40% DFA Japanese Portfolio, 35% DFA U.K. Portfolio,
15% DFA Continental Portfolio, 10% DFA Asia/Australia Portfolio net of all fees.
Jan 1993 - Present: 35% DFA Japanese Portfolio, 35% DFA U.K. Portfolio,
15% DFA Continental Portfolio, 15% DFA Asia/Australia Portfolio net of all fees.

Emerging Markets Asset Class:
January 1972 - December 1987: 50% Int'l Large and 50% Int'l Small as
described above.
January 1988 - Present: Equally weighted, rebalanced monthly. Countries:
Argentina, Brazil, Chile, Indonesia, Malaysia, Mexico, Portugal, Thailand,
Turkey.

D

Database Portfolio Management Software Providers, 244
discounters
  Fidelity, 27
  Schwab, 27
  Vanguard, 27

E

efficient frontier, 74
Encyclopedia of Associations, 213

F

Financial Analyst Journal, 49
Financial Planning Online, 268
fundamental analysis, 41

G

Gale Directory of Publications and Broadcast Media, 213
Gartner Group, Inc., 263
Garzarelli, 49
Geoffrey A. Moore, 263
Granville, 49

H

Harry Markowitz, 73

I

Ibbotson & Associates, 69
ineffectively diversified, 45
Integrated Resources, 16
International Association for Financial Planning, 8
Investment Advisors Act of 1949, 247
Investment Policy Statement, 14, 129, 131, 216, 217, 225, 227
investors
  informational, 39, 42, 43, 128
  noise, 39, 43, 45, 72, 128, 226

IRS, 190, 275, 276

J

Joel M. Dickson, 66
John B. Shoven, 66
John Caple and Company, 196
Jonathan Clements, 143
Journal of Portfolio Management, 50, 65, 66

K

Karen Maru File, 125, 204

M

Mark Tibergien, 33
market timing, 40, 42, 120, 135
Marketing to the Affluent, 199
Maximizing Wealth for Shareholders, 13
Meek and Associates, 192
Meir Statman, 48, 49, 141
Merton Miller, 73
Michael Gerber, 18, 157
Michael Solt, 49
Microsoft, 254
Modern Portofolio Theory, 6, 7, 8, 51, 52, 73, 74, 121, 129
Morgan Stanley Capital International, 71

N

NASD, 243, 246, 251
Nobel Prize, 6, 7, 73

P

Personal CFO, 145
Prechter, 49
Prince and Associates, 206
Prudent Investor Rule, 136
Public Accountant, 212

T

U

V

W

Recommended Reading:

Asset Allocation: Balancing Financial Risk; Roger C. Gibson; Hardcover; $45.00

Corporate Lifecycles: How and Why Corporations Grow and Die and What to Do About It; Ichak Adizes; Paperback; $15.26

Crossing the Chasm : Marketing and Selling High-Tech Products to Mainstream Customers; Geoffrey A. Moore; Paperback; $8.40

Cultivating the Affluent; Russ Alan Prince and Karen Maru File; Hardcover; $195 (212) 224-3233

*The Discipline of Market Leaders: Choose Your Customers, Narrow Your Focus, Dominate Your Marke*t; Michael Treacy, et al; Paperback; $10.80

The E-Myth Revisited: Why Most Small Businesses Don't Work and What to Do About It; Michael E. Gerber; Paperback; $9.00

Investment Policy: How to Win the Loser's Game; Charles D. Ellis; Hardcover; $31.50

Mastery: The Keys to Success and Long-Term Fullfillment; George Leonard; Paperback; $9.85

Networking with the Affluent and Their Advisors; Thomas J. Stanley; Paperback; $31.50

The Prudent Investor's Guide to Beating the Market; John J. Bowen, Jr., Alan B. Werba, Carl H. Reinhardt, et al; Hardcover; $27.00

The 7 Habits of Highly Effective People: Powerful Lessons in Personal Change; Stephen R. Covey; Paperback; $8.40

Stocks Bonds Bills and Inflation: 1997 Yearbook: Market Results for 1926-1996 (Serial); Hardcover; $99.00

Value-Based Selling; Bill Bachrach; Hardcover; $34.95; (800) 347-3707

Wealth Management: The Financial Advisor's Guide to Investing and Managing Your Client Assets (The Irwin/IAFP Series in Financial Planning); Harold R. Evensky; Hardcover; $45.00

All books are available at your local bookstore or at HYPER-LINK http://www.amazon.com unless a phone number is indicated.